W9-BXP-503

CREATION AND THE GOD OF ABRAHAM

Creatio ex nihilo is a foundational doctrine in the Abrahamic faiths. It states that God created the world freely out of nothing – from no pre-existent matter, space or time. This teaching is central to classical accounts of divine action, free will, grace, theodicy, religious language, intercessory prayer and questions of divine eternity and, as such, the foundation of a scriptural God but also the transcendent Creator of all that is. This edited collection explores how we might now recover a place for this doctrine and, with it, a consistent elucidation of the God of Abraham in philosophical, scientific and theological terms. The contributions span the religious traditions of Judaism, Christianity and Islam, and cover a wide range of sources, including historical, philosophical, scientific and theological. As such, the book develops these perspectives to reveal the relevance of this idea within the modern world.

DAVID B. BURRELL is Professor of Ethics and Development at Uganda Martyrs University. His previous publications include *Faith and Freedom* (2005), *Friendship and Ways to Truth* (2000) and *Deconstructing Theodicy* (2008).

CARLO COGLIATI is Spalding Fellow in Comparative Religion at Clare Hall, University of Cambridge. His research interests include modal theistic arguments in the three Abrahamic traditions; the theological significance of the notion of infinity; analogy in theology and science.

JANET M. SOSKICE is Professor of Philosophical Theology at the University of Cambridge. She is the author of *Metaphor and Religious Language* (1984), *The Kindness of God* (2008) and *Sisters of Sinai* (2009).

WILLIAM R. STOEGER is Staff Astrophysicist in the Vatican Observatory Research Group at The University of Arizona. He specializes in theoretical cosmology, gravitational physics and interdisciplinary studies bridging the natural sciences, philosophy and theology.

CREATION AND THE GOD OF ABRAHAM

EDITED BY

DAVID B. BURRELL,
CARLO COGLIATI,
JANET M. SOSKICE
AND
WILLIAM R. STOEGER

CAMBRIDGE UNIVERSITY PRESS
Cambridge, New York, Melbourne, Madrid, Cape Town, Singapore,
São Paulo, Delhi, Dubai, Tokyo, Mexico City

Cambridge University Press
The Edinburgh Building, Cambridge CB2 8RU, UK

Published in the United States of America by Cambridge University Press, New York

www.cambridge.org
Information on this title: www.cambridge.org/9780521518680

First published 2010

Printed in the United Kingdom at the University Press, Cambridge

A catalogue record for this publication is available from the British Library

Library of Congress Cataloguing in Publication data
Creation and the God of Abraham / edited by David Burrell . . . [et al.].
p. cm.
ISBN 978-0-521-51868-0 (hardback)
1. Evolution – Religious aspects. 2. Cosmogony. 3. Cosmology.
4. Creationism. 5. Abrahamic religions. I. Burrell, David B. II. Title.
BL263.C79 2010
202′.4–dc22
2010002820

ISBN 978-0-521-51868-0 Hardback

Contents

Contributors

RAHIM ACAR is an associate professor of philosophy of religion at Marmara University, Divinity School. His publications include *Talking about God and Talking about Creation: Avicenna's and Thomas Aquinas' Positions* (2005), 'Avicenna' in Chad Meister and Paul Copan (eds.), *The Routledge Companion to Philosophy of Religion* (2007), pp. 107–116, and *Dinī Çoğulculuk: İdealler ve Gerçekler* (2007) (*Religious Pluralism: Ideals and Realities*; Turkish original).

ALEXANDER BROADIE is professor of logic and rhetoric at Glasgow University and fellow of the Royal Society of Edinburgh. He has published fifteen books, the majority on the Scottish philosophical tradition. They include *The Shadow of Scotus: Philosophy and Faith in Pre-Reformation Scotland* (1995) and *A History of Scottish Philosophy* (2009).

DAVID B. BURRELL, C. S. C., Theodore Hesburgh C. S. C. Professor Emeritus in Philosophy and Theology at the University of Notre Dame, serving there from 1964 to 2007, currently serves the Congregation of Holy Cross District of East Africa, as Professor of Ethics and Development at Uganda Martyrs University. He apprenticed in Jewish–Christian–Muslim understanding in Jerusalem (Tantur Ecumenical Institute) and Cairo (Dominican Institute for Oriental Studies).

CARLO COGLIATI is Spalding Fellow in Comparative Religion at Clare Hall, University of Cambridge. His research interests include modal theistic arguments in the three Abrahamic traditions; the theological significance of the notion of infinity; analogy in theology and science. He is currently working on Aquinas' metaphysics and the foundations of logic and mathematics.

SIMON CONWAY MORRIS holds the Chair in Evolutionary Palaeobiology at the University of Cambridge, and is also a Fellow of St John's College. He was elected to the Royal Society in 1990, and is the recipient of various awards and honours, including an honorary DSc from the University of Hull. He has published extensively on the Cambrian explosion, summarized in *The Crucible of Creation* (1998), and on evolutionary convergence, as documented in *Life's Solution* (Cambridge University Press, 2003). He is also actively involved in both the public understanding of science and the science/religion debates.

DANIEL DAVIES is a research associate with the Taylor-Schechter Geniza Research Unit in Cambridge. He also lectures in religious studies at Canterbury Christ Church University. His work focuses on medieval philosophy, particularly in the Arabic and Hebrew traditions. His book, *Method and Metaphysics in Maimonides's Guide*, will appear in the American Academy of Religion series *Reflection and Theory in the Study of Religion* published by Oxford University Press.

PIROOZ FATOORCHI is a researcher at the Institute for Humanities and Cultural Studies (IHCS) and teaches various graduate-level courses at the department of philosophy of science at Sharif University of Technology (Tehran, Iran). He has done research projects on comparative philosophy of religion, epistemology, philosophy of mind, as well as science and theology.

IBRAHIM KALIN is a faculty member at the Prince Alwaleed Center for Muslim–Christian Understanding, Georgetown University. As a broadly trained scholar of Islamic studies, he has published widely on Islamic philosophy and the relations between Islam and the West. His book *Knowledge in Later Islamic Philosophy: Mulla Sadra on Existence, Intellect and Intuition* (2010) analyzes Mulla Sadra's attempt to recast knowledge in terms of existence and its modalities. His *Islam and the West* (published in Turkish) has won the 2007 Writers Association of Turkey award for best book.

ERNAN McMULLIN is the Cardinal O'Hara Professor of Philosophy Emeritus and Founder Director of the Program in History and Philosophy of Science at the University of Notre Dame. He has published widely in philosophy of science, in history of science, and in topics of joint interest to Christian theology and the natural sciences. His most recent work is *The Church and Galileo* (2005).

SIMON OLIVER is Associate Professor of Systematic Theology at the University of Nottingham and a faculty member of the Centre of Theology and Philosophy. He is author of *Philosophy, God and Motion*

(2005) and *Creation's Ends: Teleology, Ethics and the Natural* (in press), and co-editor of *Theology and Religious Studies: An Exploration of Disciplinary Boundaries* (2008).

JAMES R. PAMBRUN is Professor of Systematic Theology at Saint Paul University, Ottawa, Canada. Past Dean of the Faculty, he specializes in theological hermeneutics, theological anthropology and the theology–science dialogue. Among his recent publications are 'The Generosity of Reason: Jean Ladrière, In Recognition', *Theoforum* 38 (2007), pp. 263–307. He is currently working on a theology of creation inspired by the work of the biblical exegete Paul Beauchamp.

EUGENE F. ROGERS, JR. was educated at Princeton, Tuebingen and Yale. He taught for twelve years at the University of Virginia and is now Professor of Religious Studies at the University of North Carolina at Greensboro. His books include *Thomas Aquinas and Karl Barth* (1995), *Sexuality and the Christian Body* (1999), *Theology and Sexuality* (2002), *After the Spirit* (2006) and *The Holy Spirit* (2009).

JANET M. SOSKICE is Professor of Philosophical Theology at the University of Cambridge and a Fellow of Jesus College. Past-President of both the Catholic Theological Association of Great Britain and the Society for the Study of Theology, she is the author of *Metaphor and Religious Language* (1984), *The Kindness of God* (2008) and *Sisters of Sinai* (2009).

WILLIAM R. STOEGER, S. J., is a staff scientist for the Vatican Observatory Research Group at the University of Arizona, Tucson. His present research includes theoretical cosmology and gravitational theory, and interdisciplinary studies bridging the natural sciences, philosophy and theology. He has been a key contributor to the Vatican Observatory and the Center for Theology and Natural Science's project and series, *Scientific Perspectives on Divine Action.*

THOMAS F. TRACY is Phillips Professor of Philosophy and Religious Studies at Bates College, Lewiston, Maine. His research focuses on questions about divine action, providence and the problem of evil, and he has explored the relation between these classical issues in philosophical theology and contemporary developments in the natural sciences. His writings include *God, Action, and Embodiment* (1984) and *The God Who Acts: Philosophical and Theological Explorations* (1994).

Preface

Castel Gandolfo, the venerable summer residence of popes, has for over three hundred years been home to the Vatican Observatory. In recent years the Jesuits who run this very ancient and, at the same time, very modern institution have hosted successive gatherings of scholars exploring the interrelations between science and faith. It was during one of these that William Stoeger, S. J., and Janet Soskice got to speaking about *creatio ex nihilo*. This teaching, central to the theology of the early and medieval Church, is crucial to the traditional doctrine of God and not in any way in tension with modern science, yet its potency and sophistication, we considered, has been strangely overlooked by the modern science and religion dialogue. A conference seemed called for. *Creatio ex nihilo* has the further advantage of being a place of convergence for all the religions of radical monotheism. Because of this, Bill and Janet immediately thought to ask David Burrell, C. S. C., to be part of the planning team. David was delighted at the opportunity to bring Jewish, Christian and Muslim scholars together – philosophers as well as theologians and scientists. Carlo Cogliati's gracious response to our invitation to be *amanuensis* for the group assured genial proceedings, as his introduction displays so well.

Our hope was that bringing astute thinkers from Judaism, Christianity and Islam around a common table – some of them old hands at science and religion debates and others not – would help restore the dialectical interaction of faith and reason proper to each of these traditions. Our hopes were met beyond our wildest expectations, largely due to the composition of the group itself and the stunning setting of the Vatican Observatory whose historical gravity and sheer beauty decidedly enhanced our reflections on creation. The hospitality of the resident Jesuit community of the Vatican Observatory, especially that of the then director, Fr George Coyne, S. J., assured that our conversations would be undertaken in a receptive atmosphere.

As it turned out, Jewish and Christian interlocutors proved to be somewhat older than the Muslims, yet significant differences in age or experience made little difference to our conversations. The editors asked that the final chapters reflect the discussions of the week to allow readers to profit from our explorations, properly revised for publication. Carlo Cogliati is very much to be thanked for the bulk of the work pulling the volume together so beautifully. We also make honourable mention of Oliver Soskice, for editorial assistance at a critical moment.

Before turning readers over to the feast prepared for them, we need to announce a proper *kadish* for Professor Peter Lipton who with his wife and intellectual companion, Dr Diana Lipton, graced our gathering but was himself taken from us suddenly before the volume could be completed. May the God of Abraham be with them and with the other participants of these graced days.

DAVID B. BURRELL
AND
JANET M. SOSKICE

Introduction

Carlo Cogliati

BACKGROUND TO THE VOLUME

Creatio ex nihilo is a foundational teaching in Judaism, Christianity and Islam. It states that God created the world out of nothing – from no pre-existent matter, no space or time. This teaching is the linchpin for classical accounts of divine action, free will, grace, theodicy, religious language, intercessory prayer and questions of divine eternity – in short, the foundation for any account of a scriptural God who acts in history but yet remains the transcendent Creator of all that is.

This book is the planned outcome of a workshop on '*Creatio ex Nihilo* Today' held at Castel Gandolfo, Italy, on 9–15 July 2006, and sponsored solely by the Vatican Observatory. That consultation brought together some fourteen leading scholars of all three Abrahamic faiths to reflect on the metaphysical and theological ideas of the doctrine of *creatio ex nihilo* in light of contemporary developments in modern sciences. Each speaker was directed to a particular topic by the organisers – Bill Stoeger, S. J. (Vatican Observatory), Professor Janet Soskice (Cambridge) and Professor David Burrell, C. S. C. (Notre Dame) – and all followed their brief in presenting more questions than answers. After the conference, all participants were asked to reflect and to elaborate on the discussions their topic had raised among the delegates, and to produce a scholarly article. This collection is the final product; it explores how we might now recover a place for the doctrine, and with it a consistent defence of the God of Abraham in philosophical, scientific and theological terms.

The very involvement of Jewish and Muslim researchers, as well as Christians, in a volume of this sort is unique. The chapters cover the early patristic background, the medieval debate, modern science, and the sticking points for contemporary theology and the science/religion discussion. They can be broadly divided into three areas – historical, scientific and theological – although all the chapters aim to be in dialogue with each other in terms of different faith traditions, and across different disciplinary boundaries.

SUMMARY OF THE CHAPTERS

In 'Creation *ex nihilo*: early history', Ernan McMullin argues that the doctrine of creation from nothing only gradually took shape over more than a thousand years. He proposes to sketch in broad outline some of the main features of that long gestation period. In the Old Testament the primary focus was on salvation history, on Yahweh's covenant with Israel, and not on cosmogony or on Yahweh's role as the cosmic creator. The theologians of the early Christian Church had to face a challenge that the biblical writers had not been presented with. Various philosophical views took the presence in the world of evils of all sorts as a premise for a dualism that would set limits on God's creative power. The Fathers gradually came to realize that implicit in the Scriptures lay a rejection of any such limits. Relying primarily on the Bible, they formulated a doctrine of the Creator as all-powerful, and rejected the view that over and against Him there had been from the beginning an ungenerated principle – matter – independent of Him (the Neoplatonic view), or lesser perfect beings that were responsible for the imperfections in the world (the Gnostic view). It is with Augustine, McMullin claims, that the biblically inspired metaphysics of creation came to be fully *ex nihilo*: there is nothing that could serve as material for it; God is the Creator of all things together, to create is to create from nothing.

Janet Soskice's chapter draws our attention to the Jewish and Christian origins of the doctrine of creation *ex nihilo*. It shares McMullin's view that the Book of Genesis and the Hebrew Scriptures are little concerned with questions of metaphysics and of cosmology. The creation narratives are more concerned to establish the relationships of the people of Israel to God and to each other than to lay down a philosophical or physical account of the origin of the universe. Soskice argues that the doctrine is a response by Jewish and Christian writers of the first and second centuries AD to the Greek consensus that 'from nothing nothing comes', which threatened not only the biblical understanding of origin, but also the teaching on divine freedom and sovereignty. She shows how Hellenistic Judaism, and in particular Philo of Alexandria, plays a crucial role in such a response by repeatedly linking the metaphysical account of the creation of the world out of non-being with the biblical account of Exodus 3 where God names Himself to Moses as Being-itself.

In his chapter, David Burrell investigates the theological consequences of the act of creation by discussing Aquinas' strategy on this very matter. He shows how Aquinas invokes the Neoplatonic distinction between essential and participated being to give everything but the Creator the stamp of created: 'All things other than God are not their own existence but share in existence.' However, creation is not a mere overflow from the One, it is rather an intentional emanating, and so a gracious and gratuitous gift. For Burrell the notions of participation and analogy play a key role in understanding Aquinas' doctrine of creation, and the consequent relation between the Creator and the *creatum*. The author finds the notion of 'non-duality' very helpful to explicate such a relation: '[Every] subsistent effect is dependent on its cause for its very existence as a subsistent entity, whereas the cause is in no way dependent on the effect for its subsistence.'

Alexander Broadie's contribution, 'Scotistic metaphysics and creation *ex nihilo*', asks whether the religious claim that God created the world out of nothing is compatible with the Enlightenment claim that we human beings are world-makers. On the one hand, the author turns to Scotus to show that the world is a performance executed by the will of God and, like any performance, it lasts for only as long as the performer wills it to continue (i.e., there is no distinction in reality between creation and conservation). On the other hand, he turns to the insights of Hume and Kant to claim that certain of our mental powers have a mediating role in the process of the creation (i.e., we co-operate with God in the production of our world). The two claims – the doctrine of creation *ex nihilo*, and human beings as world-makers – are shown not to be mutually exclusive in so far as our world is the outcome of the exercise of our mental apparatus in response to a divine idea presented to us.

Daniel Davies discusses the Jewish tradition, and in particular Maimonides and Crescas. The author explains some of the common themes that run through their attitudes towards creation and the sciences. First, he argues that both thinkers subscribe to the doctrine of creation *ex nihilo* and place great importance on the notion that everything in existence depends upon God, and that dependence is non-reciprocal since God is in no way dependent on anything at all. Second, he shows that Crescas rejects Aristotelian science when certain claims (e.g., that place and space are equivalent) cannot be established with sufficient clarity, and bases his beliefs concerning what is physically possible, much more so than Maimonides, on ideas taken from theology. Finally he claims that there is, however, a common methodological approach: both are concerned to accept only theological positions which they can prove to be scientifically acceptable on science's own terms. Their attitude of respect for scientific enquiry may serve as a relevant model today in many discussions between science and religion.

Three chapters cover the Islamic tradition. Rahim Acar describes Avicenna's account of creation as one explaining the existence of the whole universe. The prime mover, first cause of motion, becomes the necessary being, first cause of existence. For Avicenna, creation as the existential relationship between God and the universe contradicts the idea of beginning to exist after non-existence. The author shows how this claim is supported by Avicenna's conception of the relationship between causes and effects (the principle of co-existence) which holds between the Creator and the *creatum*, and by his conception of the nature of things with regard to duration (the sempiternity of the universe). He then tries to show that this position, which favours the eternity of the world, may be compatible with the modern cosmological account of the Big Bang. The question of compatibility between the doctrine of creation *ex nihilo* and alternative accounts of the origin of the universe is explicitly addressed by Pirooz Fatoorchi's contribution. He examines four different conceptions of creation among Islamic philosophers and *kalam* theologians (temporal-historical, essential non-temporal, objective meta-temporal and substantive temporal non-historical). He then asks whether each of those conceptions is consistent with seven different accounts of the origin of the universe (five philosophical/theological, and two physical). The responses to those questions are the findings of his chapter. Ibrahim Kalin discusses the debate in the Islamic philosophical tradition of questioning why God created the world. According to the necessitarian model of creation, God created out of necessity in the sense that a perfect and infinitely good being cannot be conceived of existing only by and for itself. According to the libertarian or voluntarist model, God created because He chose to, and there is no further explanation to be offered. The author suggests that this dichotomous framework of necessity and volition can be overcome if we turn to Mulla Sadra's account of creation in terms of monistic theophany, an ontology of creation that begins with existence and ends with it. Both permanence and change are reduced to one single principle – existence – through a sophisticated and structured ontology to guarantee the present world order in which God acts as the direct agent of existentiation and as indirect agent of change through intermediaries.

In 'Trinity, motion and creation *ex nihilo*', Simon Oliver offers a very interesting account of creation out of nothing building on considerations of motion in relation to the divine processions and to the process of emanation. He argues that for Aquinas the principle of natural motion is analogically related to the eternal dynamism of the Trinity. Motion is not a wedge between *creatum* and Creator, but the means of creation's participation in the divine. He then shows that von Balthasar moves beyond Aquinas in describing both motion and creation as related by analogy to the eternal kenosis within the Trinitarian Godhead. Finally, he contrasts this understanding of motion, creation and Trinitarian life with the theology and cosmology of Newton. The author of the *Principia Mathematica* cannot conceive a creation out of nothing because he subscribes to an understanding of God as a single, monadic deity devoid of any relationality. The consequence is that creation – as a metaphysical and theological doctrine – stands outside the realm of reason, whereas the natural sciences are the instantiation of an inscrutable divine will and the subject of natural philosophy. This also entails a clear-cut separation between faith and reason, which had much influence in the years to follow, continuing right up to modern times.

William Stoeger, in 'The Big Bang, quantum cosmology and *creatio ex nihilo*', aims to show that the doctrine of creation out of nothing is a complementary, and not an alternative, understanding to the scientific origin of the universe, and of reality in general. First, he briefly describes the basic ideas and findings about our universe which astronomers have uncovered in recent years. Second, he argues that physics and cosmology as we know and practise them can shed a great deal of light on many questions having to do with the origin of the universe, but they are in principle incapable of providing ultimate explanations of existence and order. Lastly, he claims that such explanations are provided by the metaphysical doctrine of creation *ex nihilo*. The Creator is the fundamental source of all being and order, in whom all existing things participate. He is the necessary condition for everything, and the sufficient condition for nothing. Events and changes occur only through the created, or secondary, causes which the Creating Primary Cause sustains. Thus, Big Bang theory, quantum cosmology and creation *ex nihilo* contribute complementary and consonant levels of understanding of the reality in which we are immersed.

Simon Conway Morris asks the following question: 'What is written into creation?' Although creation *ex nihilo* as metaphysical doctrine is simply not open to scientific explorations, he argues that we are entitled to look for consistencies, such as the Big Bang and the anthropic principles of fine-tuning. He then suggests that all attempts to understand one of the most difficult and complex realities, consciousness, from a purely scientific, naturalistic or reductionistic perspective will fail. However, if we accept the proposal that there is a mental world and that the brain is 'the antenna' that makes first contact with it, then not only do we have access to new realities, but we find a world where theological discourse is not divorced from, but integral to, scientific enquiry. A world that accepts the supernatural both visible and invisible (to us), and one that is only explicable by the agency of creation *ex nihilo*.

The issue of double agency is addressed by James Pambrun. The author aims to develop a way of approaching the question of dual causality (i.e., how can we have two agents causing the same effect?) that allows an encounter to take place between theology and science with respect to the doctrine of creation *ex nihilo*. First, some historical considerations of the three main stages in the development of scientific inference – deductive, inductive and retroductive inference – can provide a more critical precision to the notion of causality. Second, the notion of verified intelligibility can further enrich the notion of causality as structural explanation of our world: the world is what is affirmed in light of the fulfilling conditions to be met given the form of intelligible relations configured by a scientific discipline. Finally, scientific enquiry and theological discourse meet when the very foundation, the very intelligibility of reality, becomes a topic for consideration in its own right. Thus, the metaphysical notion of creation *ex nihilo* speaks to the inherent intelligibility of existence as a property of every created thing in a constructive dialogue with both science and theology.

In his chapter, Thomas Tracy investigates the theological implications of the doctrine of creation *ex nihilo* for the relation of God's creative action and the diverse activity of created things. Creation out of nothing seems to entail that God alone is causally efficacious, and that the activity of creatures serves only as the occasion for divine action. If so, then it appears that there is no role for finite causes in accounting for the way things are. The challenge of this 'occasionalism' (defended both by certain Islamic and by certain Christian thinkers) can be met by the traditional distinction between primary and secondary causality. The author shows that this distinction, although helpful, needs to be modified to deal with a more complex picture of the world God has made, one which includes some events that occur by (ontological) chance. Creation out of nothing seems also to preclude creaturely freedom. On the one hand the answer offered by theological incompatibilism (human action is not free if it is determined by God) raises questions about God's sovereignty; on the other hand the answer by theological compatibilism (human action can be both free and determined by God) makes God the agent of all evil. Tracy suggests that creation *ex nihilo* may point to a third way, one which does not treat God as part of the causal nexus in which we worry about determinism and freedom, but considers God as the transcendent agent who continuously brings into being both determining efficient causes and chance events and free rational agents. In this way, a single event can simultaneously be ascribed to the activity of God and that of a free agent without raising any theological worries.

In the last contribution of this book, Eugene Rogers suggests approaching Aquinas through the topics which interest him most: a theology of science based on how human beings 'come to know'. For Rogers, Aquinas develops an account of science as discovery not from Aristotle's *epagoge*, but from his ethics, which contains his account of learning from contingency, even failure, and error. Christianity – the author claims – needs to recover a sense that natural sciences can be regarded as a religious activity. Science becomes a metaphor for heaven, a participation in the divinity. Science is a habit, a disposition of the mind. Imperfect science obtains when the earthly habit learns from contingency; perfect science obtains when the heavenly habit knows with God's own vision. The transformation from one to the other depends on the incarnation of the Son and the Grace of the Holy Spirit. Hence, the Trinity brings human beings into participation with its own activity when they come to know. That 'the invisible things of God can be known from the things God has made' warrants arguments both in cosmology and in Christology. For both, the more revealed it is, the more scientific it is. All science considers inaccessible things made accessible. And so, even the doctrine of creation *ex nihilo* has a Trinitarian deep structure: it expresses the intimacy of God to things He has created without compromise, as befits the incarnation of the Word.

INTRODUCTORY REMARKS

As we will see from the chapters in this volume, *creatio ex nihilo* was not a concept available to Greek philosophy. Aristotle thought the idea was incoherent. His conviction that 'from nothing, nothing comes' led him to insist that the universe was everlasting. His 'God' was not personal, but indifferent to human affairs, or rather, not capable of being interested in the world of chance and change. Aristotle's God was an Intelligence, a source of intelligibility but entirely incapable of awareness of, and concern with, the affairs of the created world.

Creatio ex nihilo was the product of the confluence of biblical teaching and Hellenistic Judaism, and was the means by which theologians of the early Church defended the God they saw to be revealed in Scripture: loving, living and active. The doctrine was embraced by both Jewish and Islamic medieval thinkers, and refined by Aquinas. It is understood as the ultimate ontological dependence of the existence of all things upon God as its cause, of all that which is created out of nothing upon the Creator. It is also understood as a relation:

> Creation puts a reality into a created thing only as a relation. For to be created is not to be produced through a motion or mutation ... Creation in the creature is left just as a relation to the Creator as the origin of its existence ... In its active sense creation means God's action, which is his essence with a relationship to the creature. But this in God is not a real relation, but only conceptual. The relation of the creature to God, however, is real.[1]

Thus, *creatio ex nihilo* is a metaphysical concept, not a physical event; it accounts for the existence of things, not for the change in things. This understanding of creation as a non-reciprocal relation of dependence – real from the creature's side, conceptual from God's side – allows one to reconcile the passive and the active meaning of the creative act. It establishes a true link between the finitude and the contingency of the *creatum* and the infinity and the necessity of the *Creator*, between the temporality of the world and the eternality of God. This link is rooted in Aquinas' metaphysics of being upon which the existence (*esse*) of all creatures, and their essence (*essentia*), become an 'actual existing' in relation to the Creator (*esse ad Creatorem*). By means of this existential act (*actus essendi*), God can be in an intimate relation with the created universe because 'for all things He is properly the universal cause of existence, which is innermost in all things. For this reason in sacred Scriptures the workings of nature are referred to God as to the one who works within it: "*Thou hast clothed me with skin and flesh: Thou hast put me together with bones and sinews.*"'[2,3] 'All things other than God are not their own existence, but share in existence'[4] not denying, but rather affirming His sovereignty.

The doctrine was largely taken for granted until the early modern period, when it became simply ignored or misunderstood by both scientists and philosophers, as theologians shied away from metaphysics in order to align themselves with empirical science. More recently, Darwin's theory of evolution has been taken to contradict the biblical account

[1] Aquinas, *Summa Theologiae* I.45.3; cf. also *Summa contra Gentiles* II, ch. 18; *De Potentia* III.3.

[2] Job 10:11.

[3] Aquinas, *Summa Theologiae* I.105.5. In a similar way, the Qur'an describes God as 'closer to you than your jugular vein'.

[4] Aquinas, *Summa Theologiae* I.44.1.

of creation, since its cause, natural selection, is a random process which leaves no room for divine action or intelligent design in nature. In response, certain scientists and theologians have claimed that there are certain features of life which are 'irreducibly complex', and which could not possibly be caused by natural selection. These life forms and these gaps in nature – they continue – lead us to affirm the existence of an intelligent designer and of a special act of creation. Evolutionism on the one hand and creationism on the other have come to stand for two opposing and mutually exclusive world views.[5] For some, to subscribe to evolutionism is to assert a purely scientific and secular stance. For others, to support creationism is to express religious fundamentalism and blind fideism. From the chapters in this volume it will become clear that this contrast is the result of a common confusion. Reductive evolutionists fail to distinguish between biological and philosophical explanations. And creation is first of all a metaphysical doctrine, not a scientific theory. Supporters of intelligent design and special creation argue that divine agency will manifest in the gaps of nature. But gaps of nature are still within the domain of the natural sciences, whereas the creative act ought to be seen in a proper theological perspective. Such a contrast can be overcome if we integrate the insights of *creatio ex nihilo* with our scientific understanding of life. That God created all things out of nothing leaves open the possibilities of evolutionary mechanisms like random mutation and natural selection. God's project of creation can be carried out through secondary causes, without having to posit some miraculous intervention in this or that direction to fill the gaps of nature. No biological explanation of any evolutionary theory can undermine the biblical account of creation. God's creative act exemplifies divine omnipotence and gratuitous love, and at the same time it affirms the integrity and the autonomy of the created world.

In a similar fashion, the Big Bang theory, with its idea that the universe emerged about 14 billion years ago, has been taken to confirm scientifically the revealed truth that the world has a temporal beginning in need of a divine outside agency. The physical sciences seem therefore to warrant theology. But, once again, there is a misunderstanding of the very terms in play. Creation accounts for the existence of things, not for the beginning

[5] For a detailed and illuminating discussion of these issues, see William E. Carroll, 'Creation, Evolution, and Thomas Aquinas', *Revue des Questions Scientifiques* 171:4 (2000), pp. 319–347. Here I just recall some of his findings.

of things. For Aquinas, that the universe depends for its existence upon a primary cause which is not prior in time but prior in the order of things is the conclusion of a demonstrative argument: 'Not only does faith hold that there is creation but reason also demonstrates it.'[6] But that the created world began to exist (*in principio*) or that it has always existed (*ab aeterno*) cannot be resolved demonstratively.[7] No valid inference about the nature of something in its original stage can be made from the way it is in its final form, and we only have knowledge of the final state of the world. In other words, Aquinas (following Maimonides) offers a demonstration of the undecidability of the age of the universe. And if the age of the universe is not a decidable claim, then there is no contradiction in saying that the world is either temporally or eternally created. It is by faith, and not by reason, that one knows that the world has a temporal beginning.

It becomes obvious then that the doctrine of *creatio ex nihilo* does not contradict evolutionary biology in any way, nor does it receive confirmation from contemporary cosmology. Recent developments in both disciplines raise questions of ultimacy and purpose, neither of which can be answered by science in principle. In fact all the sciences encounter similar limits – in that nothing they investigate completely explains itself. The point here is that contemporary culture, though dominated by the natural and the physical sciences, has rediscovered the need for a metaphysical account which complements our best scientific understanding of the universe we live in. The aim of this volume is to identify such an account with *creatio ex nihilo*, which we find to be also consonant with the biblical revelation of the God of Abraham.

[6] *Scriptum super libros Sententiarum* II.I.I.2, solutio.

[7] Aquinas, *Summa Theologiae* I.46.I–2.

CHAPTER I

Creation ex nihilo*: early history*

Ernan McMullin

INTRODUCTION

That God created the universe 'from nothing' (*ex nihilo*) has been a distinctive Christian claim almost from the beginning. The phrase is, on the face of it, an odd one: it is as though 'nothing' were a sort of ghostly raw material for the divine act of creating. But the '*ex nihilo*' phrase long ago was accepted as a shorthand way of saying: 'from no prior materials'. The doctrine itself only gradually took shape over more than a thousand years. In this chapter, I propose to sketch in broad outline some of the main features of that long gestation period. It lends itself readily to a threefold division: creation in the Old Testament; creation *ex nihilo* in the early Christian Church; creation of 'all together' in St Augustine.

CREATION IN THE OLD TESTAMENT

The majestic chapters with which the Bible opens could easily give the impression that cosmogony, the question of cosmic origins, was of major concern from the beginning to the writers of the Old Testament. But this was by no means the case.[1] The two 'creation' chapters date from very different periods of Israel's history.[2] Genesis 2, much the older, dates back perhaps as far as the tenth-century-BC Israel of David and Solomon. It deals primarily with the origin of man and woman, and the role of Yahweh in their making. Though Yahweh is said to have already made the heavens and the earth, nothing more is added about cosmic origins. The earth at first is arid, waiting for rain and human toil, and then the waters come and Yahweh makes man from the dust of the earth. Next comes the story of the Garden

[1] Dianne Bergant and Carroll Stuhlmueller, 'Creation according to the Old Testament' in Ernan McMullin (ed.), *Evolution and Creation* (University of Notre Dame Press, 1985), pp. 153–175.

[2] P. R. Ackroyd and C. F. Evans (eds.), *The Cambridge History of the Bible: From the Beginnings to Jerome* (Cambridge University Press, 1970), pp. 74–75.

of Eden and the making of woman. In the chapters that follow, the story continues with the Fall and the expulsion from the Garden.

There are similarities between Genesis 2–11 and the Babylonian *Atrahasis* epic, suggesting that the author of these Genesis chapters may have made use of the Babylonian source, while reworking it in order to make a series of theological points about the special relationship between Yahweh and human beings, about the relationship of the sexes and about how sin entered the world.[3] The focus of these chapters is clearly theological, not historical, and certainly not cosmological. There is already a hint of the creation theme, but no more than that. And the aside about the heavens and the earth could conceivably have been added by the later editor as a way of linking Chapter 2 to the newly added Chapter 1.

Yahweh is a constant presence in the chronicles of Israel's early history: the covenant with Abraham, the escape from Egypt, the entry into Canaan, the reign of David. He appears there not as a cosmic creator, however, but as a devoted protector of the people He had chosen as His own, a people who had to be forcefully reminded on occasion of what His favour had meant for their ancestors. The narrative centres on the relationship between Yahweh and Israel; that is what mattered above all else.[4] So long as His powers were sufficient for the great acts that marked His guardianship of Israel, that was sufficient.

In some of the earliest psalms, however, the theme of creation makes a dramatic appearance, in language that suggests a degree of Canaanite influence:[5]

> Yahweh, our Lord,
> How great your name throughout the earth!
> Above the heavens is your majesty chanted ...
> I look up at the heavens, made by your fingers,
> at the moon and stars you set in place –
> Ah! What is man that You should spare a thought for him ...[6]

Or again:

> The heavens declare the glory of God, the vault of heaven proclaims
> his handiwork.

[3] Richard J. Clifford, S. J., 'Creation in the Hebrew Bible' in R. J. Russell, W. R. Stoeger and G. V. Coyne (eds.), *Physics, Philosophy, and Theology: A Common Quest for Understanding* (Vatican Observatory Publications, 1988), pp. 151–170.

[4] B. W. Anderson (ed.), *Creation in the Old Testament: Issues in Religion and Theology* (Philadelphia, PA: Fortress, 1984).

[5] Carroll Stuhlmueller, *Psalms I and II* (Wilmington, DE: Glazier, 1983).

[6] Psalm 8:2–4. The translation here and later is from the Jerusalem Bible.

Day discourses of it to day, night to night hands on the knowledge.
No utterance at all, no speech, no sound that anyone can hear.
Yet their voice goes out throughout all the earth,
and their message to the ends of the world.[7]

And others: 'The voice of Yahweh over the waters' (Psalm 29:3); 'The heavens are yours and the earth is yours' (Psalm 89:11); 'You stretch out the heavens like a tent' (Psalm 104:3).

This is not the god of a small desert people, one god among many in a region where each tribe worshipped its own pantheon. No pantheon here, however, but a unique being who lays claim to heavens and earth, to the power of cosmic creation that sets Him apart from all others. Only such a being could have brought about the wonders that have marked off the history of Israel. Only such a being could have spoken to Moses as He did, from the burning bush or from the heights of Sinai. His name, and no other, should go out to all the earth.

A tension is beginning to show itself here between what some have called the 'inside' and the 'outside' theology of Israel.[8] On the one hand, there is the particularity of the calling of Israel, the overthrow of Israel's foes, the promise to Israel of the lands of others. Yahweh is above all *Israel's* God. On the other, there is the implicit universality of the creation theme. Yahweh is the God of all the earth, of all the nations, the God to whom all owe homage, the God who cares for all His creatures. Should Israel share Yahweh, then, with other nations? How is Israel to retain its favoured status as the nation dearer to Yahweh than all others? That tension will continue to haunt the later works of the Old Testament.

The trauma of the sixth-century-BC Babylonian exile called for reassurance on the part of the Israelites that Yahweh had not forsaken them entirely. Surely this chaos could not prevail? It is from this period that the great first chapter of Genesis dates. The literature of Babylon itself may have influenced some elements in its composition.[9] The ancient *Enuma Elish* told of how the universe began from a chaos of waters, how the gods themselves then came to be from the waters, how Marduk gained supremacy among the gods, how he separated heavens and earth, and how he finally brought order to the gods in heaven and to those who worship him on earth. The theologians of exilic and post-exilic Israel could reflect on their own

[7] Psalm 19:1–4.

[8] Donald Senior and Carroll Stuhlmueller, *Biblical Foundations of Mission* (Maryknoll, NY: Orbis, 1983), pp. 15–32.

[9] Clifford, 'Creation in the Hebrew Bible', pp. 152–154.

traditions and ask how Yahweh's people should tell their own story of cosmic origins, one in which Yahweh would play a role more in keeping with the mysterious 'I Am Who Am' of the response long before to Moses' query.

The emphasis of the six-day narrative is above all on Yahweh's role in the establishment of order, in the overcoming of darkness and of the chaos of the primal waters, in the making fertile of the earth, in the making of sun and moon not as gods but as a means of ordering time, in filling the seas and the land with living kinds, and finally in the making of humans after Yahweh's own image. There is no hint in all this of any limit to Yahweh's power or of any defect in the world thus brought about. Rather, at each step, the Lord surveys His handiwork and 'sees that it is good'. His people must not then despair; their God has overcome chaos before and can be counted on once again, this time to overcome the lesser chaos of captivity.

The Old Latin translation of the opening verse, perhaps reflecting the conviction of a later time, ran: 'In the beginning, God created the heavens and the earth. And the earth was a formless void.' Not surprisingly, this was taken in the early Church to affirm that God's act of creating was *ex nihilo*, that there was nothing before heavens and earth appeared other than the Creator Himself. And the retention of this version in the long-authoritative Vulgate translation strengthened this impression. But exegetical opinion today would favour a significantly different translation: 'In the beginning, *when* God created the heavens and the earth, the earth was a formless wasteland and darkness covered the abyss, while a mighty wind swept *over the waters*.'[10] The waters were apparently already there; there is no mention of them having been created. It was from them, through God's creative action, that the heavens and the earth emerged.[11] On the second day, a vault is created to divide the waters themselves, where the waters seem to be represented as a separate pre-existing entity.

Still, the 'Let there be' of the 'Let there be light', 'Let there be a vault', 'Let there be lights in the vault of heaven' could certainly be understood as summoning into existence rather than fashioning from something pre-existent. On the other hand, the creative acts of the remaining days do mention the materials out of which the newly created appear: 'Let the dry land appear [from the waters]'; 'Let the waters teem'; 'Let the earth

10 New American Bible. A similar translation can be found in *The Torah: A New Translation of the Holy Scriptures according to the Masoretic Text* (Philadelphia, PA: Jewish Publications, 1962); reference from Bergant and Stuhlmueller, 'Creation according to the Old Testament', p. 153.

11 Bergant and Stuhlmueller, 'Creation according to the Old Testament', p. 153 and p. 159.

produce'. It seems fair to say that the evidence for creation *ex nihilo* in these chapters is at best ambiguous. There are hints here of the doctrine but it will take a later generation to develop them further when the *ex nihilo* character of creation for the first time will become an issue.

In the Wisdom literature of this same late period, affirmations of Yahweh's creative powers became more frequent. Wisdom herself is represented as Yahweh's first creation:

> Yahweh created me when his purpose first unfolded, before the oldest of his works.
> From everlasting I was firmly set,
> From the beginning, before the earth came into being ...
> When he fixed the heavens firm, I was there ...
> When he assigned the sea its boundaries, I was by his side, like a confidant ...
> Delighting him day by day.[12]

Perhaps the most emphatic statement of His creative powers comes in Job where Yahweh responds to Job's accusations:

> Where were you when I laid the earth's foundations?
> Tell me, since you are so well-informed.
> Who decided the dimensions of it, do you know? ...
> Who pent up the sea behind closed doors? ...
> Come thus far, I said, and no farther, here your proud waves shall break.
> Have you ever given orders to the morning or sent the dawn to its post ...?
> Can you fasten the harness of the *Pleiades*, or untie Orion's bonds?
> Can you guide the morning star season by season?
> And show the Bear and its cubs where to go?
> Have you grasped the celestial laws? Could you make their writ run on earth?[13]

Attributing this statement to Yahweh himself heightens the solemnity of the affirmation it makes. By this time, the celebration of Yahweh's universal claim had become far more pronounced than it had been in the days of the patriarchs. There had been ample time to reflect on the implications of Yahweh's role in Israel's own history, what it portended for the dignity of their Lord. Prodded no doubt by their interactions with the nations whose histories had so long been entangled with theirs, the representatives of the

[12] Proverbs 68:22–23; 68:27; 68:29–30. The alternative 'like a confidant' seems preferable to the 'like a craftsman' of the Jerusalem Bible.

[13] Job 38:4–5; 38:8; 38:11–13; 38:31–33.

people of Israel had to make it quite clear that Yahweh was not to be compared with the gods of these other nations: Yahweh dwelt on another plane entirely, the single creator of all that is, claiming sovereignty over all nations, the only true God.

The closest to an explicit reference to the cosmic creation's being *ex nihilo* comes in 2 Maccabees, a late work (second century BC), where a tormented mother addresses her remaining son: 'Observe heaven and earth, consider all that is in them, and acknowledge that Yahweh made them out of what did not exist' (7:28). As it stands, this does seem like creation *ex nihilo*, but there is some doubt as to how this last phrase is to be understood, as well as to whether, on the authority of this phrase alone, one could say that the understanding in Israel of Yahweh's creative act had moved this step further.

No mention has been made so far of the New Testament. Apart from a couple of conventional references on Paul's part to God as the maker of heaven and earth (Acts of the Apostles 14:15; 17:24), the writers of the New Testament nowhere touch on the theme of creation. It seems fair to conclude that the question of whether the work of cosmic creation had proceeded *ex nihilo* had not been of particular theological concern to the biblical writers generally. After all, much of the work of creation in Genesis had clearly made use of existing materials, like the eliciting of the first vegetation from the earth or the moulding of the first human body from the dust. Whether other of the Creator's actions in setting in place the beginning world had been in fact *ex nihilo* was a question that had simply not yet called for an explicit answer. But the time for one would eventually come.

CREATION *EX NIHILO* IN THE EARLY CHURCH

The theologians of the early Christian Church faced a challenge that the biblical writers had not known. The religion of Israel had not been a missionary one: there was no incentive to make it intellectually acceptable to potential converts. Nor had there been a wider intellectual culture in possession in whose terms the religious thinkers of Israel might have been led to express the tenets of their faith. Matters would be very different for the heralds of the new Christian faith. To begin with, theirs was an essentially missionary undertaking. But the Roman world in which they were beginning to make their way was informed by a new cultural phenomenon: philosophical world views of Greek origin that claimed to rest on reason and argument rather than on tradition and faith. In this new situation, creeds would have to develop into theologies; indeed, one might almost say that it was in this situation that theology itself as a discipline was born.

Among the Greek philosophical systems, two in particular had taken root in the Roman world. The first was Platonism. It appealed to the Romans because of the literary attraction of its expression and the coherence and persuasiveness of its world view. What matters to us here is its cosmogony. In the *Timaeus*, Plato presents an account of how the world came to be, in the form of a myth or likely story. From the mathematical intelligibility and hence accessibility to Reason of some features of the sense-world, he infers the existence of a Demiurge who shaped that world according to Reason, imposing order on a Receptacle which is in some fashion resistant. Its 'shaking' makes it a source of defect and also of change which as a departure from the perfection of the Form is a sign of imperfection. The Demiurge cannot, therefore, be held responsible for the presence of defect within the world we humans inhabit. It is attributable to the recalcitrance of the material with which the Demiurge had perforce to work.

The other philosophical system was Stoicism which, though Greek in origin, flourished more especially in the Rome of the first and second centuries. For the Stoics, only bodies exist. They are constituted by two principles: a matter-principle which is inert, and God who is immanent in the world itself and acts as a fire, an intelligence, shaping world history as Fate. All things begin in a fire that contains the seeds of all that will later develop, and will end in fire in a cycle of eternal recurrence. The Stoic God worked, as it were, from within where the Platonic Demiurge worked from without.

There was much about these philosophies to which Christians could comfortably relate. Above all, their adherents had turned away from the extended pantheon of the older Roman tradition to assert the primacy of a single God, supreme and all-shaping. But for the Platonists and Stoics alike, there was a second principle over against God, not of God's making, and apparently even resistant to some extent to God's action. How was this to be reconciled with the God of the biblical tradition? This was a question that was bound to arise at some point for those Christians of the second and third centuries AD who took the contribution of philosophy to world view seriously. Gerhard May puts it succinctly: what led finally to the making explicit of the doctrine of creation *ex nihilo* was 'the attempt to do justice to the absolute sovereignty and unlimited freedom of the biblical God acting in history'.[14] To that extent, it might be said that these theologians would have seen themselves as merely drawing out what had been already implicit in the biblical account.

[14] Gerhard May, *Creatio ex Nihilo: The Doctrine of 'Creation out of Nothing' in Early Christian Thought*, trans. A. S. Worrall (Edinburgh: T&T Clark, 1994), p. viii.

Besides the impetus given by the Greek philosophical systems, there was one other development in the Roman world of the second century that was also instrumental in forcing Christian thinkers to clarify their doctrine of creation. This was the growth of Gnosticism, generally taken to have had an Eastern origin.[15] The Gnostics viewed the material world in overwhelmingly negative terms. It was something to be escaped from or, in one way or another, overcome. It could not, therefore, be the work of the supreme God. Most Gnostic theologians attributed the origin of the material world to lesser beings who, though themselves of God's making, were inimical to him. Some, however, saw matter as a primal darkness, a chaos over which God had only limited sway in bringing the world to be.

Gnosticism posed an even more direct challenge to the Christians who were trying to define themselves in this new and turbulent context. Yet it also attracted many of them by its call to asceticism and its rejection of the clearly ungodly features of the everyday world. Some prominent Gnostic theologians, like Basilides and Valentinus, regarded themselves as Christians who drew on the Old and New Testaments but who believed that these had to be supplemented by a further *gnosis* regarding the dark powers, the archons, that were responsible for so much that went awry in human society. Marcion went further. One must look to Christ for salvation but the God whom Christ preached was not the same as the God of the Old Testament, the Demiurge responsible for a defective, ultimately evil, world. The good God has created an invisible world to which the true followers of Christ must aspire.

Oddly, it would seem that it is to Basilides in the mid-second century that we owe the first quite explicit formulation of the doctrine of creation *ex nihilo* that has come down to us.[16] Unlike his fellow Gnostics, he portrays God as the Creator of all that is; there is no co-existent or defective matter over against Him. God is so far beyond any human ways of making requiring a pre-existent material that limits their product that His creating must be supposed to be *ex nihilo*. But in other respects, Basilides' teaching stayed within the broadly Gnostic tradition, meaning that his doctrinal innovation with regard to the nature of God's creation would have no immediate effect on more orthodox Christian theologians.

[15] 'A straight historical explanation of the emergence of Gnosticism and its view of the world does not seem to be possible.' May, *Creatio ex Nihilo*, p. 49. See also G. Quispel, 'Gnostic Man: The Doctrine of Basilides', *Gnostic Studies* I (1974), pp. 103–133.

[16] May, *Creatio ex Nihilo*, pp. 83–84. See also Quispel, 'Gnostic Man'.

Only in the second half of the second century did Christian theologians who separated themselves from their Gnostic contemporaries begin to take seriously the philosophy of the Greeks, worthy of notice, they suggested, because of its remote connection with the more ancient wisdom of the prophets. Justin Martyr thought it natural for a Platonist in philosophy like himself to draw on the resources of the *Timaeus* when elaborating on the account of creation in Genesis. And so he had God forming the world from a pre-existent formless matter. He did not make an issue of this; it evidently did not occur to him to challenge this typically Platonic view, though he did not hesitate to depart from Platonic precedents elsewhere. He did not, for example, link matter with defect and so passed up the opportunity of handling the problem of evil as Platonists had traditionally done. For him, the assertion in Genesis of the goodness of all that the Creator made came first. He was not making a theological point by describing the creative act as he did; shaping an indeterminate material just *was* what creating something new amounted to. Athenagoras, writing shortly after this, took the Platonic metaphor even more seriously than Justin had done when he compared the creation of the world to the action of a potter shaping his clay.

As the century waned, the clamour in Rome of competing religious proclamations grew louder. Reconstructing the variety of different writings is difficult because of the fragmentary character of the survival of the manuscript material. The Gnostic cosmogonies admitted of ever more imaginative elaboration. But they all had in common an uncompromising dualism between the matter-bound dark powers and the immaterial realities associated with the highest God. And the Neoplatonists promoted their own dualist version by emphasizing the imperfections of the matter with which the Demiurge had to cope. Tatian, a pupil of Justin, recognized the tension between this notion of an ungenerated matter and the biblical conception of an all-powerful Creator, as Justin had perhaps prepared him to see. He asserted that matter also was created by God who is the only ungenerated principle, breaking definitively in that way with the Greek philosophical tradition. But he did not go on to draw the immediate consequence that God's creation could therefore be described as being *ex nihilo*.

That was left to Theophilus of Antioch who in his *Ad Autolycum* just a few years later was the first, so far as we know, to have proclaimed creation *ex nihilo* in the full sense within the Christian tradition, arguing for it in some detail.[17] Were matter to be ungenerated, it too would be godlike,

[17] May, *Creatio ex Nihilo*, pp. 160–161.

God's overlordship in respect to all that is would be compromised, and His creative action would not differ from that of a human craftsman. Only by recognizing the creation to have been *ex nihilo* is the supremacy of the Divine will to be given full expression, and only thus can justice be done to the testimony of the Scriptures.

With the dawn of the third century, the doctrine of creation *ex nihilo* was rapidly becoming an accepted feature of Christian teaching. In his *Adversus haereses*, Irenaeus relied heavily on it in his campaign against both the Gnostics and the Neoplatonists: against them he insists that God gives existence to all things without relying on intermediaries of any kind. His will is supreme and it is also free. Irenaeus returns again and again to Scripture in support of his claims; this, rather than a philosophical system, is for him the ultimate authority. He does assert against both Neoplatonists and Gnostics that anyone who looks at the creation can see in it the goodness of the Creator but he does not deal with the philosophical issues that the *ex nihilo* doctrine raises regarding the presence of evil in the everyday world, issues that underlay both the Neoplatonic and the Gnostic initiatives in the first place.

To sum up: the inspiration for the doctrine of creation *ex nihilo* was in the first place the Scriptures rather than philosophical arguments. In the face of various world views that took the evident presence in the world of evils of all sorts as premise for a dualism that would set limits on God's creative power, the theologians of the early Church gradually came to realize that implicit in their Scriptures lay a rejection of any such limits. Relying primarily on those Scriptures, they formulated a doctrine of the Creator as all-powerful and, in consequence, rejected the view that over against Him there had been from the beginning an ungenerated principle, matter, that was not fully under His sway or lesser beings that were responsible for the multiple imperfections of the world.

With this, our story of the origins of the doctrine of creation *ex nihilo* might end. In the early third century, Tertullian and Origen simply take it as given. But one further chapter is worth adding. Almost two centuries later, Augustine of Hippo was to fill out the doctrine in ways that were, some of them, genuinely innovative.

AUGUSTINE ON CREATION

Augustine found Neoplatonism before he found Christianity again. He discovered in Plotinus a doctrine of God as the One, the Good, the Absolute, the source of all other being, a doctrine that later helped him to construct a metaphysics that would describe the God of the biblical tradition. Where Plotinus had made all else emanate from the One, Augustine had all else be the work of the One as Creator. Where Plotinus had the emanations gradually descend to the level of a matter that as non-being is over against the One and ultimately the source of evil, Augustine argued that the realities created by the Good could only themselves be good. The creative act on God's part can only be *ex nihilo*; there is nothing that could serve as material for it. To suppose otherwise would be to make God no longer the One. The warrant for the doctrine of creation *ex nihilo* was now the testimony of philosophical reason as well as of the biblical tradition.

Time is the ultimate constraint on created things: their past is no more, their future is not yet and their present is fleeting.[18] Time is the condition of the creature and thus itself came to be when creatures came to be. Thus there never was a time when creatures did not exist. God is atemporal; temporal predicates simply do not apply to Him. To call God eternal is not to imply a state that simply goes on and on; God simply is. Thus the act of creation is a single act on God's part whose product is, however, perceived by us temporal creatures as temporally extended.

How does this fit with the extended series of creation events described in the Genesis portrayal of the work of the six days? Instead of setting out to reconcile the two accounts, as he might have done, Augustine here took a bold step.[19] In a universe that is the work of a transcendent Creator, should not the potentialities of all that would come later already be present from the beginning? The idea was not new; the Stoics and, later, Basilides had made use of the metaphor of a seed to convey this same idea of all being in some sense already contained in the initial state of the cosmos. The *spermatikos logos* of the Stoics, the 'world-fire', conveyed the idea that everything that will later happen in time is already present for God, just as a seed already contains within itself the potential for the living thing that will eventually make its appearance. Augustine proposed that the *rationes seminales*, the seed-like principles, of each kind that would later appear were present from the beginning, each kind to mature when the environmental conditions were propitious.[20]

But what about the series of bringings-to-be spread out over six days that are laid out in Genesis 1? From his early days in Christian ministry,

[18] See Augustine, *The Confessions*, trans. Maria Boulding (London: Hodder and Stoughton, 1997), Books x and xi.

[19] See E. McMullin, 'Introduction: Evolution and Creation' in *Evolution and Creation* (University of Notre Dame Press, 1985), pp. 13–20.

[20] See Augustine, *The Literal Meaning of Genesis*, trans. John H. Taylor, 2 vols. (New York: Newman, 1982), vol. 1, Books iv and v.

Augustine had had to deal with the criticisms that his former co-religionists, the Manichaeans, persistently urged against the Genesis cosmogony, so clearly opposed to their own strongly dualistic one.[21] Two early commentaries on Genesis, the second unfinished, left him dissatisfied. Finally, in AD 401, he began the composition of *De Genesi ad litteram*, which would occupy him on and off for fourteen years. The work was planned as a 'literal' commentary, not in our sense of that term, but in contrast to the allegorical mode of interpretation, popular at the time, which interpreted the Old Testament as a prefiguring of the New. Thus 'literal' for him meant something like: the sense intended by the authors, Divine and human. And it could depart very far from the literal, as we would see it.

Augustine proposed that the 'days' of the Genesis account could not possibly mean days reckoned by the course of the sun; after all, the sun was not created, so the account runs, until the fourth 'day'. More plausible to set aside the notion of a temporal sequence of separate creations entirely[22] and take seriously the text in Sirach that says: 'He made all things together.'[23] As exegesis, this was obviously something of a stretch. It seems safe to say that what propelled him here were not so much specific texts of Scripture as the biblically inspired metaphysics of creation *ex nihilo* that he had been patiently developing over many years with the aid of insights drawn from both Stoic and Neoplatonist sources. This is a majestic vision:

> In the seed, then was invisibly present all that would develop in time into a tree. And in the same way we must picture the world, when God made all things together, as having all things that were made in it and with it when day was made. This includes not only heaven, with sun, moon, and stars ... but also the beings that earth produced in potency and in their causes before they came forth in the course of time.[24]

From the Creator's perspective, creation *ex nihilo* is a single atemporal act in which the origination and the conservation in being of all the potentialities as they develop are one. But from our perspective, the creation *ex nihilo* took place at the moment of cosmic origination. The later maturing of the 'seeds' to produce the various kinds was not *ex nihilo*; the materials were already there. Augustine admits that the manner in which these seed-like principles

[21] N. Joseph Torchia, O. P., *Creatio ex Nihilo and the Theology of Augustine: The Anti-Manichaean Polemic and Beyond* (New York: Peter Lang, 1999), Chapters 1–3.

[22] His tentative suggestion as to how to interpret the six-day division is that it may signify the progress in the angelic knowledge of the evolution of the infant universe.

[23] Sirach 17:1. This was the Old Latin translation of the Hebrew. Recent exegesis prefers: 'He made the entire universe' which would undercut Augustine's use of the text.

[24] *Literal Meaning of Genesis* v.45.

grow and mature is unknown to us. But then, he adds, so also is the manner in which the familiar seeds of the living world develop into the fullness of the adult form. A different kind of knowledge would be needed.[25]

The affinity between this account of origins and the evolutionary one has often been pointed out, from St George Mivart's *On the Genesis of Species* onwards.[26] Both accounts suggest a universe in which the potentialities for what will come later are already present from the beginning. But the affinity ought not to be exaggerated (as it sometimes has been). Augustine was not a transformist: each of his seed-like principles was destined to produce a single mature kind. There was no question of one kind giving rise to another. For Augustine, a Neoplatonist when it came to the relation between each kind and the corresponding Divine idea, such a transformation would have been inconceivable.

But this 'seed' that lay within Augustine's doctrine of creation is a topic to be treated elsewhere.[27] Our purpose here was to trace the notion of God's creative action from its first inchoate acknowledgement by Israel's prophets and poets to its full flowering as creation *ex nihilo* in the theologies of the early Church. Augustine's imaginative development of what it would mean for a transcendent Creator to bring a universe to be *ex nihilo* was not the end of the story. But that story is for other authors of this volume to pursue.

25 Michael McKeough, *The Meaning of Rationes Seminales in St. Augustine* (Washington: Catholic University of America Press, 1926), pp. 33–35.

26 St George Mivart, *On the Genesis of Species* (New York: Appleton, 1871).

27 Ernan McMullin, 'Darwin and the Other Christian Tradition', *Zygon* (2010).

CHAPTER 2

Creatio ex nihilo*: its Jewish and Christian foundations*

Janet M. Soskice

INTRODUCTION

Creatio ex nihilo is a central teaching in Jewish, Christian and Muslim thought – in fact, the only teaching that the medieval Jewish philosopher Moses Maimonides thought that all three traditions shared. It affirms that God, from no compulsion or necessity, created the world out of nothing – really nothing – no pre-existent matter, space or time. It is not the same thing as the 'Big Bang theory' with which it is often confused and which might roughly be defined as 'the creation of everything at the beginning of time'. Thomas Aquinas, for instance, thought that God *could* have created, *ex nihilo*, an everlasting world – that is, a world without beginning or end – although Aquinas believed, on the basis of Scripture, that the world in fact had a beginning.[1] The heart of the doctrine is the dependence of 'all that is' (for the sake of convenience I will say 'the world') on God or, more specifically, on God's free choice to create and to sustain, which comes to the same thing. Were God to cease holding the world in being for a moment it would not be.

The fact that Aquinas could consider the doctrine to be logically compatible with two different accounts of world origins demonstrates that *creatio ex nihilo* is not a cosmological or scientific hypothesis (as is the 'Big Bang theory'). It is a metaphysical position and its subject matter, so to speak, is God, although in the hands of exponents such as Thomas Aquinas *creatio ex nihilo* also has much to tell us about creatures in relation to God.

It is often claimed that the Church Fathers and medieval theologians uncritically adopted Aristotelian metaphysics when it came to creation and the doctrine of God. Those who make such claims have not considered the originality of *creatio ex nihilo*. The doctrine does not originate in Greek philosophy. Aristotle thought the idea absurd, for if there were ever a time

[1] Aquinas, *Summa Theologiae* 1a.46.2.

when nothing existed then there would be nothing now – 'from nothing, nothing comes'. In classical formulations *creatio ex nihilo* excludes both Neoplatonic emanationism in which the world flows inevitably from the Godhead and the Aristotelian cosmology in which the world and God necessarily co-exist.

Creatio ex nihilo has the odd distinction of being a *biblically compelled* piece of metaphysical theology. Once it had been clearly formulated in the second century AD, the doctrine became pivotal for reflection on a number of other teachings in the Abrahamic faiths – concerning divine action, grace, theodicy, religious language, intercessory prayer and questions of divine temporality. A long trajectory of debate, discussed in the various chapters in this volume, runs from the earliest centuries through thinkers such as Augustine, Avicenna, al-Ghazali, Maimonides and Aquinas.

The work of Thomas Aquinas, in which the doctrine of creation is pivotal, represents a pinnacle in Christian reflection on this important topic.[2] Yet to begin with Aquinas is to find oneself thrust into the midst of an already elaborate debate, and one which is awash with Aristotelian categories. Indeed the God Aquinas discusses can seem arid and remote from the God of Scriptures who loves and chastens and consoles. And although it is the 'biblical' God whom Aquinas is concerned to defend, I will in this chapter (and in keeping with the purposes of this volume) keep closer to Jewish debates on the teaching, both to add another slant and to show why it might be that *creatio ex nihilo* has been so dear to the hearts of all who worship the God of Abraham.

THE BIBLICAL ACCOUNT AND THE NAME OF GOD

It should be stated at the outset that the Hebrew Scriptures generally are little concerned with questions of metaphysics or scientific cosmology. In the first chapters of Genesis God calls light from the formless void, separating it from darkness, and names the light 'Day' and the darkness 'Night'. God divides the waters from dry land, creates the sun and moon, living creatures and, in a culmination of this creative work, humankind, male and female, in God's own image. In the Book of Genesis this sequence forms the prolegomena for the calling of Abram, renamed at that time Abraham, which marks the creation of the people, Israel, through whom God's blessings will be shed on the world. These narratives do not probe the metaphysics of space and time, or even present a consistent view on the

[2] On this see Rudi te Velde, *Aquinas on God* (Aldershot: Ashgate, 2006).

origin of matter. They are more concerned to show the relationship of all things to God and to each other, and to establish that the creation is 'good' and the work of a beneficent God. They tell us something about the created order, but also something about the nature of God.

Metaphysics makes an entry with Exodus 3, or rather with the chapter's long interpretative history. It recounts the meeting of God and Moses at the burning bush. Ostensibly the passage is not about creation at all, but about God's intention to free the Israelites from their bondage in Egypt. However, in the course of their negotiations Moses, rather oddly we may think, asks God for a name:

> God said to Moses, '*I AM who I AM*'. He said further 'Thus you shall say to the Israelites, "*I Am* has sent me to you".' God also said to Moses, 'Thus you shall say to the Israelites, "*The LORD (YHWH), the God of your ancestors, the God of Abraham, the God of Isaac, and the God of Jacob, has sent me to you*". This is my name forever, and this is my title for all generations.'[3]

The repetitions emphasize the importance of the passage. The name, which will be God's name 'for all generations', is the Tetragrammaton, YHWH. Technically this name, which is the nearest we have to a proper name for the God of Israel, has no meaning and cannot even be spoken since it lacks vowels. 'I Am Who I Am' is not strictly speaking the meaning of the Tetragrammaton but rather a gloss or a pun on the holy name, which is structurally similar to the Hebrew verb 'to be'. It is this famous gloss which was to prove so important as the Hebrew Scriptures were translated first into Greek for the Jews of the Hellenistic diaspora (*c.* third century BC onward), and then into Latin in the Christian era.

'I Am Who I Am' became, in the Greek of the Septuagint, *ego eimi ho on*, and in the Latin of the Vulgate, *ego sum qui sum*. The metaphysical resonance of this sacred name, so translated, was irresistible both to early Christians and to Hellenistic Jews such as Philo of Alexandria, to whom I shall return. The name given to Moses seemed an ideal meeting place of scriptural revelation and Greek metaphysics, and came to be seen as implying an identification of God with Being. From here it is a short step to saying that only God is being itself (which is not at all the same thing as saying that God is 'the greatest being'), that only God is eternal, that all creatures are dependent on God, that even space and time are creatures – all adjunct theses of *creatio ex nihilo*.[4]

[3] Exodus 3:14–15, *NRSV* (my italics).

[4] To suggest that God was the 'greatest being' would lead to ontotheology, a view which could not be attributed to Augustine or Aquinas.

It should be pointed out that these metaphysical readings are not dictated by the Hebrew of the Book of Exodus. Quite the opposite. The gloss which we translate 'I Am Who I Am', or *ego sum qui sum*, is better rendered as something like 'I am with you and will be with you'. Martin Buber and Franz Rosenzweig were particularly exercised, at the beginning of the twentieth century, by the distortions which entered when this Hebrew name of promise – a promise to be with the people on their journey in the wilderness – was made into a proposition of metaphysics. One of their targets on this score was Moses Mendelssohn; another was Maimonides. Consideration of their dispute over the Name and its gloss can open up some matters at stake in the theology of *creatio ex nihilo*.

Buber and Rosenzweig, as translators of the Bible from Hebrew into German, were faced with the question of how to render the Tetragrammaton, a difficulty which had already vexed previous translators. In the early nineteenth century Moses Mendelssohn had faced the same problem when he, with others, compiled the commentary known as the *Biur*, a precursor to modern biblical criticism. Mendelssohn did not follow the precedent of other Germano-Jewish translations, which used simply God/Gott to render the Tetragrammaton, and chose instead, to the subsequent dismay of Rosenzweig, to use 'the Eternal' – a choice nourished by the gloss on the name, 'I Am Who I Am.'

The decision in favour of an abstract philosophical term to translate the Tetragrammaton was, according to Rosenzweig, 'a mistake and moreover one which was to influence all Jewish piety of the Emancipation, even in orthodox circles'.[5] He felt that Mendelssohn, in opting for 'the Eternal', deferred to the rationalizing spirit of the Enlightenment on the one hand, and to Maimonides on the other, in presuming that the notion of a being necessarily existent must imply a providential one.

Rosenzweig and Buber wanted to move away from the static sense of Divine Being mediated to the West, especially to the Christian West, by the Greek of the Septuagint and the Latin Vulgate. Their own translation of the famous gloss of the Tetragrammaton favoured the dynamic sense of *becoming*, of *appearing* and of *happening*.[6] Of the incongruity of a *metaphysical* answer to Moses' request for a name, Rosenzweig wrote,

> what meaning for the despairing and wretched Israelites would be offered by a lecture on God's eternal necessity? They, like this timid leader himself, need rather

[5] In M. Buber and F. Rosenzweig, *Scripture and Translation* (Bloomington, IN: Indiana University Press, 1994), p. 100.

[6] Buber and Rosenzweig, *Scripture and Translation*, p. 104.

an assurance of God's being-among-them: and unlike their leader, who hears it directly from God's mouth, they need this in the form of a clarification of the old, obscure name, sufficient to establish that the assurance is of divine origin.

In the narrative context, then, the only justifiable translation is one that makes prominent not God's being eternal but his being present, his being present for and with you now and in time to come.[7]

Yet Rosenzweig conceded that, despite his 'wrong choice' in translation, Mendelssohn did show great religious insight on the Name. In his commentary, and at the first use of the Tetragrammaton in Genesis 2:4, Mendelssohn forbears to say *anything at all*, simply telling his readers to consult his later commentary on Exodus 3:14, 'for there is the place to discuss it'.[8] This suggests that for Mendelssohn, as for the medieval commentator Rashi, the significance of the Name is to be read 'backwards and forwards', so to speak, from the revelations to Moses at Horeb/Sinai. The Name and its glossed meaning cannot be separated. When he reached Exodus 3:14 Mendelssohn paraphrased in this way:

> God spoke to Moses: 'I am the being that is eternal.'
> He said further: 'Say to the children of Israel,
> The eternal being, which calls itself, I-am-eternal, has sent me to you.'[9]

His comment on this was the following:

It says in a midrash,

The Holy one, Blessed be He, said to Moses: 'say to them, "I am the one who was, and now I am the same and will be the same in the future."' And our teachers, may their memory be a blessing, say further: 'I will be with them in this need, who will be with them in their bondage in the kingdoms to come.' (Cf. Berakhot 9b)

Their meaning is the following: 'Because past and future time are all present in the creator, *since in Him there is not change and dependence and of His days there is no passing – because of this all times are in Him called by a single name, which embraces past, present and future alike. Through this name he indicates the necessity of existence and at the same time the continuous and abiding character of providence.* He says, then, by this name, "I am with the children of men, to be well disposed and to have mercy on whom I will have mercy. Say then to them, to Israel, that I am He who

[7] Buber and Rosenzweig, *Scripture and Translation*, p. 105. My colleague, Graham Davies, has pointed out to me that the Hebrew of Exodus 3 suggests the present presence and future presence but that it is more difficult to find 'past presence' in it. Pre-critical readings were less bothered by adding the suggestion of the past.

[8] Buber and Rosenzweig, *Scripture and Translation*, p. 105.

[9] Buber and Rosenzweig, *Scripture and Translation*, p. 101.

was, is, and shall be, and who practices lordship and providence over all. I shall be with them in this need and shall be with them whenever they call to me."'[10]

Mendelssohn explicitly joins omni-temporality, necessary existence and providence – ideas at the heart of *creatio ex nihilo.* The word which, he believed, best caught all of these meanings was 'the Eternal'. But his own comments show that Mendelssohn considers the name 'Eternal' to be far more than 'a lecture on God's eternal necessity'; it has to do with God's concern for the plight of the children of Israel as they labour in bondage in Egypt and will wander homeless in the Sinai desert. Citing a string of Jewish sources – Onkelos, Saadia Gaon and Maimonides – he says that the holy name in fact has three meanings: one concerning providence, another eternity and the third existential necessity. All of these are captured by the Name and its gloss, and Mendelssohn sees no conflict between them.

By ancient and entirely biblical warrant Jews, Christians and Muslims hold to an 'intentional creation'.[11] Unlike Aristotle's deity, whose existence is everlastingly coterminous with the equally everlasting and unchanging world, or the god of Neoplatonism whose 'creation' was a necessary emanation and in no sense volitional, the God of Israel creates freely, intentionally and without compulsion. The God of the Bible – according to Maimonides and Aquinas – freely creates all that is, including space and time, and is thus in no sense a 'creature' of space and time. The intimacy which God has with the world is the intimacy of a Maker, and Artisan, whose actions are free and deliberate and who is everywhere and always (omnipresently and eternally) present to His creation.

To Rosenzweig's insistence that, 'in the narrative context . . . the only justifiable translation (of the Name) is one that makes prominent not God's being eternal but his being present, his being present for and with you now and in time to come', a Maimonidean might reply (and a Thomist certainly would reply) that this intimacy, this providence, is precisely what it means for Jews and Christians, but not for the philosophers, to say that God is Eternal.[12] 'Eternity' is thus not another idea alongside and possibly in

[10] Buber and Rosenzweig, *Scripture and Translation*, pp. 102–103 (my italics).

[11] David B. Burrell, 'Freedom and Creation in the Abrahamic Traditions', *International Philosophical Quarterly* 40 (June 2000), pp. 161–171, at p. 167.

[12] By way of showing that not all contemporary Jewish scholars disparage 'eternity' when considering this passage, but rather want it in its proper context, consider Herbert Brichto commenting on 'I Am Who I Am' of Exodus 3:14, in *The Names of God: Poetic Readings in Biblical Beginnings* (New York: Oxford University Press, 1998), p. 24:

> This Hebrew sentence then is an exposition of the name to come . . . its meaning is . . . all of the following: 'I am what I am, I am what I was, I am what I shall be, I was what I am. I was what I was,

conflict with that of providence, but is in the Jewish and the Christian understandings part of the meaning of providence or, better, part of what it means for Jews and Christians to say that God is the Creator. God's undivided presence to everything in particular is in sharp contrast with what 'divine eternity' meant for classical Greek philosophy.

THE JEWISH AND CHRISTIAN FOUNDATIONS

Sophisticated pagan theology was monotheistic and, indeed, far from feeling they had learned of monotheism from the Jews, Greek intellectuals praised Judaism for being a 'philosophical' cult precisely because it was, like their own philosophical cosmology, monotheistic. Greek philosophy arrived without reliance on any concept of revelation at a remarkable consensus concerning the unity of the divine essence and the nature of the divine attributes.[13] Such were findings of their science, for 'natural theology' was an aspect and requirement of science and a formal discipline, akin to mathematics. The Christian Fathers regarded the austere and non-mythic discipline of Greek natural theology as a quarry to be mined, but with caution.

Greek natural theology was directed to cosmological questions and overwhelmingly concerned with *arche*, that is with the search for origins and originating principles, temporal or other. The object of Greek science was to explain the world around us – the facts of motion, cause and consequence – in as economical a manner as possible. Fable and anthropomorphism were generally shunned, except as illustration. 'God', while important as a theoretical category, was not a proper name. Lloyd Gerson goes so far as to say that the term 'god' in Greek philosophy does not denote a person so much as an explanatory principle 'analogous to the hypothetical entities of modern science like black holes or neutrinos'.[14] To fulfil the requirements of their science Greek philosophers needed an *arche* which is single. To stop infinite regress this *arche*, which might also be called 'god', was held to be necessarily existent. What *could not* be said was that this 'god' was in any sense free or a volitional agent.

In philosophical terms, the development of *creatio ex nihilo* by Jewish and Christian writers was a riposte to the Greek consensus that from nothing

I was what I shall be, I shall be what I was . . .' In other words, the name Ehye . . . has the connotations in the one-word name of eternity, timelessness, without beginning or end, and in the exposition of changelessness, enduring dependability.

[13] Lloyd P. Gerson, *God and Greek Philosophy: Studies in the Early History of Natural Theology* (London: Routledge, 1990).

[14] Gerson, *God and Greek Philosophy*, p. 2.

nothing comes – *ex nihilo nihil fit* – which threatened not only their understanding of cosmic origins but also teaching on divine freedom and sovereignty. Yet exactly when the doctrine is first unequivocally stated is a matter of some debate. Jewish thinkers were exposed to Greek ideas from the time of Alexander the Great's conquests in the fourth century BC. Gerhard May argues, conservatively, that the notion that *creatio ex nihilo* is a product of Hellenistic Judaism cannot be sustained, and dates its clear formulation well within the early Christian period, arising out of Christian debates.[15] The important point, however, is that, even if the doctrine does attain clear formulation only in response to 'pagan' philosophy, it does not reflect absorption of Hellenistic ideas but is rather a critical response. As May says, 'The driving motive which underlines the Christian doctrine of *creatio ex nihilo* is the attempt to do justice to the absolute sovereignty and unlimited freedom of the biblical God acting in history . . . Christian theology has developed its doctrine of *creatio ex nihilo* from its own presumptions, albeit . . . within the ambit of the philosophical teaching of world-formation.'[16]

While both Aristotle's thesis on the eternity of the world and Stoic pantheism were rejected by early Christianity and Hellenistic Judaism, for some time there remained an ambiguity as to matter itself.[17] The Bible at times seems to speak of God moulding a pre-existent matter. The first verse of Genesis where the earth is described as 'formless void' (leaving it unstated as to whether formless void exists 'prior' to creation) is susceptible to such a reading as is Wisdom 11:7 where we learn of 'the hand that from formless matter created the world'. Philo of Alexandria and some of the earliest Christian writers seemed untroubled by such a reading and saw in it no threat to divine sovereignty, and the rabbis were in general content to let variant understandings live at peace with one another. On the other hand, we find in texts like 2 Maccabees (composed around the beginning of the first century BC) sentiments that seem to rule out any notion of the God of Abraham as a demiurge moulding pre-existing matter: 'my child, observe heaven and earth, consider all that is in them, and acknowledge that God made them out of what did not exist, and that mankind comes into being in the same way' (2 Maccabees 7:28).[18] It is hard not to see here a statement about the singularity of God's creative power. Yet an argument can be made for an independent Jewish strand of development for the ideas which fed

[15] Gerhard May, *Creatio ex Nihilo: The Doctrine of 'Creation out of Nothing' in Early Christian Thought* (Edinburgh: T&T Clark, 1994).

[16] May, *Creatio ex Nihilo*, p. viii. [17] May, *Creatio ex Nihilo*, p. 3.

[18] G. May, pushing hard at his case that *creatio ex nihilo* first arises in distinctly Christian confrontations with Greek philosophy, treats such verses as paraenetic and pre-ontological.

into the developed teaching. Menahem Kister sees interest among the Jewish sages in the question of whether the world was created 'out of primordial elements, out of Matter (*ex hyles*) or out of nothing (*ex nihilo*)' as early as the second century BC, in the Book of Jubilees.[19]

Old Testament references to divine creation are not, of course, restricted to Genesis but suffuse the worship of the Psalms and other books – 'the sea is his, for he made it and the dry land, which his hands have formed' (Psalm 95:5). The Psalms and the Book of Isaiah, both heavily drawn upon by early Christians, regularly link God's power as Creator with God's faithfulness and ability to redeem, as in Psalm 121:1–2:

> I will lift up my eyes to the mountains:
> From where shall come my help?
> My help shall come from the Lord
> Who made heaven and earth.

In Isaiah 45:8 an extended address from the Lord works on the same theme:

> Shower, O heavens, from above,
> and let the skies rain down righteousness;
> let the earth open, that salvation may spring up,
> and let it cause righteousness to sprout up also;
> I the LORD have created it.

And in the midst of a stirring address on the need to turn to God and be saved (Isaiah 45:18):

> For thus says the LORD,
> who created the heavens
> (he is God),
> who formed the earth and made it
> (he established it;
> he did not create it a chaos,
> he formed it to be inhabited!):
> I am the LORD, and there is no other.[20]

'Greek influence' on Jewish thought should not be understood as acquiescent absorption of Greek categories – we must speak also of abreaction. The second and first centuries BC were periods of persecution for the Jews. The plunder of the Temple of Jerusalem in 169 BC by the Seleucid king Antiochus IV Epiphanes provoked strong anti-Hellenistic reactions, and

[19] Menahem Kister, '*Tohu wa-Bohu*, Primordial Elements and *Creatio ex Nihilo*', *Jewish Studies Quarterly* 14 (2007), pp. 229–256, at p. 229.

[20] This chapter will be echoed famously in Paul's 'Christ hymn' of Philippians 2.

produced many Jewish martyrs. It appears to be this period, and the death of these martyrs, that first gave rise to serious debates in Judaism about the resurrection of the dead. It is then not surprising that what many take to be the first clear statement of something akin to *creatio ex nihilo* occurs in strongly anti-Hellenistic 2 Maccabees (a book which, nonetheless, it should be noted was written in Greek) and in the context of martyrdom. A mother, having witnessed the martyrdom of six sons, encourages her youngest in this way: 'my child, observe heaven and earth, consider all that is in them, and acknowledge that God made them out of what did not exist, and that mankind comes into being in the same way ... make death welcome, so that in the day of mercy I may receive you back in your brothers' company' (2 Maccabees 7:28–29). The same connection between the power to create from what does not exist and the power to raise the dead will be made by Jewish and Muslim writers: Paul, in Romans 4:17, speaks of Abraham 'in the presence of the God in whom he believed, who gives life to the dead and calls into existence the things that do not exist'.

By the second century AD both Christian and Jewish writers were stating positions which differentiated their own, biblically informed, view of creation from that of the philosophers.[21] The background Platonism (or more properly Neoplatonism) of the time held that matter exists eternally and is not the result of a creation. If this was unacceptable, even more so was the Neoplatonic conviction that 'being necessarily proceeded from the One', an assertion entirely at odds with the idea that God creates freely.[22] Over and against the formally necessitated 'creation' of the Platonists and in order to preserve divine freedom and creaturely contingency, rabbis and theologians formulated *creatio ex nihilo* – not as a departure from the biblical account but as its clarification and defence. Thus we find Rabbi Gamaliel II (*c*. 90/110) in dialogue with a philosopher who says: 'Your God was indeed a great artist, but surely He found good pigments which assist him.' Rabbi Gamaliel replies: 'God made the colours, too!'[23] Although such statements are rarer in writings of the rabbis than in those of early Christians, Jews and Christians shared a motive – to protect God's sovereignty, freedom and action in the world.[24]

Philo, our main source for Hellenistic Judaism in the first century AD, is interesting here. He is not entirely consistent, but the basic tenets of *creatio ex nihilo* are already present in his writings: God has created the world out of

[21] The actual historical prompt for this may have been the need to rebut Gnostic heresies, as May demonstrates, but the net effect is a position quite distinct from philosophical cosmology.

[22] May, *Creatio ex Nihilo*, p. 5. [23] May, *Creatio ex Nihilo*, p. 23. [24] Genesis Rabah 1:9.

non-being, *creating* as well as *moulding* formless matter. God, he believes, has created time itself.[25] He rejects outright the Greek idea that the universe is eternal, which he believes is incompatible with providence. The cosmos is wholly dependent on God and God is in no sense dependent on the cosmos.

Philo repeatedly links these metaphysical notions with Exodus 3, a passage in which he understands God to have named himself to Moses as 'being itself'. Philo was, of course, a Hellenized Jew, but this identification of God with the source of being cannot simply be attributed to Hellenistic leanings. The Palestinian Targums, emerging from a Semitic milieu, provide us with the following glosses on the 'ehyeh esher ehyeh' (I Am Who I Am) of Exodus 3:15:

- Pseudo-Jonathan (14a): He who spoke and the world came into being, spoke and everything came into being.
- Fragmentary Targum (14a) v: He who said to the world, 'Be', and it came into being, and who will again say to it: 'Be', and it will be.
- Neofiti margin 2: I have existed before the world was created and have existed after the world has been created. I am he who has been at your aid in the Egyptian exile, and I am he who will be at your aid in every generation.[26]

All of these link the 'I Am' of Exodus to 'the Creator of all that is', as will Thomas Aquinas. It is of related interest that Numenius, a pagan philosopher of the second century AD who shows a detailed interest in the Exodus story, credits Moses and the Jews with the revelation that the First God is '*ho on*' – 'Being itself'.[27]

The great medieval philosophers who worked on *creatio ex nihilo*, al-Ghazali, Maimonides and Aquinas, all contrast the God of Abraham not just with the god of Plato but with the god of Aristotle, whose texts had for centuries been lost to the Christian West. Maimonides was especially aware of the decisive gulf between the views of the philosophers (including Aristotle, whom he admires almost without qualification) and *creatio ex nihilo*, the teaching (as he believes) of Moses. Here is how Maimonides delineates the matter:

[25] See *Legum Allegoriae* III; *De Fuga et Inventione* 46; *De Vita Mosis* II.267. He is somewhat ambiguous as to whether God creates primary matter in *De Opificio Mundi*.

[26] I am grateful to my colleague Graham Davies for these references. See his 'The Exegesis of the Divine Name in Exodus' in Robert P. Gordon (ed.), *The God of Israel* (Cambridge University Press, 2007), pp. 139–156.

[27] See M. F. Burnyeat, 'Numenius of Apamea on *Exodus* and Eternity' in George H. van Kooten (ed.), *The Revelation of the Name YHWH to Moses: Perspectives from Judaism, the Pagan Graeco-Roman World, and Early Christianity* (Leiden: Brill, 2006), pp. 145–148.

Those who follow the Law of Moses, our Teacher, hold that the whole Universe, i.e., everything except God, has been brought by Him into existence out of non-existence. In the beginning God alone existed and nothing else ... He produced from nothing all existing things such as they are, by His will and desire. Even time itself is among the things created; for time depends on motion, i.e., on an accident in things which move, and the things upon whose motion time depends are themselves created beings, which have passed from non-existence into existence. We say that God *existed* before the creation of the Universe, although the verb *existed* appears to imply the notion of time; we also believe that He existed in infinite space of time before the Universe was created; but in these cases we do not mean time in its true sense. We only use the term to signify something analogous or similar to time. For time is undoubtedly an accident, and, according to our opinion, one of the created accidents.[28]

Despite the formality of his statement, Maimonides is here speaking of a God of 'will' and 'desire'.[29] This God is Creator of all, including space and time, and not part of that which is created. This has implications for religious language especially when we predicate common terms like 'exist', of God, as Maimonides points out. 'To exist' normally implies 'existence in time', but this cannot be the sense in which God 'exists' since God exists apart from and 'prior' to creation. Time, too, is God's creature.[30]

Despite deference to Aristotle in matters sub-lunary, Maimonides could not for religious reasons accept the eternity of the world.[31] In Jewish understanding, but not in Aristotle's, God could exist without any universe.

[28] Moses Maimonides, *Guide for the Perplexed*, trans. M. Friedlander (New York: Dover Publications, 1956), Part II, Chapter 13, p. 171.

[29] Maimonides believes that terms are used of God and creatures equivocally, however, a position with which Aquinas will take issue in his developed theory of analogy. Maimonides' view of the workings of providence is also a good deal more restrictive than that of the Christian writers (and of some Jews). Alexander Broadie speaks of Maimonides' providence as 'of a highly elitist sort', only pertaining to human beings (*Guide* III.17, p. 471) and then more attentive to those greater in perfection. Here Moses ranks high (*Guide* III.17, p. 475). See Alexander Broadie, 'Maimonides and Aquinas on the Names of God', *Religious Studies* 23 (1987), pp. 167–168. But as Broadie points out, however restrictive it is, Maimonides does want to insist on God's providential care for and knowledge of individuals, something entirely alien to Aristotle's theology.

[30] Similar observations on the collapse of our tensed and temporal language were made much earlier by Augustine in Chapters 11 and 12 of the *Confessions*. Here Augustine peppers his account of time and creation with liberal mention of the 'penury of human understanding' and our correlative tendency to 'excessive wordiness' but draws no explicit contrast with the philosophers.

[31] Maimonides, like al-Ghazali, seems to presume that *creatio ex nihilo* entails a beginning in time, that is, they seem to disallow the possibility that the Creator may have freely created an everlasting universe. Aquinas, as already mentioned, allows this last possibility, although he believes that, as a matter of fact, the universe is not everlasting. David Burrell puts it nicely in 'Freedom and Creation', pp. 168–169:

Maimonides simply presumes (as did Ghazali) that an everlasting universe leaves no room for free creation; in this he conflates *creatio ex nihilo* with *creatio de novo* – that is, not simply that nothing is presupposed to creation but that it takes place such that there is an initial moment of time. Aquinas

Furthermore, for Aristotle no questions can be asked about the purpose of the universe or the final cause of the heavens – there is no 'purpose' at that level in Aristotle's system. But these were questions which Maimonides felt the followers of Moses must ask. Aristotle's prime mover is as much a part of the cosmic order as that which is moved. There is no room for divine freedom or divine knowledge of particulars and, since the system is fixed, seamlessly ordered and without beginning or end, no room for miracles. Maimonides, despite his admiration for Aristotle, considered Aristotle's particular 'eternal universe' must be rejected on religious grounds, and *creatio ex nihilo* defended as a fundamental principle of the Jewish religion. It is, as he puts it, 'a high rampart erected around the Law'.[32] 'According to our theory, taught in Scripture, the existence and non-existence of things depends solely on the will of God and not on fixed laws.'[33] By reason of this teaching on creation, Maimonides' God is personal whereas Aristotle's deity, which consists entirely of intellection directed upon itself, is not. Yet at the same time Maimonides' God is also far less comprehensible, at least by philosophical means. For whereas the lineaments of Aristotelian divinity are deducible from the universe of which it is prime mover and with which it makes a whole, Maimonides' God (and that of Aquinas) is altogether 'other' than that which God creates. For Maimonides and Aquinas, God need not have created *at all* and so can never, even in an exalted sense, be a part of the system. The dependence is altogether one way – the created order is completely dependent upon God, but God is not dependent upon the created order. The Creator is not only an 'uncaused cause' (an ascription which could be predicated as well of Aristotle's deity) but, as Creator, is not 'part' of creaturely causality while at the same time holding it at every

declares his indebtedness to both by concurring with Maimonides that neither position – everlasting or temporal creation – admits of proof, and yet he refuses to foreclose the conceptual possibility of a free creator (in the biblical or Qur'anic sense) creating everlastingly ... He does concede that postulating an initial moment would make the case more evident ... but, strictly speaking, the case for creation *de novo* rests solely with revelation ... (There is no conceptual difficulty with an eternal God creating an everlasting universe, precisely because one can distinguish the *eternity* which characterizes God alone from a temporality without beginning.)

[32] Maimonides, *Guide* II.17, p. 181. José Faur sets out Maimonides' views in the following way in *Homo Mysticus: A Guide to Maimonides's Guide for the Perplexed* (Syracuse: Syracuse University Press, 1999), p. 89 (citing Maimonides' *Treatise on Resurrection* 30):

> The only possible relation between absolute monotheism and a world brimming with diversity is Creation *ex nihilo*, repudiating an ontological relation between God and the Universe ... 'Belief in the creation of the world,' wrote Maimonides, 'necessarily requires that all the miracles are possible.' Consequently, 'Whoever believes in the eternity (of the world) does not belong at all to the congregation of Moses and Abraham.'

[33] Maimonides, *Guide* II.27, p. 202.

moment in being. God is in no sense a being among beings.[34] This God is more 'other' than Aristotle's or Plato's, but also more intimate. Maimonides' God can have knowledge of particulars in a way the Greek deity cannot.

Maimonides is above all concerned to affirm the freedom of both God and human beings. This freedom would not be a possibility in the changeless universe of Aristotle, and nor would providence – at least not the sort of providence that allows the Eternal God to change the life of Israel by such actions as the gift of the Law at Sinai. God can 'act' in the world without this being intervention in the accustomed sense of that term because God is not one among many players in the unfolding of time, but present to all time as its Creator.[35] It is on similar grounds that Aquinas will insist that creation is not a 'change' since change takes place between one state of affairs and another, or between one moment and another. But there is no time 'before' God creates time; 'Hence, since there is no process of change in creation, a thing is simultaneously being created and is created.'[36] God holds all that is in being, as gift. *Creatio ex nihilo* thus does not conflict with scientific explanation, since it is a belief about God as the foundation of the causal order itself, and not a link in the chain of scientific explanation. José Faur states it neatly: 'Causality is the effect, not the grounds, of creation.'[37]

For Aristotle 'God' and the universe are both eternal in a sense which might better be called 'everlasting'. The God of Jews, Muslims and Christians is eternal in virtue of being the Creator of time, and not a creature of time. Nor is this, in the history of Abrahamic apologetic, a mere philosophical nicety. On this understanding depend the classical theological teachings on divine and human freedom, of divine omnipotence, of miracles and of intercessory prayer. It is because God stands in radical and free relation to creation that God is intimate with it in the way no element of the created order could be (omnipresence, eternity). Since God as the 'cause of being' is a cause of a different order from the causal

[34] For an account of some of the more recent misunderstandings of *creatio ex nihilo*, especially those which see God's freedom and agency in contrast to that of creatures, see Kathryn Tanner, *God and Creation in Christian Theology: Tyranny or Empowerment* (Oxford: Blackwell, 1988).

[35] This point is made by José Faur in *Homo Mysticus*, p. 93. Faur also points out the link with divine omnipotence.

[36] Aquinas, *Summa Theologiae* Ia.54.2.

[37] Faur, *Homo Mysticus*, p. 113. Catherine Keller, in *The Face of the Deep: The Theology of Becoming* (Oxford: Routledge, 2003), takes *creatio ex nihilo* to be a *change* – which Aquinas expressly insists it is not. She thus finds the teaching (of which she is, on her terms, understandably critical) presents us with 'a great supernatural surge of father-power, a world appearing-zap-out of the void' and above all a setting of stasis (pp. 5–6). While some theologians do talk in this way, the considerable merit of a sophisticated handling of *creatio ex nihilo* is to exclude this kind of anthropomorphism and to facilitate precisely what Catherine Keller is after – a theology of becoming.

agency of any creature, God's causation 'does not compete with a creature's causation – human freedom is preserved'.[38] God may 'act' in the miraculous without that being in violation of the created order.[39]

Although God does not need creation to be God, the creation nonetheless stands in a real, if contingent, relation to God. God's *creatures* are gratuitously created from no compulsion but God's abundant love. Although the idea that God must need us if we are to need him has some initial attractiveness, even anthropomorphically speaking it is curious if not morally repellent to believe that God created the world from deficit or emotional need. In classical philosophical theology it is because God is always already abundance and fullness of life that creation is *wholly* gift and grace. Out of no need but from pure love and delight God creates all that is created. Aristotle's prime mover and 'necessary existent' is not what is disclosed at Sinai.

The books of the Pentateuch show no metaphysical longing for first principles. It would be unreasonable and anachronistic to suppose that they did. But it is not unreasonable to read them as attesting to the disclosure or revelation of the One who is and was and will always be, a God of loving-faithfulness who has created and will redeem. This is what subsequent Jewish and Christian reflection has done, and it was in order to secure this distinctive insight that Abrahamic understandings of divine eternity and of *creatio ex nihilo* were developed. Providence is here not derived from some pre-existing philosophical commitment to a 'necessary existent' – the order is, if anything, the other way around: Scripture and its narratives come first, the text of Torah and the 'I Am Who I Am.' The eternal God, ever free to act and be present to the people, is known as eternal God through his everlasting, providential concern.

FINAL THOUGHTS

What might *creatio ex nihilo* mean for the dialogue of theology with modern science? I suggest three points. First, *creatio ex nihilo* is a metaphysical claim, not an empirical one, and does not dictate a particular cosmology. It is thus

[38] Burrell, 'Freedom and Creation', p. 169.

[39] We have the stuff of many great philosophical debates here. My purpose here is to show that thinkers like Augustine, Maimonides and Aquinas were trying precisely to defend the freedom of God and of humankind as they saw it in Scripture by developing their ideas about God's eternity, and not supplanting that God with a philosophical ghoul. On the coherence of *creatio ex nihilo* and human freedom see Burrell, 'Freedom and Creation', and also his *Aquinas: God and Action* (University of Notre Dame Press, 1979). An elegant recent treatment of Aquinas on the matter is found in Rudi te Velde, *Aquinas on God*, and see David Burrell's contribution to the present volume. For a defence of the classical outline of divine eternity as fully compatible with and indeed necessary for the idea of a God who acts, see Eleonore Stump and Norman Kretzmann, 'Eternity' in Thomas V. Morris (ed.), *The Concept of God* (Oxford University Press, 1987), pp. 219–252.

not in competition with scientific explanation, nor potentially defeasible by it. Second, *creatio ex nihilo* leaves worldly causality in place. God is not a 'cause among causes' but holds the whole in being, and God's acting, for instance, in response to prayer, would not be a violation of the causal order. Finally, *creatio ex nihilo* frees us to be religious materialists. Christians and their critics display persistent temptation to a dualism in which the world is accompanied by a spooky spiritual realm. Taking on board *creatio ex nihilo* makes us see that the decisive distinction is not between 'the spiritual' (as somehow closer to God) and 'the material' (as somehow inert), but between the Creator and creatures. This view suffuses the writings of early theologians such as Athanasius for whom 'spirit' and 'soul' are as much creatures as are bodies. God creates all that is, visible and invisible. The angels are creatures as much as are the elephants. This has rich potential for a meeting with modern science, where it is increasingly evident that matter, as congested energy, is just as much a mystery as anything we might call spirit or soul.

CHAPTER 3

The act of creation with its theological consequences

David B. Burrell, C. S. C.

INTRODUCTION

It is certainly remarkable that it took the fledgling Christian movement four centuries to respond to its central faith question concerning Jesus: who and what is he? Moreover, the long-standing quest for clarity regarding Jesus doubtless overshadowed more explicit reflection on the first article of the creed as well: 'I believe in God, the Father almighty, creator of heaven and earth.' As Robert Sokolowski observes: 'The issue the church had to settle first, once it acquired public and official recognition under Constantine and could turn to controversies regarding its teaching, was the issue of the being and actions of Christ.' Yet he goes on to insist:

> [While] the Council of Chalcedon, and the councils and controversies that led up to it, were concerned with the mystery of Christ, ... they also tell us about the God who became incarnate in Christ. They tell us first that God does not destroy the natural necessities of things he becomes involved with, even in the intimate union of the incarnation. What is according to nature, and what reason can disclose in nature, retains its integrity before the Christian God [who] is not a part of the world and is not a 'kind' of being at all. Therefore, the incarnation is not meaningless or impossible or destructive.[1]

Moreover, what Sokolowski calls:

> the Christian distinction between God and the world, the denial that God in his divinity is part of or dependent on the world, was brought forward with greater clarity through the discussion of the way the Word became flesh. The same distinction was also emphasised as a background for the Trinitarian doctrines

This chapter has appeared in Thomas Weinandy, Daniel Keating and John Yocum (eds.), *Aquinas on Doctrine* (London: T&T Clark, 2004), pp. 27–44. The editors wish to thank the publishers for allowing its publication.

[1] Robert Sokolowski, *God of Faith and Reason* (Washington, DC: Catholic University of America Press, 1995), pp. 34–36. For a dramatic account of the sinuous journey to Chalcedon, see Thomas Weinandy, *Does God Change?* (Still River, MA: St. Bede's, 1985).

and for the controversies about grace . . . Thus many of the crucial dogmatic issues raised in the relationship between God and the world, and the positions judged to be erroneous would generally have obscured the Christian distinction between the divine and the mundane.[2]

So creation not only comes first, as it were, in our God's transactions with the world; it is also true that the way we understand that founding relation will affect our attempts to articulate any further interaction. For were the One who reached out to us 'in Christ' not the Creator of heaven and earth, the story would have to be told in a vastly different (and inescapably mythic) idiom, as indeed it has often been on the part of Christians so preoccupied with redemption that creation is simply presumed as its stage-setting.

Moreover, and understandably enough, since the narrative of incarnation and redemption captures the lion's share of the tripartite creed associated with the initiation rites of baptism, so creation can appear a mere preamble. Moreover, an adequate treatment of the unique activity which constitutes creating, as well as the quite ineffable relation between creatures and creator which it initiates, will tax one's philosophical resources to the limit, so more timid theologians prefer to finesse it altogether. Yet, as Sokolowski reminds us, we cannot afford to do this since the interaction among these shaping mysteries of faith is at once palpable and mutually illuminating. Nor can Christians treat the Hebrew Scriptures as a mere preamble to their revelation of God in Jesus, since the God whom Jesus calls 'Abba' is introduced in those very Scriptures. They too reflect similar structural parallels between *creation* and *redemption*, with the engaging story of God's affair with Israel beginning at Genesis 12 with Abraham, while the initial chapters detailing God's creation of the universe seem designed to offer that particular story universal grounding.[3] By the time Aquinas came to engage these issues, a third Abrahamic voice[4] clamoured for recognition, though reflecting a new scripture. The Qur'an's account is far more lapidary: 'He says "be" and it is' (6:73), yet the pattern is repeated. The heart of the drama turns on Mohammed's God-given 'recitation'; Allah's identifying Himself with 'the Creator of the heavens and the earth' (2:117) assures us that we are not merely trafficking with an Arabian deity. So the forces conspiring to elaborate the Christian 'doctrine of creation' were at once historical and conceptual, scriptural and philosophical, with discussions from other faiths

[2] Sokolowski, *God of Faith and Reason*, p. 37.

[3] For a more detailed discussion of creation in the Old Testament, recall E. McMullin's chapter, section 2, of this volume.

[4] Hence the title of the present volume, *Creation and the God of Abraham.*

shaping the context.[5] Both Jewish and Christian readings of Genesis had taken the equivocal language regarding pre-existent stuff as part of the inherently narrative structure of the work, insisting that God created the universe *ex nihilo*; that is, without presupposing anything 'to work on', as it were. So the philosophical task will be to articulate 'sheer origination', while the theological goal will be to show this action to be utterly gratuitous. If creator and creation are to be what the Hebrew Scriptures presume them to be, neither stuff nor motive can be presupposed. Here is where what Sokolowski has identified as 'the distinction' proves so critical: creation can only be creation if God can be God without creating. No external incentive nor internal need can induce God to create. In the remaining part of this chapter I wish to focus on Aquinas' account of creation and its theological consequences.

AQUINAS' STRATEGIES

Aquinas' capacity to integrate philosophical with theological demands is displayed in the initial article in the *Summa Theologiae* on creation: 'Must everything that is have been caused by God?'[6] Relying on his identification of God as that One whose very essence is to exist, Aquinas shows why one must 'necessarily say that whatever in any way *is* is from God'. For if 'God is sheer existence subsisting of its very nature [*ipsum esse per se subsistens*], [and so] must be unique, ... then it follows that all things other than God are not their own existence but share in existence.'[7] So the Neoplatonic distinction between *essential* and *participated* being is invoked to give everything but the creator the stamp of *created*. Very little, if anything, is said here about causation, but the elements are in place to press for a unique form of it, even though another way of posing the initial question employs Aristotle explicitly: 'whether God is the efficient cause of all beings?' An objection asks about those 'natural necessities' which Aristotle presumed simply to be, or always to have been: 'since there are many such in reality [spiritual substances and heavenly bodies which carry no principle of dissolution within themselves], all beings are not from God'. Aquinas deftly diverts this objection by recalling the primacy of existing: 'an active cause is

[5] For an explicitly interfaith appraisal, see the articles in David B. Burrell and Bernard McGinn (eds.), *God and Creation* (University of Notre Dame Press, 1990). For a narrative sketch of the interaction among the chief medieval protagonists, see my *Knowing the Unknowable God: Ibn-Sina, Maimonides, Aquinas* (University of Notre Dame Press, 1986), as well as *Freedom and Creation in Three Traditions* (University of Notre Dame Press, 1993).

[6] Aquinas, *Summa Theologiae* 1.44.1 (hereafter, *ST*). [7] *ST* 1.3.4.

required not simply because the effect could not be [i.e., is contingent], but because the effect would not be if the cause were not [existing]'.[8] So even 'necessary things' will require a cause for their very being: this is a radical revision of Aristotle, depending on the Avicennian distinction of *essence* from *existing*. What it suggests is that Aquinas was seeking for a way of understanding created being using Aristotelian metaphysics, yet the 'givens' of that philosophy will have to be transformed to meet the exigency of a free creator. Put another way, which anticipates our elucidation, the *being* which Aristotle took to characterize substance must become (for Aquinas) an *esse ad creatorem* (an existing in relation to the creator). This is another way of saying that 'all things other than God are not their own existence', either in the radical sense on which this chapter insists, distinguishing creatures from the creator, or even in a more attenuated sense in which the being which they *have* cannot be 'their own' in the sense of belonging to them 'by right' or by virtue of their being the kind of things they are (which was Aristotle's view). Everything other than God receives its being from the Creator as a gift. Yet such derived or participated things are no less real than Aristotle's substances, since now there is no other way to be except to participate in the *ipsum esse* of the Creator. So the nature of the creating act depends crucially on our conception of the One from whom all that is comes.

Now if that One is most properly identified as 'He who is' since 'the existence of God is his essence and since this is true of nothing else', then we are in the presence of One whose characteristic act will be 'to produce existence [*esse*] absolutely . . . which belongs to the meaning of creation' defined as 'the emanation of the whole of being from a universal cause' or 'universal being'.[9] That being's 'proper effect', then, is the very existence of things.[10] One implication of this unique form of causation is that

> creation is not a change, except merely according to our way of understanding, [since] creation, whereby the entire substance of things is produced, does not allow of some common subject now different from what it was before, except according to our way of understanding which conceives an object as first not existing at all and afterwards as existing.[11]

So creating is not a process answering the question: *how* does God create? God creates intentionally, that is, by intellect and will, though these are identical in God, so Aquinas has no difficulty adopting the metaphor of 'emanation' to convey something of the act of creation: God's consenting to the universe coming forth from God – that One whose essence is simply

[8] *ST* 1.44.1, ad. 2. [9] *ST* 1.13.11; 1.3.4; 1.45.5; 1.45.1; 1.45.4, ad. 1. [10] *ST* 1.45.5. [11] *ST* 1.45.2, ad. 2.

to-be.[12] The revelation of God's inner life as Father, Son and Spirit will in fact allow Aquinas to say more, while respecting the absence of process. For it is this revelation which directs us to

> the right idea of creation. The fact of saying that God made all things by His Word excludes the error of those who say that God produced things by necessity. When we say that in Him there is a procession of love, we show that God produced creatures not because He needed them, nor because of any other extrinsic reason, but on account of the love of His own goodness.[13]

The act of creating is not a 'mere overflow' (or emanation) from this One whose very nature is to-be. It is rather an intentional emanating and so a gracious gift. Yet the mode of action remains utterly consonant with the divine nature, hence the natural metaphor of *emanation*.

The other metaphor which Aquinas invokes is that of the artisan: 'God's knowledge is the cause of things; for God's knowledge stands to all created things as the artist's to his products', with the implication that 'natural things are suspended between God's [practical] knowledge and our [speculative] knowledge'.[14] The deft way Aquinas employs Aristotle's distinction between *practical* and *speculative* knowing here allows him to utilize the metaphor of the artisan critically, and so avoid pitting divine and human knowing against one another. Since God's knowing brings things into being and sustains them, we need not worry ourselves whether God's knowing 'what will have happened' determines future contingent events, since the knowing which God has of what will have taken place is not propositional in character. God knows what God does; the model is practical knowing. Taking a cue from Aquinas' strategy regarding God's knowledge of singulars, we must say that divine knowledge extends as far as divine activity, for God does not work mindlessly. Yet we can have no more determinate model for divine knowing than that.[15] Yet the artisan metaphor for creation might lead one to suspect that the product could subsist without any further action on the part of its maker.

So emanation will need to be invoked to remind us of the revolution which the presence of a creator and the act of creation has worked in Aristotle: the very being (*esse*) of creatures is now an *esse-ad*, 'a relation to the creator as the origin of its existence'.[16] Aristotle's definition of substance as 'what subsists in itself' can still function to distinguish substance from accident, but the being inherent to created substances proceeds from

[12] *ST* I.19.4, ad. 4. [13] *ST* I.32.1, ad. 3. [14] *ST* I.14.8, and ad. 3.
[15] *ST* I.14.11. See also my extended treatment of these issues in *Freedom and Creation*, pp. 105–119.
[16] *ST* I.45.3.

another, from the source who alone subsists eternally as the One whose essence is to be. And if substances must now be denominated 'created substances', the causality associated with creating can hardly be comprehended among Aristotle's four causes. For the two contenders, efficient and formal, each fail since an efficient cause without something to work on would be unintelligible to Aristotle, while trying to fit the creator into Aristotle's formal cause would directly foster pantheism, as Aquinas notes in *ST* 1.3.8. So a 'cause of being' must be *sui generis*, as we shall see, confirming 'the distinction' of creator from creation, while the founding 'non-reciprocal relation of dependence' will be unique as well, and best characterized by the borrowed expression 'non-duality'.[17] So the practical knowing involved in creating will be more like *doing* than *making*, suggesting James Ross' prescient image of the 'being of the cosmos like a song on the breath of a singer', while emphasizing that 'God's causing being can be analogous to many diverse things without even possibly being the same as any one of them.'[18]

WHAT A FREE CREATION PORTENDS

We now begin to see the philosophical thickets into which the assertion of faith that God freely creates the universe can lead us. And rightly so, since that affirmation grounds all the other Abrahamic faiths as well. Indeed, both al-Ghazali and Moses Maimonides staunchly resisted the necessity endemic to the picture of creation as emanation which they encountered in the philosophy of their time, for fear that it would preclude the very possibility of revelation. Nothing short of a free creation can ground a free revelation, and, with it, a free human response to the One from whom all that is comes forth.[19] Aquinas will enlist the resources of Neoplatonism to offer a philosophically coherent account of the creator as the One causing being, allowing him to insist that 'the proper effect of the first and most universal cause, which is God, is existence itself [*ipsum esse*]'.[20] Yet since this effect is that of an agent thoroughly intentional and free, he also insists that 'what God principally intends in created things is that form which consists in the

[17] See Sara Grant's comparative study of Aquinas and Shankara for this creative proposal to find a positive way to express the relation attendant upon 'the distinction', *Towards an Alternative Theology: Confessions of a Non-dualist Christian*, with introduction by Bradley J. Malkovsky (University of Notre Dame Press, 2002). More in the last section of this chapter.

[18] James Ross, 'Creation II' in Alfred Freddoso (ed.), *The Existence and Nature of God* (University of Notre Dame Press, 1983), pp. 115–141, at p. 128.

[19] This is the burden of my *Freedom and Creation*.

[20] *ST* 1.45.5.

good of order of the universe [*bonum ordinis universi*]'.[21] Calling the 'good of order of the universe' a 'form' is clearly as much of an accommodation of Aristotelian terminology as calling the creator 'the efficient cause of all being', yet the stretch must begin somewhere.[22] As always, one notices the transformation in the ways Aquinas employs these notions once they have been introduced; it is the language in use which counts. And since mention of 'good' invites a discussion of 'evil', Aquinas' concluding remarks to this section on 'the distinction among creatures', including 'the distinction between good and evil', are especially illuminating. He is confronted with the Manichean argument that 'we should postulate some supreme evil which of itself is the cause of evils [since were one to] allege that evil has an indirect cause merely, not a direct cause . . . it would follow that evil would crop up rarely, not frequently, as it in fact does'.[23] His response is forthright:

> As for the reference to evil being present in the majority of cases [*in pluribus*], it is simply untrue. For things subject to generation and decay, in which alone we experience physical evil, compose but a small part of the whole universe, and besides defects of nature are minority occurrences in any species. They seem to be in a majority only among human beings. For what appears good for them as creatures of sense is not simply good for them as human, that is as reasonable beings; in fact most of them follow after sense, rather than intelligence.[24]

This sharp exchange can be parsed as Aquinas' countering the claim that there is more evil than good in the universe by means of a distinction: in the natural world – despite cataclysms, miscarriages and other 'defects of nature' – there is manifestly more good than evil in creation. Here his faith perspective is reinforced by his Aristotelian cosmology, as it would be even more by the intricacies unveiled by modern science. The human world, however, reflects the opposite state of affairs, to which Aquinas assigns a cause here, only to explore it later (in *ST* I–II.77 and 85). What might well startle us, however, is the matter-of-fact assertion that our cultural world displays more evil than good. Aquinas would have had no truck with modernity's claim about human perfectibility, so he hardly needed the chastening of the twentieth century to disabuse him. He did feel the need to account for our role in systematically distorting creation, however, though our experience with the way in which claims of human perfectibility have distorted the natural environment of humans could expand exponentially on his. Yet, ironically enough, that hubris peculiar to humans can at least in part be traced to the way we find his earlier claim,

[21] *ST* I.49.2. [22] *ST* I.44.1. [23] *ST* I.49.3, obj. 5; I.48–49. [24] *ST* I.49.3, ad. 5.

that 'things subject to generation and decay . . . compose but a small part of the whole universe', so quaint. For a universe bereft of intelligences, whether they be identified as heavenly bodies or angels, can only place human beings at its pinnacle, thus leading us to read that fatal line in Genesis as licensing us to transform the natural world to serve our needs. Aquinas' lapidary explanation for this propensity of ours – that most of us 'follow after sense rather than intelligence' – recalls the 'good of order of the universe' as well, as he notes that this propensity also contravenes our given nature, since 'what appears good for them as creatures of sense is not simply good for them as human'. Moreover, this is a humanity firmly placed within the 'good of order of the universe' and hence included within a vast world of nature, indeed inserted at the point where the material and the spiritual dimensions of that universe intersect. An awesome picture indeed, and one Aquinas could glean from his Aristotelian cosmology, yet can only be available to us by faith.

A PLATONIC LEGACY

Another arresting feature of Aquinas' account for us is the way he links *being* with *good*, as we have seen. Here we need to turn to the celebrated *Liber de Causis*, an Islamic adaptation of Proclus published in Arabic as *al-kitab al-Khair* (*Book of the Pure Good*), on which Aquinas commented.[25] Aquinas found in this manifestly Neoplatonic text an idiom for expounding the elusive category of 'cause of being' to explicate the act of creation. We might pose the question this way: how is it that the One, whose proper effect is things' very being, effects that? The 'first cause infuses all things with a single infusion, for it infuses things under the aspect [*sub rationem*] of the good'.[26] Aquinas concurs, reminding us that it had already been shown that 'the first cause acts through its being, . . . hence it does not act through any additional relation or disposition through which it would be adapted to and mixed with things'.[27] Moreover, 'because the first cause acts through its being, it must rule things in one manner, for it rules things according to the way it acts'.[28] The following Proposition 21 links this 'sufficiency of God to

[25] An annotated English translation of the commentary by Vincent Gualiardo, Charles Hess and Richard Taylor, *Commentary of the Book of Causes* (Washington DC: Catholic University of America Press, 1996). See my 'Aquinas' Appropriation of *Liber de Causis* to Articulate the Creator as Cause-of-Being' in Fergus Kerr (ed.), *Contemplating Aquinas* (London: SCM Press, 2003), pp. 55–74.

[26] *Book of Causes*, p. 123 (p. 110). All references to the *Book of Causes* give the page reference to the English translation, followed by the page reference to the Latin text in brackets.

[27] *Book of Causes*, pp. 123–124 (p. 111). [28] *Book of Causes*, p. 124 (p. 111).

rule' with divine simplicity, 'since God is simple in the first and greatest degree as having his whole goodness in a oneness that is most perfect'.[29] Hence Proposition 23 can assert: 'what is essentially act and goodness, namely, God, essentially and originally communicates his goodness to things'. With such a One there can be no anxiety about 'control'; indeed, the simile which the proposition on divine rule elicits is that 'it is proper for a ruler to lead those that are ruled to their appropriate end, which is the good'.[30] Thus to 'infuse things under the aspect of the good' is precisely to bring all things to be in a certain order, inherent in their very existing, so there is nothing 'external' about divine providence, no imposition – neither 'inasmuch as it establishes things, which is called creation; [nor] inasmuch as it rules things already established'.[31] Indeed, the initial diversity comes from the first cause, who 'produces the diverse grades of things for the completion of the universe. But in the action of ruling . . . the diversity of reception is according to the diversity of the recipients.'[32] Yet, since the original order comes from the One, the One in ruling will 'effortlessly' adapt itself to the order established in creating. Another way of putting all this, and one which should dissolve most conundra regarding 'divine action', is to remind oneself that the creator, in acting, acts always as creator; and this proposition elucidates Aquinas' contention that *creating* and *conserving* are the same action, differing only in that conserving presupposes things present.

However, the manner of that action will ever escape us, for its very simplicity belies any *manner* at all – no 'relation or disposition' – the best we can do is to remind ourselves that it ever acts by constituting the order which inheres in each existing thing, in the measure that it is.[33] And 'order' is a consummately analogous term, so we can never be sure we have detected the originating divine order in things, though our conviction that there is one, inscribed in their very being and our intentional attitudes towards them, will continue to fuel our inquiry. Crude classifications – inanimate, animate, intentional – can be supplemented by refined mathematical structures and symmetries (as in DNA), but each stage of the analytic tool will be serving our innate desire to unveil the activity present in these infused 'goodnesses' which constitute our universe. Moreover, to grasp something of that constitutive ordering is to come closer to its source,

[29] *Book of Causes*, p. 125 (p. 112), p. 126 (p. 113). [30] *Book of Causes*, p. 134 (p. 118).
[31] *Book of Causes*, p. 137 (p. 122). [32] *Book of Causes*, p. 137 (p. 123).
[33] Since essence measures *esse*, it is pointless to oppose essence to existing in things that are.

because every knowing substance, insofar as it has being more perfectly, knows both the first cause and the infusion of its goodness more perfectly, and the more it receives and knows this the more it takes delight in it, [so] it follows that the closer something is to the first cause the more it takes delight in it.[34]

All is not light or delight, of course, because in truth we cannot ourselves hope to *know* 'the first cause and the infusion of goodness'. Indeed, 'the most important thing we can know about the first cause is that it surpasses all our knowledge and power of expression', for 'our intellect can grasp only that which has a quiddity participating in "to-be" [while] the quiddity of God is "to-be itself"'.[35] Indeed, that is why Aquinas can concur that 'the first cause is above being inasmuch as it is itself infinite "to-be"'.[36] Yet, since 'what belongs to higher things [is] present in lower things according to some kind of participation', we can be said to share, as beings, in this inaccessible One.[37]

A PLATONIC COROLLARY: PARTICIPATION

It is but a short step from this treatment to the central theme of participation in Aquinas' account of created being. Indeed, recognizing how central participation is to Aquinas' metaphysics of created being recalls Josef Pieper's penetrating observation that creation is 'the hidden element in the philosophy of St. Thomas'.[38] And registering the implications of Pieper's remark should lead one to re-assess the easy demarcation between philosophy and theology so redolent of twentieth-century Thomism.[39] In a recent monograph of stunning proportions, Rudi te Velde[40] offers a fresh presentation of this theme, recapitulating the earlier work of Cornelio Fabro and Louis Geiger. He begins his consideration of Aquinas' use of this Platonic notion with the apparently innocent question posed by Boethius in *De hebdomadibus* (on which Aquinas commented): how can things be said to be *good*? By participation or by substance? It is the disjunction that will bother Aquinas, and his commentary will make clear that Boethius must pose it that way because for him 'participation refers to an accidental property of a substance', depending as it does 'on the Aristotelian categorical

[34] *Book of Causes*, p. 130 (p. 116), p. 138 (p. 123). [35] *Book of Causes*, p. 51 (p. 47), p. 52 (p. 43).
[36] *Book of Causes*, p. 51 (p. 47). [37] *Book of Causes*, p. 30 (p. 17).
[38] 'The Negative Element in the Philosophy of St. Thomas' in *The Silence of Saint Thomas* (New York: Pantheon, 1957), pp. 47–67.
[39] See my 'Theology and Philosophy' in Gareth Jones (ed.), *Blackwell Companion to Modern Theology* (Oxford: Blackwell, 2002), pp. 34–46.
[40] Rudi te Velde, *Participation and Substantiality in Thomas Aquinas* (Leiden: Brill, 1995).

division of being into substance and accident'.[41] Boethius' solution – that things are good 'in virtue of [their] relation to the first Good' – leaves us asking 'in what sense created things are good by participation, such that they are nevertheless also essentially and not just accidentally good'?[42] So the issue is joined: 'participation' will need to be explicated by an ontology richer than the received distinction of substance/accident, although the mode of participation operative in that very distinction will offer us some hints as to how to understand it in a fuller way.

This is exactly the reason [for] calling the likeness between God and creatures 'analogous', as well as the rationale for developing Dionysius' causal notion of participation to the point where it can satisfy the criterion of one action which gives both existence and order, being and diversity.[43] Both the unitary act of creation and the diversity inherent within things demand the developed notion of participation, the entire purpose of which is to render so unique an act as intelligible as we can make it.

Aquinas does all this by transforming 'participation' as he found it, offering an interpretation of the Neoplatonic hierarchy which will not include God as part of it, while incorporating the Aristotelian notion of form in such a way as 'to reconcile his metaphysical gradualism based on participation with the substantiality of created beings'.[44] Both Hellenic streams will be transformed to show that there is 'but one transcendent source of participation from which all things derive their distinct perfection'.[45] And the unity of those perfections in God, to offer a rich evocation of divine unity as metaphysical simpleness, completes the account by returning to the plenitude of Aquinas' understanding of *esse*.

CREATOR AND CREATURES – A NON-DUALITY?

A more theological commentary on these matters can be found in the slim volume of Teape lectures by Sara Grant, recently re-issued by Bradley Malkovsky. As she puts it:

> In India as in Greece, the ultimate question must always be that of the relation between the supreme unchanging Reality and the world of coming-to-be and passing away, the eternal Self and what appears as non-Self, and no epistemology can stand secure as long as this question remains unanswered. [It is indeed this

[41] te Velde, *Participation and Substantiality*, pp. 14 and 17.
[42] te Velde, *Participation and Substantiality*, pp. 18 and 20.
[43] te Velde, *Participation and Substantiality*, p. 116.
[44] te Velde, *Participation and Substantiality*, p. 210.
[45] te Velde, *Participation and Substantiality*, p. 211.

startling contention which this chapter has been exploring.] . . . A systematic study of Shankara's use of relational terms made it quite clear to me that he agrees with St. Thomas Aquinas in regarding the relation between creation and the ultimate Source of all being as a *non-reciprocal dependence relation*; i.e., a relation in which subsistent effect or 'relative absolute' is *dependent on its cause for its very existence as a subsistent entity*, whereas the cause is *in no way dependent on the effect for its subsistence*, though there is a *necessary logical relation between cause and effect*; i.e., a relation which is *perceived by the mind* when it reflects on the implications of the existence of the cosmos.[46]

Her final observation about a 'necessary logical relation' is quite compatible with regard to creating as a free action of the creator, for its import is intended to capture Aquinas' identification of 'creation in the creature [as] nothing other than a relation of sorts to the creator as the principle of its existing'.[47]

So the very existence (*esse*) of a creature is an *esse-ad*, an existing which is itself a relation to its source. As we have noted, nothing could better express the way in which Aquinas' formulation of the essence/existing distinction transforms Aristotle than to point out that what for Aristotle 'exists in itself' (substance) is for Aquinas derived from an Other in its very in-itselfness, or substantiality. Yet since the Other is the cause of being, each thing which exists-to the creator also exists in itself: derived existence is no less substantial when it is derived from the One-who-is, so it would appear that one could succeed in talking of existing things without explicitly referring them to their source. 'The distinction', in other words, need not *appear*. But that simply reminds us how unique a non-reciprocal relation of dependence must be: it characterizes one relation only, that of creatures to creator.

If creator and creature were distinct from each other in an ordinary way, the relation – even one of dependence – could not be non-reciprocal; for ordinarily the fact that something depends from an originating agent, as a child from a parent, must mark a difference in that agent itself. Yet the fact that a cause of being, properly speaking, is not affected by causing all-that-is does not imply remoteness or uncaring; indeed, quite the opposite. For such a One must cause in such a way as to be present in each creature as that to which it is oriented in its very existing. In that sense, this One cannot be considered as *other* than what it creates, in an ordinary sense of that term; just as the creature's *esse-ad* assures that it cannot *be* separately from its source.[48] So it will not work simply to contrast creation to emanation, or to

46 *Towards an Alternative Theology*, p. 35. 47 *ST* 1.45.3.
48 See my exchange with Tom Flint in *Freedom and Creation*, p. 112, esp. note 33.

picture the creator distinct (in the ordinary sense) from creation by contrast with a more pantheistic image. Indeed, it is to avoid such infelicities of imagination that Sara Grant has recourse to Shankara's sophisticated notion of 'non-duality' to call our attention in an arresting way to the utter uniqueness of 'the distinction' which must indeed hold between creator and creation, but cannot be pictured in any contrastive manner.[49] Nor does Aquinas feel any compunction at defining creation as the 'emanation of all of being from its universal cause [*emanatio totius entis a cause universali*]'.[50] Indeed, once he had emptied the emanation scheme of any mediating role, he could find no better way of marking the uniqueness of the causal relation of creation than using the term 'emanation' to articulate it.[51] For once the scheme has been gutted, that *sui generis* descriptor should serve to divert us from imaging the creator over against the universe, as an entity exercising causal efficacy on anything-that-is in a manner parallel to causation within the universe.[52] While the all-important 'distinction' preserves God's freedom in creating, which the emanation scheme invariably finesses, we must nevertheless be wary of picturing that distinction in a fashion which assimilates the creator to another item within the universe. Harm Goris has shown how close attention to the uniqueness of the creator/creature relation, with its attendant corollary of participation as a way of articulating this *sui generis* causal relation, can neutralize many of the conundra which fascinate philosophers of religion.[53]

Although it may seem that we have strayed far from Aquinas in invoking Shankara's hybrid term of 'non-duality', we should have realized by now how Aquinas helps himself to various ways of expressing the inexpressible: the 'distinction' as well as the 'relation' between creatures and their creator. Both prove to be foundational to any attempt to grasp our transcendent origins as gift. Bible and Qur'an conspire to highlight the Creator's freedom; philosophy proves helpful to theology in finding ways to think both creature and Creator together.

[49] Kathryn Tanner develops a sense of transcendence that is expressly 'non-contrastive', illustrating that suggestive category through the history of some key questions in philosophical theology, in her *God and Creation in Christian Theology: Tyranny or Empowerment* (Oxford: Blackwell, 1988).

[50] *ST* 1.45.1. [51] See my *Knowing the Unknowable God*, pp. 86–91.

[52] As in William Hasker's treatment of the issues in his *God, Time, and Knowledge* (Ithaca, NY: Cornell University Press, 1989).

[53] Harm Goris, *Free Creatures of an Eternal God* (Leuven: Peeters, 1996).

CHAPTER 4

Scotistic metaphysics and creation ex nihilo

Alexander Broadie

INTRODUCTION

In the High Middle Ages all the major theologians of the Christian West teach that God created our world *ex nihilo*, that is, that first there is God and no world, and then, by an act of divine will, there is a world which is, in some sense, at a distance from and therefore other than God. During the Age of Enlightenment the concept of the creation of the world modulates to a distant key, for we find philosophers propounding the thesis that the world is the product of an act not of the divine but of the human mind. It may seem bizarre to hold that each of us produces the world in which we live, and presumably therefore produces it on the side, without our even noticing that we are engaged in such a stupendous act. Nevertheless there are powerful arguments in support of the claim; I shall give prominence to doctrines of David Hume and Immanuel Kant, doctrines according to which certain features of the world, features which give rise to our perception of the world as objectively valid, are the product of our own mental powers.

A question therefore arises as to the relation between on the one hand the religious claim that God created the world and on the other hand the Enlightenment claim that we human beings are world-makers. The two claims may seem mutually incompatible. Here I shall argue that they are not incompatible and in particular I shall argue for the coherence of the claim that human beings co-operate with God in the act of creation. By this means I hope to explicate the relation of otherness in which our world stands to God. So far as my narrative concerns Enlightenment insights, I have already indicated that Hume and Kant will play guiding roles. As regards the religious doctrine concerning God's creation of the world, I shall focus on John Duns Scotus and it is to him that I now turn. Since it will be necessary to employ the concept of the relation between the being of God and the being of the world my point of departure is Duns Scotus' doctrine of being.

SCOTUS ON BEING AND MODES OF BEING

Being has many modes. Among them are infinity, finitude, necessity and contingency; and medieval theologians of the Christian West were united in their judgment that the creator's being is both necessary and infinite and that the being of *creata* is contingent and finite. Since there can be no greater metaphysical difference than that between the being of the creator and of the *creatum*, does this imply that the term "being" cannot have precisely the same sense when predicated of creator and *creatum*? In accordance with my broadly Scotistic frame of reference I shall be supposing that the concept of "being," one and the same concept, can be truly affirmed of both the creator and his *creata*. Scotus argues that, since I can believe that God exists and be in doubt about whether God's being is infinite or is finite, I must therefore be able to predicate of God a being that is neutral as between infinity and finitude.[1] Likewise, though believing that there is a God I can be in doubt as to whether God's being is uncreated or created and I therefore predicate of God a being that is neutral as between these alternatives. I can say this of *creata* also. For example, though I am certain of the being of the starry heavens, I might be in doubt as to whether their being is uncreated and whether their being is infinite. I therefore predicate of the starry heavens a being that is neutral as between these various alternatives. Thus I predicate being, in precisely the same sense of being, of God and *creata*. That the concept of "being" can be affirmed in this way is the main tenet of Scotus' doctrine of the univocity of being.[2]

All this is of course compatible with there being immense metaphysical differences between the being that is proper to the creator and the being that is proper to *creata*, and it is compatible also with there being aspects of the creatorial being which are necessarily beyond the reach of our intellects. Furthermore the doctrine of univocity of being does not imply that there can be anything whose being is in reality neither infinite nor finite, neither necessary nor contingent, neither uncreated nor created. The doctrine of

[1] *Ordinatio* I.3.I.I–2, n. 27, in John Duns Scotus, *Opera Omnia*, ed. C. Balić *et al.* (Civitas Vaticana: Typis Polyglottis Vaticanis, 1950–), vol. III, p. 18.

[2] Scotus does not in fact give a definition of "univocity" though he does present two necessary conditions for the deployment of the term. (1) If the propositions "X is an A" and "X is not an A" are mutually contradictory then "A" is employed univocally in the two propositions. And (2) granted that the following is a valid syllogism: "Every B is C and every A is B, therefore every A is C," then the middle term "B" is being used univocally in the two premises (*Ordinatio* I.3, nn. 25–30, in *Opera Omnia*, vol. III, pp. 16–20). Though these criteria of univocity would be inadequate as definitions it is not clear that Scotus intended them as definitions rather than as necessary conditions for the correct deployment of the term "univocal."

univocity of being means no more than this, that it is possible to form a unitary concept of being under which can be brought the creator and *creata*. In that sense, and in that sense alone, can there be being which is neutral in respect of these various modes. That is to say, being *simpliciter* exists at the conceptual level and not otherwise. From which it follows that the doctrine of univocity of being is not metaphysical but logical.

I have two reasons for considering here the doctrine of the univocity of being. The first is that I shall be operating within a broadly Scotistic theological framework during this metaphysical speculation on the relation in which the being of the world stands to the being of God, and it is necessary to be clear that the doctrine of the univocity of being is a central feature of Scotus' theology. It should be added at once that from a Scotistic perspective the doctrine is of importance for the whole enterprise of natural theology in view of the fact that the discipline sees itself as a science and therefore as something that advances by a process of discursive reasoning. If the meanings of terms are not invariant through the course of an argument then the argument is invalid. Hence natural theology, as a science, is bound to respect the rules concerning the fixity of meanings of terms.[3]

My second reason for invoking here the doctrine of univocity of being is that creation is held to be the creation of being. Aquinas affirms this doctrine,[4] so also does Scotus, and I should like now to focus on it. Of course not every creative act is a production of something *ex nihilo*. We human beings create material things and cannot produce them *ex nihilo*; we need to employ an antecedently existent matter. Fortunately we do not need to create matter since God has already done that for us; we engage instead therefore in the task of working creatively on what, by divine provision, is already in being. But if we have not produced the being of the material things that are the products of our creative acts, is our contribution to those products less valuable than it would have been if we had also contributed their being? The creative person produces something of value by working creatively on antecedent matter, and the aim is to put a value into the world. Matter must be available to us in order for there to be something that is the bearer of the value that is the product of the creative person's creativity and that is the truest representative of their creative power. It is, after all, the value contributed by the agent's creative imagination that has value in itself

[3] *Lectura* I.3.I.I–2, n. 113, in *Opera Omnia*, vol. XVI, p. 266. "*Item, nisi ens importaret unam intentionem, univocam, simpliciter periret theologia*" (Moreover, unless being implied one univocal intention, theology would simply perish).

[4] For Aquinas' discussion of creation and its theological consequences, see D. Burrell's chapter in the present volume.

and the being of what bears the value has value in only an instrumental way as bearer.

I am not working here against the doctrine, traceable at least to Plato, that there is no being without value; that is, in a metaphysical sense, merely to be is already to be good. My point instead is that being is for the sake of the good and not vice versa. But if there is no creative act that does not put value into the world then why is it appropriate to say that creation is creation of being rather than that it is creation of value? Why specify being and not the *causa finalis* of being? Put otherwise, it is appropriate to ask what is so good about being as such. If *per impossibile* a creative act could produce a being that were absolutely valueless then there would be no more point to producing that being than to producing nothing. Likewise there would be no more point to creating a valueless thing that lasted for a long time (or indeed forever) than to creating one that lasted for a mere moment.

However, though there is reason to identify an act as creative in virtue of its final rather than material cause (if it is appropriate to think of being as a material cause), from one point of view it is not important whether we privilege finality rather than materiality for, on a Scotistic reading, there is no difference in reality between the two transcendentals *being* and *good*. Neither of these as such, that is, as unqualified or indeterminate, can be proper to anything for, as indeterminate, they are not part of the metaphysical form of anything. We have already noted that there is in reality no indeterminate being, and we should now also note that there is in reality no indeterminate good. Indeterminate good exists solely as a concept in the mind, a concept under which everything that is good can be brought. On this basis, it is not metaphysically significant whether we identify creation as creation of being or as creation of value, and I shall therefore continue to abide by the tradition that focuses on creation as creation of being.

Let us proceed, then, by supposing that God has ideas and that these include the idea of the world that he created. But God's creation of the world is not his creation of the idea of a world. The idea is in the divine mind and this surely must not be said of the world itself. The world is neither God nor any part of God. It is other than him in a way in which no idea in the divine mind can be either other than that very mind or other than God. The created world cannot, however, just be that same idea but *outside* the divine mind, for the world, as having contingent and not necessary being, has a different mode of being from that of any idea within the divine mind.

Here we face the smallest hint of the immensity of the difference between divine creativity and human. We too have ideas which we then externalize, and in the process of externalization we modify what is already external, by deploying our knowledge, such as it is, of the laws of nature. Our *creatum* becomes other than ourselves by being placed in the public domain where it can have a continuity not otherwise possible for it. It acquires an otherness marked by the fact that our *creatum* is able to continue to be even when we cease to think about it.

None of this can be said of God's creation of the world. For reasons given earlier we have to suppose his creative act to be one through which the world comes to be other than he, but plainly his creative act does not require deployment of knowledge of the laws of nature, for since there was no nature there were no laws of nature either. Nor may we suppose that before the creation there was a place into which God's *creatum*, the world, could be inserted. There was nothing other than God, nothing either out of which to make the world or into which to place the world.

We must allow, I think, that something of the world had being in the divine mind prior to the creation. But the fact that an idea of the world is in the divine mind cannot alone serve to explain the being of the world. We cannot begin to set a limit to the activity of the divine mind, nor therefore set a limit to the number or kinds of its products, and in particular we must allow the possibility that God is able to conceive an infinite number of possible worlds, worlds perhaps differing infinitely from each other; the fact that these ideas are in the divine mind does not imply that they must therefore come to have being separate from God. Whether they come into being separate from God must depend in some measure on an act of the divine will.

SCOTUS AND CONTINGENT BEING

Let us suppose therefore that just as God has an idea of the world, considered as having *esse intentionale* in God's mind and therefore as being in no sense other than God, so also the divine will produces the world, considered as having *esse naturale* and therefore as being in some sense other than he. Yet it cannot be entirely other since the world is formally identical with the divine idea of it even though the world, as other than God, must have a different mode of being from the idea. But what is the nature of the otherness that the natural world has in its relation to God? I shall offer an answer to this question and, as a first step towards the answer, shall explore the fact that the world is a product of an absolutely free act of the divine will.

At the heart of Duns Scotus' concept of free will is the concept of "being open to contraries or opposites."[5] Whatever it is that I freely will, I could at the same moment have willed something else or could have willed nothing. This is in contrast to the alternatives open to purely natural substances, for there are no alternatives open to them. Whatever it is that they do, they could not then and there have done anything else instead. *Natura ad unum voluntas ad opposita.* Though the sun can bleach things and blacken things, can melt things and can bake things hard, these contraries are not open to it at each moment and in respect of each of the objects on which it acts. In short, whatever it does it does necessarily, and, on a traditional understanding, that is the mode of operation of things in nature.

Though we think that the sun has awesome power, it is powerless; for whatever it does it is powerless not to do, and what it does not do it is powerless to do, whereas we are free to act otherwise than we do. It is true that we act under the constraints of nature in that our bodies cannot break natural law, and in acting on the world we must act in the light of our grasp of the laws of nature. But we can form concepts of alternative possible futures for us, and it is not nature that determines which future we shall will to make our present; it is our free will itself that determines the outcome. The will is therefore not a mere passivity in relation to causally active agents which operate on the will from outside. The intellect, which for Scotus has only a natural form of causality, can propose a project to the will in light of external circumstances, but the will, always open to contraries, is free to say no to intellect, however reasonable intellect's project may be. Intellect proposes but will disposes. The will, therefore, has an indeterminacy in respect of its acts. It is, however, not an indeterminacy consequent upon uncertainty as to which external active principle will determine the will's act; but instead it is an indeterminacy constituted by its real openness to contraries so that the will itself, and nothing else, determines its own acts. With such considerations in mind, Scotus speaks of the "superabundant sufficiency" of our will.[6] From entirely within its own resources, and in no way coerced by anything outside it, the will determines its next act from among the many possibilities available to it. Hence in performing a free act we produce an actual state of affairs which is synchronic with states of affairs that are possible but counterfactual.

Scotus classifies the actual state of affairs produced by a given act of free will as "contingent," by which he means that some other act, also open to

[5] See A. Broadie, *The Shadow of Scotus* (Edinburgh: T&T Clark, 1995), Chapters 2 and 3.

[6] *Quaestiones in Metaphysicam* IX.15.

the agent, would have produced another state of affairs instead, another state which, though unactualized, was no less possible than was the state of affairs that was actualized.[7] There is therefore, for Scotus, a kind of negativity with which actual products of freely willed acts are permeated. The negativity is not merely the fact that the product, which had not been in being, comes to be in being, nor even is the negativity the fact that the product will in due course cease to be. The negativity resides in the fact that even while the freely willed product has being the product is accompanied by invisible siblings, the counterfactual states of affairs that were no less possibilities than is the state of affairs that was chosen from the various alternatives.

For Scotus nothing exists contingently except by an act of free will and all contingent beings therefore have a being that is on the edge of non-being. It is for this reason that Scotus expresses a preference for speaking of contingency in adverbial rather than predicative terms. He writes: "I do not call everything contingent which is not necessary and which was not always in existence, but only that whose opposite could have occurred at the time that this actually occurred. That is why I do not say that something is contingent but that something is caused contingently."[8] We are, therefore, to conceive of contingency primarily in terms of a kind of causing, namely such a causing as is characteristic of the operation of a free will. As products of an act of free will contingent beings are in being only because something happened, an act of will, that equally well might not have happened, and contingent beings therefore carry with them throughout their temporal span this original possibility of never having come into being.

The world itself, God's *creatum*, is no less contingent for being the product of the divine will than is an artifact which is the product of a human will. It is the same kind of contingency that is at issue. Since our world is one of infinitely many possible worlds that God could have created, our world is permeated by non-being insofar as other worlds that God could

7 Scotus does not seek to demonstrate *propter quid* that anything is contingent (a demonstration *propter quid* being a demonstration which reveals *why* something is so). He holds on the contrary that such a demonstration is not possible, since the existence of contingent things is a manifest fact. He invokes in his support Avicenna who affirms that those who deny a first principle should be flogged or exposed to flames until they concede that being burned is not the same thing as not being burned, nor is being flogged the same as not being flogged. See Scotus, *Ordinatio* 1.38.2, in *Opera Omnia*, vol. VI, p. 415. As to the lack of a demonstration, Scotus does not spell out this fact in detail, beyond noting that, while the existence of a contingent being can serve as the premise of a proof that there must be a necessary being, the reverse proof does not work.

8 John Duns Scotus, *A Treatise on God as First Principle*, trans. and ed. Allan B. Wolter, O. F. M. (Chicago: Forum Books, 1966), p. 84 (4.18).

have created but did not were, in the moment he created our world, no less possible than the world he did create. Hence, if I may so put the point, our actual world is synchronic with all the possible worlds that could have been created but that in fact are counterfactual while remaining possible. Our world was created out of non-being; its being is permanently on the edge of non-being – for throughout its being it remains something that might equally not have been created – and it remains in being for only as long as God wills, that is, it remains in being with the time span that God willed it to have in willing the world. This point requires development and I shall now turn to that task.

Scotus argues that creation and conservation are really the same, or more precisely he argues that the relation in which a creature stands to God as creator is really the same as the relation in which the creature stands to God as conserver. Where the creature or *creatum* in question is the world itself, Scotus' doctrine implies that God created the world as having a given time span and that having created the world he does not have the further task of conserving what he has created – it is by the one creative act that the world, with its time span, has being. Perhaps the allotted time span of the world is finite, but even if its time span is infinite the world remains permanently on the edge of non-being in virtue of its having been created (and therefore also in virtue of its being conserved) by an act of free will.[9] Plainly there is no room in Scotus' schema for the idea that once the world exists it can generate a momentum of its own in virtue of which it is able to maintain itself in being by its own efforts. Left to survive by its own efforts the world would vanish on the instant – it lacks the means even to try to make the effort to survive. Even less does Scotus subscribe to the doctrine that once the world has been created it has to be re-created moment after moment. For he does not hold that God created the world more than once, as if once was insufficient. For God to re-create would be for subsequent creating to be exercises in copying, and there is something bizarre in the idea of God copying something. Scotus' doctrine is clear: There is no distinction in reality between creation and conservation of the world, because the original (and one and only) act of creation of the world was of a world which has a time span.

As already indicated, whether the time span be finite or infinite the world is surrounded by and permeated by nothingness. I am reminded of the

[9] Scotus held that there is no real distinction but only a distinction of reason between God's creation of the world and his conservation of it. See A. Broadie, "Scotus on God's Relation to the World," *British Journal for the History of Philosophy* 7 (1999), pp. 1–13.

distinction, made by St. Anselm of Canterbury, between God who truly exists and we creatures who scarcely exist.[10] The distinction between *vere esse* (truly being) and *vix esse* (scarcely being) corresponds precisely to the distinction between that whose being is necessary and that whose being is contingent.

CREATION, CO-OPERATION AND THE AGE OF ENLIGHTENMENT

Throughout its time span the world is absolutely dependent upon the divine will. This doctrine is according to the mind of Scotus; but it is also according to the mind of Aquinas who teaches that being is an act, by which I think he means that for the world to be is for God to be doing something. The world is a performance executed by the will of the divine performer and, like any performance, it lasts for only as long as the performer wills it to continue. How then can the world be at a distance from or other than God? Nevertheless this chapter is premised on the belief that our world cannot be either God or any part of him, and it is therefore necessary for me to confront the question of how the otherness of the created world is to be explained. In response I shall now deploy insights of David Hume and Immanuel Kant, insights that will give me space in which to argue that certain of our mental powers have a mediative role in the process of the creation of the world. We do not merely perceive the world; we perceptibilize it. We do not merely understand the world; we intelligibilize it. I shall therefore argue that our status, the status of us finite free spirits, is that of co-operators with God in the production of our world. I now turn to those Enlightenment insights.

According to a common and defensible interpretation of Hume's *Treatise of Human Nature*, he takes as his starting point the existence of mental entities, perceptions of the mind, which either are impressions or are copies of impressions, which he terms "ideas." Hume argues that whatever there is must be reducible to these mental entities, these "fleeting existences," as he describes them. Yet there is a world, which seems external, permanent and

[10] "Since that which [creatures] were does not now exist, and that which they will be does not yet exist, and that which they are in the fleeting, knife-edged and scarcely existent present scarcely exists, since, therefore they are as mutable as this they are rightly said almost not to exist and scarcely to exist." *Monologion*, Chapter 28; in *S. Anselmi Opera Omnia*, ed. F. S. Schmitt, O. S. B., 6 vols. (Edinburgh: Nelson, 1940–1951), vol. 1, p. 46, ll. 12–16 (my translation). In *Proslogion* Chapters 2, 3, entitled "*Quod vere sit deus*" (That God truly is), Anselm constructs a proof of the proposition that God is such that it is impossible for him not to be.

independent of us who perceive it. But if perceptions are all there is, how is such a world possible? Hume's answer is that the world that we perceive is in fact the product of our own imaginative activity by which, with the help of empirically acquired concepts, we impose coherence upon the chaotic swirl of our impressions and ideas.[11] In this sense he regards us as active in the creation of our world, and not as mere recipients of it.

Hume was classed by some contemporaries as denying the being of the external world. Yet he affirms: "We may well ask, *What causes induce us to believe in the existence of body?* but 'tis vain to ask, *Whether there be body or not?* That is a point, which we must take for granted in all our reasonings."[12] Hume holds therefore that the belief in the existence of an external world is irresistible. But what he wants to know is not whether we believe in the external world but how we come by that belief; and in the course of answering this question he in effect characterizes the world's mode of being. The external world is a product of our mental powers working on our perceptions; its being is therefore intentional and nothing more than that. In short, there are not two worlds, one discovered by looking *ad intra* and the other discovered by looking *ad extra*; there is just one world, which is in reality *ad intra* but read or interpreted as *ad extra*. Not surprisingly therefore he speaks of our world, the world known to us through our senses, as a "fiction."[13] It is also not surprising that some philosophers thought him a skeptic on the question of whether the world exists. On the other hand Immanuel Kant is generally not seen as a skeptic regarding the being of the external world, and yet he argues that categorial features that we think of as features constitutive of the world, such as the relations of substance and accident, of cause and effect, and of reciprocity between agent and patient – that all these are in the world because our faculty of understanding has constituted the world in that way.[14] Kant is therefore often interpreted as holding that the objective validity of the world is the product of our own rational activity operating on what is given in sensory experience. In their different ways therefore both Hume and Kant regard human beings as world-makers.

It is not my business here to defend the detailed argumentation of either of these two great thinkers. However, an informed philosopher cannot now philosophize as if there had not been an Enlightenment; and in particular the doctrine of naive realism has not been tenable since Enlightenment

[11] David Hume, *A Treatise of Human Nature*, ed. L. A. Selby-Bigge, 2nd edn. with text revised and notes by P. H. Nidditch (Oxford: Clarendon Press, 1978), I.IV.ii.

[12] Hume, *Treatise*, I.IV.ii, p. 187. [13] Hume, *Treatise*, pp. 200, 201, 205 and 209.

[14] Kant, *Critique of Pure Reason*, trans. N. K. Smith, 2nd edn. (1781; London: Macmillan, 1787), Part II, Division I, Book I, Chapter I, "Of the Pure Concepts of the Understanding."

philosophers investigated the question of the extent to which what we like to think of as reality is in fact external to and independent of us. The conclusion some reached, that largely, if not totally, the external world is the product of our own mental activity, is supported by powerful arguments, arguments which cannot simply be ignored; and especially they cannot be ignored in discussion of the creation of the world since the concept of the mode of being of the world must be an essential element in the narrative.

Although the doctrines of Hume and Kant regarding the mode of being of the world might be judged incompatible with the doctrine of God as creator of the world, I wish to argue to the contrary. I began this chapter by assuming a creator-God and I had to face the problem, the subject of this chapter, of how he could make a world that is at a distance from or other than he. On the one hand there is the world which is an idea in God's mind and on the other hand there is the world which we inhabit and which is at least partly a consequence of our own sensory, conceptual and imaginative activity. This distinction can be expounded in terms of the world as an idea that God presents to us and also as something that we receive or to which we respond, a divine idea made available to us and accessed by the mediation of our reception apparatus, and especially by forms of intuition, by concepts and categories, such as those investigated by Hume and Kant, in terms of which we render perceptible and intelligible that which is presented to us. The joint product of God's activity and our receptivity is the world in which we live.

One implication of the above narrative is that we are not required to suppose two divine acts, one *ad intra* and the other *ad extra*, by which God re-produces with *esse naturale* an idea that already exists with *esse intentionale* in his mind. There is no need for such duplication. God has the idea, and we respond, as no doubt intended, by making of his idea our world, the world in which we live. The idea in the divine mind is, so to say, a world in waiting, a world waiting to become ours. It is *a* world but to become what we understand to be *the* world it requires to be received by us with our human sensory and intellectual apparatus, both a priori and empirical.

Our world is ours not in virtue of our having created it *ex nihilo* but in virtue of the exercise of our mental faculties on something presented to us by God. It might well be said, in a Kantian spirit, that the world is intelligible to us because we have intelligibilized it; but I also note the fact that our intelligibilizing activity must be supposed to make an objectively valid world out of something which is appropriate for or amenable to just such mental activity. A question therefore arises as to why it happens that there is present to our faculties an object of precisely the kind that our faculties need if they are to produce our world.

This point can also be made in respect of Hume. For though Hume says a good deal about the way impressions work as points of departure for our production of our world, he provides no explanation, nor thinks that we are ever in a position to provide one, regarding the origin of impressions; they are among the ultimate data of his system. That impressions are of such a nature, and that they present themselves in such a way, that it is possible for us to read them as if what they really are is an external, permanent and independent world – all this is something that does not give Hume pause. It gives me pause, but my starting point is not Hume's. He begins the exposition of his philosophy by talking about things in his head, impressions and ideas, and by defining his ontology in terms of those things, thus prompting the question of how, from such a starting point, Hume could ever reach the real world. Hume's answer, as we have seen, is that he manages to be in the world because the world is his construct.

I, on the other hand, began by taking for granted God's creation of the world and I wondered how the world could, in any sense, be other than or at a distance from God. My answer is that the otherness is explicable in terms of our perceptibilizing and intelligibilizing activity upon that which God has presented to us. God's creative act is the presentation to us of his idea of the material world. He presents it and we receive it. But reception is not a form of pure passivity. What we have been presented with would not exist for us, exist as our world or indeed as anything else that is ours, unless we made sense of the gift, and making sense of it is something that we have to *do*. And *we* have to do it. No one else can do it for us. So the perceptibilizing and the intelligibilizing come from within us. It is our contribution to the existence of an objectively valid world. Until we finite spirits have received the divine idea there is no material world except in the sense of a world with *esse intentionale* awaiting *esse naturale* by our co-operative act. In that sense our world is indeed a human construct; but it would not exist unless we had something out of which to construct it – and of course the "something" has to have a nature that is appropriate for that end. If it did not have such a nature, we could no more make our world out of it than we could sign our name on the surface of the ocean.

To sum up: I have sought here to effect a reconciliation between on the one hand traditional teaching on creation *ex nihilo* and on the other hand Enlightenment teaching on human beings as world-makers, and I have argued that insofar as our world is the outcome of the exercise of our mental reception apparatus in response to a divine idea presented to us, we finite spirits co-operate in the work of God.

CHAPTER 5

Creation and the context of theology and science in Maimonides and Crescas

Daniel Davies

INTRODUCTION

Moses Maimonides (1138–1204) is probably the most famous medieval Jewish philosopher. His *Guide for the Perplexed* has inspired Jewish philosophy since its appearance at the end of the twelfth century.[1] Hasdai Crescas (*c.* 1340–1410) has been described as his most important philosophic critic.[2] He wrote *The Light of the Lord* in response to Maimonides as part of an overall project to provide an alternative philosophical and *halakhic* system, a project which ultimately remained incomplete.[3] Despite great differences between their belief systems and world views, there are certain attitudes that can be identified in the approach of both thinkers to scientific and philosophical inquiry. The question of *creatio ex nihilo* is one which can be used to showcase those similarities and also some differences. In this chapter I will explain some of the common themes that run through their attitudes towards creation and the sciences. First, they both place importance on the notion that everything in existence depends upon God. That dependence is non-reciprocal[4] since both argue that God is in no way dependent upon anything at all. Second, I will show that there is, to a certain extent, a common methodological approach: they are both concerned to accept only theological positions which they can show to be scientifically acceptable on science's own terms. Both of these points are true of the writings of Maimonides and Crescas, even though they disagree over the nature of the things that God sustains in existence.

[1] The best English translation of the *Guide* is by Shlomo Pines, *The Guide of the Perplexed* (Chicago University Press, 1963).

[2] Warren Zev Harvey, *Physics and Metaphysics in Hasdai Crescas* (Amsterdam: J. C. Gieben, 1998), p. xi.

[3] In this chapter the references to the *Light* are taken from Shlomo Fisher's edition, *Sefer Or Hashem* (Jerusalem: Sifre Ramot, 1990).

[4] A very similar idea is found in Aquinas, as elucidated by D. Burrell's chapter in the present volume. Recall the discussion of 'non-duality', borrowing Sara Grant's terminology.

THAT EVERY EXISTING THING DEPENDS UPON A CAUSE

Because of the terminology, discussion of the doctrine of *creatio ex nihilo* as dependence upon God in the context of Jewish philosophy is liable to become confused before it even begins. It is often the case, though not always, that creation from nothing (*beriat yesh me'ayin*) is considered in opposition to creation from something (*beriat yesh miyesh*). Accordingly, opinions vary as to whether the world is originated (*meḥudash*) or eternal (*qadmon*).[5] The question addressed in these terms is whether or not the world, or something out of which the world was formed, has existed for an infinite past time. However, it remains the case that the importance of the question may be connected to the issue of whether there is a God upon which everything that exists depends. As Crescas says,

> there is nothing which is a necessarily existing being in view of itself apart from God. Everything other than God, however it is posited, originated or everlasting, exists contingently in view of itself and proceeds from God . . . God does not overflow and give to a receptacle since God gives the existence to the receptacle. When we say 'creation from nothing' we mean nothing other than this.[6]

What is at issue in this notion is more often elaborated explicitly when the discussion focuses on God's existence. God alone is considered to be uncaused. Everything else depends upon God, but God in no way depends upon anything. In Maimonides' view, this is such an important point that he expresses it at the very beginning of his *halakhic* code, the *Mishneh Torah*:

> The basic principle of all basic principles and the pillar of all sciences is to know that there is a first being who brought every existing thing into being. All existing things, whether celestial, terrestrial, or belonging to an intermediate class, exist only through its essence. Should it be supposed that it does not exist, it would follow that nothing else could possibly exist. Were it supposed that all other beings were non-existent, it alone would still exist. Their non-existence would not invoke its non-existence for all beings need it, but it needs none of them.[7]

[5] The bracketed terms are examples of Hebrew expressions for the relevant notions. Maimonides and many other Jewish thinkers wrote their philosophy in other languages. In the *Guide*, Maimonides uses a variety of Arabic expressions to describe creation from nothing. See Kenneth Seeskin's *Maimonides on the Origin of the World* (Cambridge University Press, 2005) for an extensive recent account of Maimonides' view.

[6] *Light* 3.1.1.5.

[7] A translation of this passage can be found in Isadore Twersky's *A Maimonides Reader* (New York: Behrman House, 1972), p. 43.

Crescas explains that belief in God is not itself one of the commandments; it is impossible, he says, to command belief since belief is not something which can be controlled by human will: it is not an object of choice. Crescas argues that if a proof for God's existence is compelling one cannot choose to disregard it.[8] The important point for the purposes of this chapter, though, is that Maimonides thought God's existence to be a matter that could be known, and that it is incumbent upon everyone subject to the law to understand how. Although Crescas does not think it a matter for legislation, he agrees that God's existence can be proven.[9] What exactly it might mean to say that God is the 'uncaused cause' is fleshed out when Crescas advances the only rational proof of God's existence which he considers persuasive. In a clear echo of Avicenna's 'proof from contingency', Crescas explains that all contingent existence must derive from an uncaused cause.[10] He dedicates a short chapter to the proof, which he expresses as follows:

> Whether causes and effects are finite or infinite, there is no escaping the conclusion that there must be something which is the cause of the aggregate of all of them. For were they all effects, they would be possible of existence with respect to themselves and would need something to cause the preponderance (*makhrī'a*) of their existence over their non-existence. That which brings their preponderance about is the cause of the entirety of effects and that is what we call God.[11]

To clarify the argument, the conclusion may be understood as a consequence of the following two principles: first, that there is a distinction between the essence and existence of all things in the world, and, second, that the activity of possessing existence is an effect which must be caused by an agent itself possessing existence. Once both these are granted, Crescas is entitled to draw the conclusion that there must be a necessary being to account for all contingent beings.

The distinction between essence and existence expands on the idea that every being can be conceptually divided into its component parts. For

[8] *Light*, introduction.

[9] It may be the case that he does not attach as much force to rational proofs of God's existence as Maimonides, though.

[10] For more on the proof itself and discussion of the debate over how to interpret Avicenna's text see Toby Mayer's 'Ibn Sīnā's "Burhān al-Siddīqīn"', *Journal of Islamic Studies* 12:1 (2001), pp. 18–39. The argument is clearly in the background of the *Guide* as Alexander Altmann shows in 'Essence and Existence in Maimonides' in Joseph A. Buijs (ed.), *Maimonides: A Collection of Critical Essays* (University of Notre Dame Press, 1988), pp. 148–165. Nevertheless, in his explicit demonstrations for God's existence he uses it in a slightly different way from Avicenna. See also Josef Stern's 'Maimonides' Demonstrations: Principles and Practice', *Medieval Philosophy and Theology* 10 (2001), pp. 47–84.

[11] *Light* 1.3.2.

example, a dog may be thought of as a quadruped or as furry. It may also be thought of as part of the genus animal. To define the essence of the dog, by assigning it a species as well as a genus, is to answer the question of what that thing is. That the definition signifies the essence is clear from the terms often used for 'essence' or 'nature' in both Arabic and Hebrew, *māhiyyāt* and *mahūt*: both could be translated as 'whatness', or quiddity. So the dog's essence as a whole, its definition, is among these components since its essence can be considered apart from its existence.[12] The same is true of all things in the created universe. This much is clear from the observation that answering the question of what something is does not answer the question of whether or not that thing exists. Consequently, when explaining what something is by giving it a definition, no account is taken of whether the thing exists or not.[13] Likewise, asserting that a particular thing exists does not give any information about what that thing is but, rather, that it is. In light of the distinction between essence and existence, then, it is clear why things do not explain their own existence. What a thing is has no bearing upon whether or not that thing exists. Therefore, when considered only with regard to its own essence it might or might not exist: it is possible. The existence of a thing depends, then, upon existence somehow attaching to the essence, or being added to it. Since such existence does not come from the essence of the thing in question, it must be caused by something else. Things that are caused to exist by something else are contingent on the act of the agent: they are possible of existence with respect to themselves since they exist because of something other than their own essences.

Before considering briefly what it might mean to say that existence is caused by an existing being, which is what is involved in the second principle mentioned above, a few words on causation in general are appropriate. In the Aristotelian view, properties are caused by other things already possessing those properties. A substance possesses accidental qualities and is considered to be the substrate of those qualities. That is one sense in which it is *prior* to its accidental qualities. If a particular substance could possess a particular property, it is said to possess it either potentially, if the property is not present, or actually, if it is. So, for example, metal is a certain temperature and is therefore capable of being either hot or cold, or anything in between

[12] For an account of the history of this distinction's development and the use to which Avicenna puts it see Robert Wisnovsky's *Avicenna's Metaphysics in Context* (London: Duckworth, 2003), pp. 145–180.

[13] A number of difficult questions surround this whole issue. For example, can universals exist and how? What is the existential status of thoughts or imaginary beings? Richard Frank's article raises some of them and discusses certain responses. 'The Non-existent and the Possible in Classical Asharite Teaching', *Mélanges de l'Institut Dominicain d'Études Orientales* 24 (2000), pp. 1–37.

the extremes. It possesses the potential to receive such contraries because temperature is one of its accidental features. While it is hot, it is hot in act but remains potentially cold. It is not hot by virtue of its own essence though, but is caused to be hot by something else imparting heat to it. That cause would itself have to be hot, otherwise it would not be able to impart heat to the metal.[14] It could not be caused to be hot by an altogether different property. For example, being grammatical or ignorance of grammar would not be able to cause heat since 'knowledge of grammar' could not be connected to heat except accidentally through sharing a common subject.

The claim in Crescas' argument from contingency is that existence is similar to other properties in as much as it is derived. It therefore comes to be in the existing thing because it is caused by something else already possessing existence. Even then, the question of where the cause derives its existence from still remains. It may itself be an effect in which case it would also derive its existence from something other than its own nature. Similarly, each prior cause may be considered an effect. Crescas argues that whether or not all things are effects and the causal chain is infinite, the question of the existence of the aggregate of beings, and therefore of existence per se, still stands. If all existing things derive their existence, and existence is caused only by something that exists in act, there must be an existent that exists *in actu* in its own right and from which all existence is derived to begin with. Such a thing would have existence as part of its essence: it would exist necessarily and would be that to which everything that exists contingently ultimately traces its existence.

A problem arises in likening the manner of causation by which a thing exists to that by which an already existing thing changes into something else. The problem lies in the fact that in the case of the latter, there is already an existing substrate which receives properties. By contrast, in the former case, there is no existing thing waiting to receive existence and therefore nothing which could act as a substrate. There is no potential thing upon which existence can act. For this reason Crescas sees shortcomings in Maimonides' comment that 'existence is an accident happening to that which exists. It is therefore something added to the nature of the existing thing.'[15] If existence attaches to something as an accident, and does so in the same way as other

[14] This principle of ancient and medieval physics may not be true but it helps to illustrate the argument used here. According to the system I am discussing, heat in the sub-lunar world is caused by the element fire. It should be noted that the argument does not necessarily depend on medieval physics. For a recent argument that God should be considered a necessary being see Barry Miller's *A Most Unlikely God* (University of Notre Dame Press, 1996).

[15] *Guide* 1.57. Crescas identifies two different approaches. See H. A. Wolfson's 'Crescas on the Problem of Divine Attributes: Chapter II', *Jewish Quarterly Review* 7 (1917), pp. 175–221, at p. 195.

accidents, that something would be prior to its own existence. However, in order for the subject to exist in the first place it requires the property of existence. That would then make it reliant on one of its accidents and thus posterior to the accident. In that case, says Crescas, the accident would be more properly called the 'essence' than the essence itself, in as much as it is presupposed by the existence of the essence and therefore prior to it. Crescas therefore prefers to avoid characterizing existence as an accident, though he still maintains that existence is distinct from essence.

On Crescas' account, then, if the word 'God' does indeed mean 'the cause of the aggregate of existing things', existence must be part of God's nature and God would therefore be that which exists by virtue of its own essence. That is to say, God would exist necessarily. In order to be the cause of the aggregate of existing things, a being must have existence in its own right, otherwise it would simply be a part of the aggregate that it is supposed to cause. It would be part of the universe of contingent existence and, as such, its existence would be derived. The question of the origin of existence would remain. As explained above, Crescas argues that there is no escaping the leap to a being necessary of existence in itself because the question remains to be asked even if the causal chain is infinite. It is then possible to conclude, with Maimonides, that 'that which has no cause for its existence, which is God alone, because this is the meaning of our saying that it exists necessarily, its existence is its essence and its truth, and its essence is its existence'.[16]

The divine unity and the non-reciprocal nature of creation are also thereby secured: unity because there can be no composition in God, even of the most basic kind between essence and existence, and the non-reciprocal nature of creation because God's existence is independent of all other things. Although Crescas argues that God cannot be Creator without creating something, it does not follow that God cannot be God. Ascribing creativity to God requires there to be something created, but ascribing necessary existence to God does not. In that context, to be God is to be the necessarily existing being. To be God, it is not essential to be a creator, although from the perspective of creatures, God is the cause of all things.[17]

THEOLOGY AND THE LIMITS OF SCIENTIFIC INQUIRY

So far I have explained that the notion that every existing thing is derived from God and dependent upon God alone, and therefore created *ex nihilo*, is an important metaphysical doctrine for both Maimonides and Crescas.

[16] *Guide* 1.57. [17] Wolfson, 'Attributes', p. 180.

On matters of physics, though, they differ greatly. One of Maimonides' positions on what is within the remit of human knowledge can be illustrated by his discussions of a first moment. He argues that such a moment cannot be demonstrated through reason[18] and is critical of some theologians (*mutakkalimūn*) who try to establish a first moment by way of rational argument because he argues that their methodology is poor and they confuse the relationship between physics and theology.[19]

In Maimonides' view, fundamental mistakes in approach can be identified when *kalām* thinkers try to establish a first moment using a proof which looks similar to that employed above to prove God's existence. Their argument begins with the premise that the existence of the world is possible. Since there is no more reason that possibly existent things should exist than not exist, there must be a preponderating factor (*tarjiḥ*) causing them to exist. In that case, since the world is possible, there must be a preponderating factor causing its existence. Such a factor is God. Therefore, the world is created.[20]

Maimonides detects a number of problems with this argument. It plays on an ambiguity in the word 'possible' and for that reason can be construed in a few different ways. The first takes 'possible' in the sense which the *kalām* give to it, i.e., imaginable.[21] In this case, the argument begs the question (*petitio principii*) since it assumes a first moment. A second way in which the argument may be understood would take 'possible' in the sense that philosophers give to it, i.e., contingent. In this case the argument is guilty of irrelevance as it simply does not show what the *kalām* want it to. Rather than demonstrating a first moment it would simply show that the world is contingent upon a preponderating factor. Maimonides himself argues that such a conclusion is necessary whether or not there was a first moment of time. A third way understands 'possible' in different senses in the two premises. In this case the argument is invalid since it employs the fallacy of the ambiguous middle.[22] Because it uses the same word in different premises the argument appears valid. However, since the word is used with different meanings in each of the premises, it is not. There is no middle

[18] A similar position is embraced by Aquinas. See his discussion in *Summa Theologiae* 1.46.2.

[19] Maimonides' characterizations of the theologians should not be taken as authoritative. He criticizes an important group of early Islamic theologians but his critique by no means applies to Islamic theology in general, nor to all aspects of *kalām*. For an explanation of Maimonides' own use of dialectic see Joel L. Kraemer's 'Maimonides' Use of (Aristotelian) Dialectic' in H. Levine and R. Cohen (eds.), *Maimonides and the Sciences* (Dordrecht: Kluwer Academic Publishers, 2000), pp. 111–130.

[20] *Guide* 1.74. [21] *Guide* 1.73, Premise 10.

[22] This is Harvey's reading. See his *Physics and Metaphysics*, p. 85. It may be supported by Maimonides' stating that the word *tarjiḥ* should only be used when there is a substratum.

term connecting the premises to one another and therefore no conclusion can be drawn from them. One of Maimonides' general criticisms of the *kalām* philosophical and scientific systems applies here. He argues that they do not understand the difference between demonstration and other kinds of proofs. Their reasoning is faulty because they are not sufficiently trained in logic, which is, in Maimonides' view, a crucial tool for physical investigation.

Although their argument sounds similar to Crescas' argument for God's existence, no refutation of Crescas' argument can be drawn from this critique of the *kalām*. The *kalām* argument is designed to prove a first moment whereas Crescas tries to prove God's existence.[23] Maimonides is making a very different point here. He is supporting the scientists of his day, who affirmed a rationalist, Aristotelian view of the physical world, over those who base their understanding of the physical world on preconceived, uncritical theological ideas. Another of Maimonides' criticisms of the *kalām* is evident here, that they presume theological beliefs and decide their physics accordingly.

Nevertheless, Maimonides' attitude to the philosophers of his day is one of respect rather than slavishness. He states that Aristotle correctly examined everything that exists in the sub-lunar sphere. The only mistake he made, says Maimonides, involves asserting that the world is everlasting. Even on this point, though, Maimonides mitigates Aristotle's error. He argues that Aristotle himself did not consider his own argument that the world is everlasting to be demonstrative.[24] Rather, Aristotle judged it to be the most likely position to be true.[25] It is an opinion (*ra'y*) rather than a result of demonstration (*burhān*).

Because Aristotle did not offer a demonstrative proof for his position that the world is everlasting, Maimonides does not consider himself obliged to adopt it. However, he does need to avoid the charge levelled against the *kalām* and not beg the question. In order to do so, he must give the Aristotelian position its due credit. Only if he can successfully show that Aristotle's position does not have a stronger claim than creation *de novo* does he think that there might be reason to consider the latter to be true. Furthermore, the discussion of Aristotle's view must take place on Aristotle's terms, those of rational philosophy, not on the basis of any theological evidence since 'whoever prefers one of the two positions because

[23] Harvey notes the similarity and the likelihood that Crescas took the wording for his own proof from Ibn Tibbon's translation of the *kalām* argument.

[24] *Guide* 2.20. [25] *Guide* 2.23.

of his upbringing, or for some advantage is blind to the truth'.[26] If on weighing up the evidence for each of the different positions he finds that there is no rational proof favouring one over another, Maimonides needs to find other reasons to adopt a position, or suspend judgement.[27] This he does by using evidence that leads to proofs which are weaker than strict demonstrations, but are all that can be asked for in this context.[28]

To set the groundwork for ascertaining whether the apparently most likely position has in fact been shown to be the case, then, Maimonides must consider whether arguments in its favour manage to achieve what they set out to do. He argues that they do not; all such arguments infringe the rules of demonstration their supporters adhere to. By extrapolating from the way in which things within the created universe work to the creation of the universe as a whole, Aristotle and his followers push their arguments beyond their legitimate boundaries. They take arguments that hold in the world of generation and corruption and apply them to something else: the creation of that world. However, creation is not an instance of generation. It is the act which allows for its possibility. There is therefore no way of knowing that those same arguments will hold for creation as well. That is why Aristotle and his followers fail to demonstrate their opinion. By contrast with the *kalām*, Maimonides only feels able to assert that Aristotle might have erred once he has already examined Aristotle's opinion in detail. Furthermore, he accepts that should the examination establish that Aristotle's position has been demonstrated it would have to be accepted.[29]

In this context Crescas' role is very different from the one he played above. Instead of supporting an idea found in the *Guide*, Crescas enters the frame as one who criticizes the bases of Maimonides' science: Aristotelian physics. His scientific world view is entirely different from that of Maimonides. It is for this reason that Crescas thinks Maimonides' arguments for God's existence fail. Likewise, Maimonides' arguments about creation are insufficient, says Crescas, since they are based upon false scientific premises. Much of the *Light* is dedicated to a critique of the

[26] *Guide* 2.16. [27] *Guide* 2.16.

[28] It should be noted that many different interpretations of Maimonides and ways of reading his *Guide* have been advanced over the centuries. Interpretations of his account of creation reflect these differing approaches to the *Guide*. Often, the discussion revolves around the question of whether or not Maimonides really did think that there was a first moment. For a history of 'esoteric' readings of Maimonides, see Aviezer Ravitzky's 'The Secrets of the "Guide to the Perplexed": Between the Thirteenth and Twentieth Centuries' in I. Twersky (ed.), *Studies in Maimonides* (Cambridge, MA: Harvard University Press, 1990), pp. 159–207.

[29] *Guide* 2.25. Ultimately, Maimonides argues that there are *philosophical* reasons for rejecting Aristotle, though they are not decisive. For more on this see Seeskin's *Origin*, pp. 121–153.

peripatetic philosophical and scientific system. He advances positions very different from those of Maimonides, many more of which are based on theological premises. So, for example, Crescas cites a *midrashic* passage stating that God walks around in 18,000 different worlds and says that this passage authoritatively teaches that there are many worlds. Furthermore, he argues that if God's power is infinite, God must be able to create an infinite number of worlds, both simultaneously and throughout the passage of time, which, in his view, is also infinite. Limiting the number of worlds that God is capable of creating would place a limit on God's power. Therefore, he argues, it is likely that there are an infinite number of existing worlds.[30] Furthermore, he says that the present world is probably one of an infinite number of past and future worlds.

Crescas claims that Aristotle and his followers uncritically take place and space to be equivalent. He claims that when they try to prove that the two are the same, they assume them to be so. The argument is therefore circular and begs the question.[31] Here some clarification is required. Aristotle would be entitled to assume that place and space are equivalent if it is a primary notion that they are. A primary notion is something that is automatically understood and accepted by anyone who understands it. For example, 'the whole is greater than the part' must be accepted by any who know the definitions of the terms. If place and space are defined so that their equivalence is automatically understood when their definitions are understood, Aristotle's conclusion would be acceptable. The way in which Aristotle defines them indicates that this is his intention.[32] Crescas' point seems to be that Aristotle's definitions cannot be established with sufficient certainty. No evidence could be drawn from the world to show conclusively that there is no space unoccupied by some body. All evidence offered must take the world as its backdrop, in which it is granted that place is filled with body, and so will fall short of an absolutely certain demonstration. While it makes sense to say that all space within the physical world is occupied by some body, and to that extent the space in which things in the world are is limited to their particular place, the same claim cannot be made of the world as a whole. No reason can be given from within the world as to why the world as a whole is not in a place surrounded by space. For that reason, by

30 Crescas' statements on this matter conflict with one another. See Harvey, *Physics and Metaphysics*, p. 8.

31 Harry Wolfson translated the relevant passages. See his *Crescas' Critique of Aristotle* (Cambridge, MA: Harvard University Press, 1971), pp. 179–191.

32 Aristotle does not say as much but al-Kindi explicitly states that there can be neither void nor plenum outside the universe and that can be established by a purely intellectual argument. See Peter Adamson's *Al-Kindi* (Oxford University Press, 2007), p. 89.

ruling out the possibility of an extra-cosmic vacuum on the basis of definitions taken from within the world, Aristotle's position begs the question. Furthermore, a number of problems engendered by Aristotle's view disappear once a three-dimensional vacuum is posited.[33]

So Crescas rejects Aristotelian science and bases his beliefs concerning what is physically possible, much more so than Maimonides, on ideas taken from theology. However, it is important to see that he does not consider himself to be violating the principles of inquiry that Maimonides employs. Before he feels entitled to offer *midrashic* evidence to support, for example, the assertion that there are probably other worlds apart from this one in existence, he considers himself obliged to establish on scientific grounds that other worlds could exist. He does this by arguing that Aristotle and his followers are unsuccessful in their attempts to argue against the possibility of a vacuum. Crescas is less optimistic than Maimonides over what philosophy can show to be true. Therefore he thinks that theological premises have much more to say independently of philosophy than does Maimonides. Crescas makes little if any attempt to offer a new scientific system, but, rather, argues that the bases of Maimonides' views are inadequate, thereby throwing doubt upon Maimonides' entire project. Crescas' purpose was to defend what he considered correct theological views in the face of the dominant understandings of the world. It is nevertheless crucial that he only argues on the basis of theological views once he feels he has established that philosophy cannot show such views to be incorrect.[34] That is one reason why, in the *Light*, Crescas spends more time on the critique of the widespread scientific system of his time than on constructing a new one.

CONCLUSION

Both Maimonides and Crescas find themselves bound to accept what is rationally demonstrated. They represent an attitude of respect for science and a willingness to consider scientific doctrines on the terms of science

[33] Crescas' contribution to this idea has been overstated, though there is a definite distinction to be made between his view and that of Maimonides. For a recent account of Crescas' influence and aims, and a critical account of previous assessments, see Y. Tzvi Langermann's 'East and West in Hasdai Crescas: Some Reflections on History and Historiography' in Y. Tzvi Langermann and J. Stern (eds.), *Adaptations and Innovations: Studies on the Interaction between Jewish and Islamic Thought and Literature from the Early Middle Ages to the Late Twentieth Century, Dedicated to Professor Joel L. Kraemer* (Dudley, MA: Peeters, 2007), pp. 229–248. For further on the idea and its development see Edward Grant's *Much Ado about Nothing: Theories of Space and Vacuum from the Middle Ages to the Scientific Revolution* (Cambridge University Press, 1981).

[34] Many medieval scholars thought that there are matters about which science can be absolutely certain.

which may serve as a relevant model today. Furthermore, the argument that there must be a creator of everything since nothing exists by virtue of its own nature is common to both. That shows that it is an argument capable of supporting diverse scientific world views. Since its veracity depends upon considerations of the nature of existence as a whole, not simply the nature of existing things, it may also survive other scientific revolutions and thereby be applicable even now.[35]

[35] I am grateful to José Faur and to the editors of this volume for comments on an earlier draft.

CHAPTER 6

Creation: Avicenna's metaphysical account

Rahim Acar

INTRODUCTION

In the Middle Ages, followers of Abrahamic religions – inheritors of the Greek and Hellenistic philosophical legacy – struggled to come up with a philosophically and theologically satisfactory account of creation.[1] The Greek and Hellenistic philosophical heritage provided at least three major ways of relating the universe to God. The universe owes to God (i) its order; (ii) its movement; or (iii) simply its existence. The first two alternatives may be traced back to Plato[2] and Aristotle[3] respectively. The third alternative may be associated with Platonists, especially with Plotinus, and it seems to emerge as an interpretation of Plato's position. A fourth alternative must be added to the triplet. It is that the universe owes to God not simply its existence but its existence after non-existence. This is the conception of creation which was favoured by the majority of medieval philosophers and theologians in the Western and Islamic worlds.

Avicenna (980–1037) shares concerns of his fellow philosophers and theologians affiliated with any of the three Abrahamic religions, with regard to creation taught by religion. Two major points of controversy in Avicenna's position can be identified. The first is the necessity of the universe, and the second is whether the universe began to exist. Regarding both issues, Avicenna's position caused severe debates and objections.[4] Avicenna's position falls within the third alternative which indicates that the universe should

[1] Richard Sorabji, *Time Creation and the Continuum* (Ithaca, NY: Cornell University Press, 1983), pp. 193–196. See also Gerhard May, *Creatio ex Nihilo: The Doctrine of 'Creation out of Nothing' in Early Christian Thought*, trans. A. S. Worrall (Edinburgh: T&T Clark, 1994), Chapter 1, pp. 1–38.

[2] Plato, *Timaeus*, trans. Donald J. Zeyl, in John M. Cooper (ed.), *Complete Works* (Indianapolis, IN: Hackett Publishing, 1997), pp. 1,224–1,291, 28–29a.

[3] Aristotle, *Physics* VIII.1, trans. R. P. Hardie and R. K. Gaye, in Richard McKeon (ed.), *The Basic Works of Aristotle* (New York: Random House, 1941), pp. 213–394.

[4] Reactions to Avicenna's position in the Islamic world and the Western world are a well-known issue. For example, see Louis Gardet, *La Pensée Religieuse d'Avicenne (Ibn Sīnā)* (Paris: J. Vrin, 1951),

be related to God only with regard to being, not with regard to time. He also argues against the fourth alternative. Conceiving creation as a metaphysical account explaining the existence of the whole universe, he emphasizes that the idea of creation is not compatible with the idea of beginning to exist after non-existence. Consequently, for him the universe cannot have begun to exist *de novo*. Despite the difficulties inherent in Avicenna's position with regard to philosophical objections as well as orthodox religious teachings, his conception of creation might still be viable depending on one's understanding of the nature of the universe.

AVICENNA'S ACCOUNT OF CREATION

For Avicenna the idea of creation is a metaphysical account of things, in the sense that it concerns the universe *qua* being. It is also a metaphysical account in the sense that it concerns the being of the whole universe, not simply of the things to which time and beginning after non-existence can be applied. In Arabic there is a whole range of terms concerning the existence or emergence of things. These include *ibdāʿ*, *iḥdāth*, *khalq* and *takwīn*.[5] All these terms are found in the Qur'an and they may be more or less rendered in English as 'creation'. Avicenna prefers the term '*ibdāʿ*' over the terms '*iḥdāth*' and '*khalq*' to express the idea of creation. He affirms that '*ibdāʿ*' means to give being in the most inclusive sense. It is the most inclusive term indicating the dependence of creation upon God, because it is applicable not only to material and temporal things but also to immaterial and incorruptible beings. Material things that are subject to generation and corruption emerge after non-existence. Avicenna considers their non-existence before they emerge as relative non-existence. Even though they actually come to exist after non-existence, their material and remote auxiliary causes exist. When any such material-generable thing begins to exist, its relative non-existence is removed. The term *ibdāʿ* indicates more than the removal of the relative non-existence. It denotes the elimination of absolute non-existence. This is creation in the proper sense.[6] It does not denote only the existence of things that come to exist after non-existence, but it denotes

Chapter 2; Beatrice Zedler, 'Saint Thomas and Avicenna in the "De Potentia Dei"', *Traditio* 6 (1948), pp. 105–159; see also Herbert Davidson, *Proofs for the Eternity, Creation and the Existence of God in Medieval Islamic and Jewish Philosophy* (Oxford University Press, 1987).

5 For a discussion of Avicenna's terminology concerning creation, see Jules Janssens, 'Creation and Emanation in Ibn Sina', *Documenti e Studi Sulla Tradizione Filosofica Medievale* 8 (1997), pp. 455–477.

6 Avicenna, *Kitāb al-Shifāʾ, al-Ilāhiyyāt*, ed. George C. Anawati *et al.*, 2 vols. (Cairo: Organisation Générale des Imprimeries Gouvernementales, 1960), VI.2, p. 266.12–15 (hereafter Avicenna, *Metaphysics*). See also, Avicenna, *Metaphysics* VIII.3, p. 342.15–19.

first and foremost the existence of ungenerable (*samradī*) things, which are placed above generable things in the hierarchy of being.

Avicenna explicitly states that creation is out of nothing. Since creation is the prevention of absolute non-existence, it is opposed to the idea that things are created out of some thing. The non-existence of things denoted by the expression 'absolute non-existence' is not simply the non-existence of their form, or their matter. But any element making up things, the whole being of things, is non-existent.[7] This certainly sets creation apart from generation and the conditions applicable to generation. The act of making something out of something else is not creation in the true sense. But it is generation. Via generation, things come to exist after non-existence. Their emergence after non-existence is not traced directly to the efficient cause. It also requires a material cause. If creation were out of something, this thing would have the status of the material cause, and the act of making things exist would be like prevention of relative non-existence, like causing movement. Thus it would be rather a weak action.[8] The act of creation differs from causing movement in this respect: it is the making of things out of nothing. Creation concerns the being of the world as a whole including all kinds of things in it. And the cause making things exist 'deserves to be a cause more [than others]. This is so because it prevents the absolute non-existence of things. It is the one that gives complete [*tāmm*] being to things.'[9]

Avicenna's discussion of the term *iḥdāth* indicates his contention that the idea of creation should be considered in atemporal terms. The Arabic term, *iḥdāth*, means 'making something exist after not having existed'. It is usually preferred by Muslim theologians to express the relation of the world to the Creator and the beginning of the universe.[10] The posteriority in this account is taken to mean temporal posteriority, since the posteriority of the universe, implied by the term *iḥdāth*, is not the posteriority of nature or existential posteriority. By noting the temporal connotation of the term *iḥdāth* Avicenna states that it can be used to express the idea of creation only if the implication of temporal posteriority is taken out.[11]

Although Avicenna rejects the terminology implying a temporal posteriority of the universe, he acknowledges its existential posteriority. The existence of the universe is posterior to its non-existence. It simply indicates

[7] Avicenna, *Metaphysics* VIII.3, p. 342.6–11. [8] Avicenna, *Metaphysics* VI.2, p. 267.4–9.

[9] Avicenna, *Metaphysics* VI.2, p. 266.11–12.

[10] For the Muslim theologians' conception of creation, see Harry Austryn Wolfson, *The Philosophy of the Kalam* (Cambridge, MA: Harvard University Press, 1976), Chapter 6, pp. 355–465.

[11] Avicenna, *Metaphysics* VI.2, p. 266.16–17 and p. 267.1–3.

that things do not exist by themselves, they have an origin. In this sense, creation

> is making something after absolute non-existence, because the effect, in itself, has non-existence, and it has existence on account of its cause. And, in the mind, the thing that something has by itself is essentially, but not temporally, prior to the thing that it has on account of something else. Thus every effect is an existence [or existent] after non-existence, in the sense of essential posteriority.[12]

Precisely speaking, the posteriority of creation in this sense does not mean that the universe began to exist after non-existence. It basically confirms existential dependence of creation upon the Creator.

Avicenna's metaphysical account can also be identified via his conception of the metaphysical efficient cause. Avicenna defines efficient cause as 'the cause that brings out [*tufid*] a being different from itself'.[13] The efficient cause is different from the material cause in that it is not a substratum out of which the effect is made. The effect exists on account of the efficient cause and it is potentially included in the efficient cause in an accidental sense.[14] The effect emanates from its efficient cause, and none of them can receive each other.[15] Avicenna distinguishes two senses of the efficient cause. When the term efficient cause is used in the context of metaphysics, it denotes the cause of being. When it is used in the context of physics, it signifies the cause of movement. In both cases, the effect is something distinct from the cause. But in the first case the efficient cause does not use anything else in order to produce the effect. In the second case, the efficient cause moves something, already an existent, to become something else.[16] On this distinction, God is the metaphysical efficient cause of the universe, as he makes everything exist out of nothing.

THE PRINCIPLE OF CO-EXISTENCE

For Avicenna creation as the existential relationship between God and the universe contradicts the idea of beginning to exist after non-existence at the universal level. His arguments to defend this position are traced (i) to his conception of the relationship between causes and effects and (ii) to his conception of the nature of things with regard to duration. Since God is the metaphysical efficient cause of the universe, the way one understands the relationship between causes and their effects plays an important role in

[12] Avicenna, *Metaphysics* VI.2, p. 266.12–15.
[13] Avicenna, *Metaphysics* VI.1, p. 257.10.
[14] Avicenna, *Metaphysics* VI.1, p. 257.7–11.
[15] Avicenna, *Metaphysics* VI.1, p. 259.11–14.
[16] Avicenna, *Metaphysics* VI.1, p. 257.13–17.

delivering a consistent understanding of creation as divine action. Similarly, whether or not time or beginning to exist is applicable to all things making up the universe helps determine one's answer to the question of whether the universe can begin to exist after non-existence via creation.[17]

Avicenna adopts the Neoplatonic scheme of emanation in order to explain the causal network running through his cosmogony and to draw the map of the universe. For him all things come to exist through emanation from God. Emanation is not a process unfolding gradually in time, or an event that has happened once for all. It is the result of eternal divine action, and it holds always. Only one intellect immediately emanates from God. Then from the first intellect emanates the soul and body of the outermost heaven and the second intellect. This emanation comes down to the tenth intellect, and the sub-lunar world, in which we live. The last heavenly intellect emanates the matter in the sub-lunar world and the forms appearing in matter.[18]

Avicenna firmly maintains that causes and effects must co-exist. His emanative scheme posits a vertical order of causes beginning from God coming down to material beings. In the hierarchy of causes and effects, there is a gradation and ranking. Causes are prior to their effects. God, the cause making the whole universe exist, is prior to everything. However, the ranking between causes and effects does not have anything to do with time. The ranking between them concerns their being. The cause that gives being to its effect is prior to it with regard to being. The effect is posterior to its cause with regard to having existence.[19] But there cannot be a temporal gap. For Avicenna, since causes necessitate their effects, when the cause exists the effect must exist. 'They both are together [*ma'an*] in time

[17] It might be proper to relate these two arguments of Avicenna for the sempiternity of the universe to Thomas Aquinas' agnostic position (which agrees with Maimonides' as D. Davies' chapter in this volume has outlined). Avicenna's two arguments are based upon the ideas that (i) God and the universe must be simultaneous and (ii) not everything in the universe can begin to exist. Thomas Aquinas argues that on rational grounds it is possible that the universe exists everlastingly, but this cannot be demonstrated either by an argument from the side of God or by an argument from the side of the universe. The first counters Avicenna's simultaneity argument. Aquinas argues that it cannot be demonstrated from the side of God, because God creates by will; divine will concerning creation is not necessary. Hence from the side of God we cannot demonstrate that the universe is sempiternal. Aquinas' second reason counters Avicenna's argument that not everything within the universe can begin to exist. Aquinas argues that from the side of creatures there is nothing requiring that the universe be sempiternal. See Thomas Aquinas, *Summa Theologiae: Latin Text and English Translation, Introductions, Notes, Appendices, and Glossaries*, ed. Thomas Gilby (New York: McGraw-Hill, 1964–1980), Ia.46.2 (hereafter *ST*). See also *On the Power of God* (*Quaestiones de Potentia Dei*), trans. English Dominican Fathers (London: Burns Oates & Washbourne, 1932–1934), III.17 (hereafter *De Potentia*).

[18] Avicenna, *Metaphysics* IX.4, pp. 406–407.

[19] Avicenna, *Metaphysics* IV.1, pp. 164.18–165.14.

[*zamān*], or in perpetuity [*dahr*], or something else.'[20] This might be called the principle of co-existence. It requires that when the cause exists, the effect must exist, but it does not require that both cause and effect are on a par with regard to existence. While the effect has its being on account of the cause, the cause does not owe it to its effect.

Granted that the principle of co-existence holds between God and the universe, Avicenna's argument for the beginninglessness of the universe runs as follows: 'if anything is essentially [*li dhātihi*] always [*dā'iman*] the cause for the being of some other thing, it is always the cause for it [i.e., this other being] as long as it [*dhātuhu*] [i.e., the cause] is an existent [*mawjūda*]. If it exists always [*dā'iman*], then its effect exists always [*dā'iman*].'[21] Since God is the essential cause of the universe and God exists always, the universe must exist always. If so, the universe cannot have begun to exist after non-existence.

To this argument, one may reply, recalling the difference between natural and voluntary agents, and questioning the nature of divine creative action, whether it is a natural action or a voluntary action. It would constitute an objection to the validity of the principle of co-existence between God and the universe. This is how, for instance, Thomas Aquinas counters Avicenna's stipulation of co-existence of God and the universe. God as a voluntary agent can plan that the universe begins to exist after non-existence.[22] Avicenna does not mention such a distinction exactly. But he provides a host of arguments to prevent such a distinction. One of them is that the cause is the cause of the existence of its effect, not its non-existence.[23] Avicenna considers the existence and the non-existence of the effect as separate units. The existence of the effect is due to its cause; its non-existence is also due to its cause. The cause of the non-existence of the effect is the non-existence of the cause. Since the cause is the cause of the existence of the effect it does not have anything to do with the non-existence of the effect.[24] If the effect cannot come to exist without preceding non-existence, the effect is not simply due to the designated cause. The preceding non-existence must have a part in it, which he deems absurd.

Avicenna thinks that if the universe begins to exist after non-existence, the posteriority of the universe is a temporal posteriority.[25] Accordingly he

[20] Avicenna, *Metaphysics* IV.1, p. 167. [21] Avicenna, *Metaphysics* VI.2, p. 266.9–12.

[22] Aquinas, *De Potentia* III.17, ad. 4; *ST* Ia.46.1, ad. 9. [23] Avicenna, *Metaphysics* VI.1, p. 260.1–4.

[24] Avicenna, *Metaphysics* VI.1, p. 260.5–11.

[25] In fact, the implication of time by the assumption that the universe began to exist after non-existence is considered by the defenders of this view as well. They qualify this time period implied by the assumption as imaginary and negligible. See for example, al-Ghazālī, *The Incoherence of the Philosophers*, ed., trans. and annotated by Michael Marmura (Provo, UT: Brigham Young University, 1997), pp. 30–36; Aquinas, *ST* Ia.46.1, ad. 8; *De Potentia* III.17, ad. 20.

brings in a host of *reductio ad absurdum* arguments to reject that the universe can begin to exist after non-existence. These may also be considered against the natural and voluntary agent distinction, since on this distinction God, as a voluntary agent, can make the universe begin to exist after non-existence so that the existence of the universe does not have to follow the existence of God. For Avicenna, if the universe is supposed to begin to exist after non-existence, this implies a time period before the universe. Then one may meaningfully ask why God did not create earlier. Again one may ask how this time period before the existence of the universe, when there is nothing movable, could be identified. Since time is supposed to be the measure of movement, if there is nothing movable, there is no movement. Thus position of time implies position of something movable. And Avicenna also asks whether God is prior to the universe by being or by time. If the universe begins to exist after non-existence, God is prior to the universe by time, and this implies that the universe is temporally posterior to God. Granting the existence of time before the universe implies granting the existence of something temporal. This, however, implies that God is prior only to the actual universe, but not to everything. Hence if we define the universe as anything other than God, temporal posteriority of the universe is self-defeating.[26]

Whether the principle of co-existence between the cause and the effect holds between God and the universe may be questioned based on our everyday experience. If God and the universe must co-exist, then everything would have been forever, and nothing new could emerge, no change could occur. But this is contrary to our everyday experience. Before tackling this objection, I need to have a look at Avicenna's position regarding the nature of the things making up the universe, since it is also closely connected with the issue of the validity of the principle of co-existence between God and the universe. Based upon the nature of things making up the universe, he provides a second major argument for the beginninglessness of the universe. After delineating Avicenna's view of and argument based on the nature of things making up the universe, I will come back to the issue of the applicability of the principle of co-existence between God and the universe.

THE SEMPITERNITY OF THE UNIVERSE

For Avicenna the universe as a whole is sempiternal, not subject to change or to a beginning of its existence, because the sempiternal part of the

[26] Avicenna, *Metaphysics* IX.1, pp. 379–380.

universe encompasses the temporal part to which beginning to exist is applicable. Avicenna divides being into three categories with regard to duration.[27] First there are things in time. These are changeable things. They begin to exist and cease to exist. Their beginning and their end are different. The second category includes things that exist with time but not in time. It is called perpetuity (*dahr*), and encompasses time. The existence of the heavenly sphere is an example, since time originates from the movement of this sphere. Time itself is of this kind. Such existence is the relation (*nisba*) of the permanent to the changeable. The third category is existence of the permanent with the permanent and it is called sempiternal (*sarmadī*); it encompasses perpetuity.[28] Broadly speaking, sempiternal and perpetual things – composed of heavenly intellects, heavenly souls and heavenly spheres – make up the supra-lunar realm. Heavenly intellects are sempiternal, i.e., they are permanent and are related to permanent things; heavenly spheres are perpetual, i.e., they are permanent but related to changeable things. As a whole, however, supra-lunar beings are atemporal, not subject to generation and corruption. The sub-lunar part of the universe is spatio-temporal. It is the realm of things that begin to exist and pass away.[29] On this division of being with regard to duration and the relationship between different realms of being, the universe as a whole is sempiternal. This is

[27] This division is not something specifically belonging to Avicenna. It is traceable to Neoplatonic sources. Proclus is one of these Neoplatonic authors who might be credited with the fusion of the triple division in the medieval Muslim as well as Christian world. For a comparison of Avicenna's conception of perpetuity (*dahr*) to that of Proclus' view, see Fazlur Rahman, 'Mir Damad's Concept of Huduth Dahri', *Journal of Near Eastern Studies* 39 (1980), pp. 139–153. In the medieval Christian world, a similar division of being into three is found. See, for example, Aquinas, *ST* Ia.10.4–5; Thomas Aquinas, *Commentary on the Book of Causes*, ed. and trans. Vincent A. Guagliardo, Charles R. Hess and Richard C. Taylor (Washington, DC: The Catholic University of America, 1996), pp. 148–160.

[28] Avicenna, *Ta'liqāt* (Qum: the Islamic Seminary of Qum, AH 1379/1421), pp. 170–171. Avicenna is not clear whether all three kinds of being refer to three categories of creatures, heavenly intelligences, heavenly spheres and things subject to generation and corruption in the sub-lunar world, or whether *sarmad* refers to God, and *dahr* and time refer to ungenerable and generable things respectively. Fazlur Rahman prefers the latter alternative. See his 'Ibn Sina's Theory of the God–World Relationship', in David Burrell and Bernard McGinn (eds.), *God and Creation* (University of Notre Dame Press, 1990), pp. 38–52, at pp. 43 ff. Based on this interpretation, Fazlur Rahman discusses the difficulties resulting from putting together heavenly intelligences and heavenly spheres in the same category in terms of duration. However, in the *Metaphysics* part of the *Shifa*, Avicenna explicitly uses the term *sarmad* to refer to the duration of things included in the universe (*Metaphysics* VIII.3, p. 342.16). Interpreting these three kinds of existence based on duration as referring to three categories of beings making up the universe may eliminate some problems which Fazlur Rahman discusses. On the interpretation of Avicenna's position suggested here, the correspondence of the Arabic terminology and the Latin terminology may look as follows: *tempus* can refer to *zaman*; *aevum*, or *sempiternus*, may correspond to *dahr* and *sarmad* together; and *aeternitas* may correspond to *qidam*.

[29] Rahman, 'The God–World Relationship', p. 42.

because the realm of temporal beings is encompassed by the realm of perpetual beings, and it is, in turn, encompassed by the realm of sempiternal (*sarmadī*) beings.

Based on the nature of things making up the universe here outlined, Avicenna argues for the sempiternity of the universe. For Avicenna the universe cannot have begun to exist, because beginning to exist is applicable only to some of the things in the universe. To explain Avicenna's intention, let us compare a palm tree grown up out of a seed to a heavenly intellect. The palm tree is a vegetable, composed of form and matter. Some portion of matter received the form of palm tree at a definite time, under certain material conditions through generation. A heavenly intellect, however, is not a material and temporal thing. If it exists, it exists atemporally and permanently; it cannot come to exist through generation. The fact that the palm tree can come to exist through generation and the heavenly intellect cannot do so is traced to their quiddity. Putting it in general terms, if the quiddity of an effect is such that it can exist only as something material and temporal, then it may begin to exist after non-existence. The preceding non-existence of the effect is not traceable to the cause making it exist. Beginning to exist after not having existed (*ḥudūth*) does not have anything to do with the power of the cause, but it concerns the quiddity of the effect. It is not something that can be done irrespective of the quiddity of the effect. On this division of being, within the universe, there are things the quiddities of which require that they cannot exist, except after preceding non-existence. These are the things in the realm of generation and corruption. Some other things in the universe, however, cannot begin to exist temporally after not having existed. These consist of things in the supra-lunar realm, which are not subject to generation and corruption. On account of their whatness, i.e., quiddity, some things in the universe must exist necessarily (*wājibun darūratan*) 'after temporal non-existence' (*'adam*), and some others must exist necessarily 'not after temporal non-existence'.[30] Since the sempiternal part of the universe – which cannot exist after temporal non-existence – encompasses the part that can begin to exist after temporal non-existence, the universe as a whole is sempiternal, i.e., cannot begin to exist after non-existence but has always existed.

One may ask why God's creative act should be limited by the quiddities of things, if God is the free creator of the universe, and if creation is out of nothing. To answer this question Thomas Aquinas' analysis of the

[30] Avicenna, *Metaphysics* VI.1, p. 262.6–14.

constraints upon God's creative activity may provide guidance. Aquinas states that with respect to the divine creative act

> [n]ecessity arises from the end when the intention of the end cannot be fulfilled, either not at all or not conveniently, without this or that thing. It remains therefore that necessity in God's works cannot arise except from the form which is the end of operation ... thus we might say, for instance, supposing that God intends to make a man, that it is necessary and due that he give him a rational soul and an organic body, without which there is no such thing as a man.[31]

For Avicenna, given that the thing God wills is the existence of things, and given the existence of things that are not subject to generation and corruption, those that are possible by themselves must exist without any temporal gap.[32] He provides an argument based on the concept of possibility paralleling the one based on the duration of things. For him, every existent other than God is possible if considered without reference to its efficient cause, ultimately God, and necessary on account of its cause. Otherwise none of them would exist. He argues that, in order for something to exist, its existence must be possible. Nothing impossible can exist or can be made to exist. In this regard he divides things into two categories: those that need a substratum to exist and those that do not need a substratum. The possibility of things whose existence is possible through a substratum is found in their substratum. All material things belong to this category – their possibility is found in matter. However, things that exist without a substratum are possible by themselves. While the possibility of things that exist without a substratum cannot be temporally prior to their existence, the possibility of things that exist through a substratum is prior to their existence. When the proper conditions hold they begin to exist after non-existence.[33] But those that can exist without a substratum exist without beginning to do so.

SOME OBJECTIONS

Having discussed Avicenna's argument for the sempiternity of the universe based on the nature of things making up the universe, now I may go back to where I left the applicability of the principle of co-existence between God and the universe. As we saw earlier, according to that principle when the cause exists, the effect exists too. This may not hold between a designated cause and its effect, if the cause is not the cause of the effect by itself, or the

[31] Aquinas, *De Potentia* III.16. [32] Avicenna, *Metaphysics* IX.1, p. 378.14–16.
[33] Avicenna, *Metaphysics* IV.2, pp. 177–182.

effect is something subject to generation and corruption. However, in so far as creation is concerned, the rule of co-existence is valid between God and the universe because (i) God is essentially the cause of the universe by himself and (ii) not all things making up the universe can begin to exist after non-existence. Avicenna is quite aware that not all causes are simultaneous with their effects. An efficient cause may be the cause of its effect simply by itself. Then when the cause exists the effect exists. But if an efficient cause is not simultaneous with its effect, either its effect begins to exist after the existence of the cause, or the effect may survive its cause. The first alternative entails that the cause is not the sufficient cause of its effect by itself, and the second that the cause is the cause of the beginning of the effect, but not of its remaining in existence. If God and the universe are not simultaneous, this means that there is a temporal gap between them. Avicenna attributes the view that stipulates a temporal gap between the efficient cause and its effect to the majority of people, which refers to Muslim theologians.[34] Since God is the essential and sufficient cause of the universe there cannot be a temporal gap between them. Given the existence of the effect, if it does not follow from, and is not in accordance with, the existence of the cause, the cause must be potential cause at first and then become actualized. The actualization of the cause later on implies both the insufficiency of the cause and also the occurrence of something new to the cause. For example, the cause may have just recently decided to act, or something external may have compelled it to do so.[35] Thus if such a conception of efficient cause is granted, thereby requiring that there be a temporal gap between the cause and its effect, God cannot be the simple, eternal and perfect efficient cause of the universe. In other words, such a conception of efficient cause contradicts the conception of God shared by the majority of medieval philosophers and theologians. On this conception, God is fully perfect, eternal and simple. Occurrence of something new or additional to the divine being so that he creates the universe contradicts all these divine properties.

Another objection regarding the validity of the principle of co-existence between God and the universe may be raised based on the difference between them in terms of duration. Avicenna states that the co-existence of the effect and the cause concerns their duration but it does not require that they are on the same order of being. 'They exist together [*ma'an*] in time, or in perpetuity [*dahr*], or something else. But they are not together

[34] Avicenna, *Metaphysics* VI.1, p. 263.3–11. See also, Avicenna, *Ishārāt* V, pp. 147–148.
[35] Avicenna, *Metaphysics* VI.1, p. 263.12–18.

with respect to having [*ḥuṣūl*] existence.'[36] How can we apply this to creation? Since Avicenna grants that God is eternal, then the universe must be eternal. However, he adamantly rejects that anything other than God may be eternal. If both the effect and the cause have the same kind of being, such as being temporal or sempiternal, then it is conceivable that both the cause and the effect 'exist together'. However, if the cause and effect are not of the same order of being, how can they be simultaneous or co-existing? It seems that this is a dilemma, which is just as difficult to conceive as how eternity encompasses time.[37] Although asserting a relationship of co-existence or simultaneity between the eternal God and the non-eternal universe is problematic for Avicenna in this context, it is not a difficulty that affects only Avicenna's discussion of creation. It is a difficulty that is faced by many philosophers and theologians, especially with regard to their effort to offer a philosophically coherent articulation of the eternal divine knowledge of temporal things, God's intervention in history and his response to prayers.

A radical objection may be raised against Avicenna's atemporal explanation, which does not leave room for the beginning of the universe, on the basis of modern cosmological account. One may wonder whether Avicenna's metaphysical account is still relevant, since the map of the universe drawn by Avicenna and the one drawn by modern cosmological theories are quite different. With reference to the modern cosmological theories assigning a beginning to the universe, we may object to Avicenna's second argument based on the nature of things making up the universe. This, in turn, affects whether the principle of co-existence between God and the universe is valid. For Avicenna the universe was divided into two: the realm of things that are subject to generation and corruption and the realm of things that are not subject to it. Time and beginning to exist after non-existence are applicable to things that are subject to generation and corruption. But those things above the sphere of the moon were not temporal (not made of matter but of ether). Contrary to this, in modern cosmology, not only the things in the sphere of the moon but many more things, beyond the so-called sphere of fixed stars, are temporal things that began to exist after the Big Bang, the leading cosmological account of the

[36] Avicenna, *Metaphysics* IV.1, p. 167.2–3.

[37] What eternity is and how an eternal being can co-exist with temporal things is an important issue of debate. For an attempt to explain the simultaneity of eternity and time, see Eleonore Stump and Norman Kretzmann, 'Eternity', *Journal of Philosophy* 78:8 (1981), pp. 429–458. David Burrell questions the success of their arguments. For him their arguments fail because we cannot understand eternity in positive terms. It can be understood only by one who is eternal. For further details, see his 'God's Eternity', *Faith and Philosophy* 1:4 (1984), pp. 394–402.

beginning of the universe.[38] Clearly, there is a difference of scope between the realm that Avicenna thought to be subject to time and beginning to exist and the one acknowledged in modern cosmology. According to the Big Bang theory, the universe began to exist some 12–15 billion years ago, and Avicenna argued that the universe cannot have begun to exist after not having existed. Avicenna argues that time cannot have a beginning; Big Bang theory dictates that time began some 15 billion years ago. While Avicenna argues that beginning to exist requires movement or change, according to the Big Bang theory there cannot be any movement before the Big Bang event, and time began only then.

Does this contrast between Avicenna's position and this modern cosmological account amount to falsification of Avicenna's position? Answering this question falls beyond the scope of this chapter. It requires a careful study of their basic concepts, their similarity as well as dissimilarity. Nevertheless, it is proper to make some general remarks indicating a possible way to overcome the opposition between them. Avicenna's position and the Big Bang model concerning the beginning of the universe may not be opposed to each other. Although Avicenna's map of the universe and the modern cosmological one are different, Avicenna's arguments can be adapted to the new data. First, his statements about the things that are subject to generation and corruption, which are located in the sub-lunar realm, can be extended to all material things, going far beyond the sphere of the fixed stars. This would broaden the scope of things that are subject to generation and corruption so as to include the supra-lunar heavenly bodies. Second, one should also pay attention to the different senses of the term universe[39] common to Avicenna's theory and to the Bing Bang model. While Avicenna's account is a metaphysical explanation using elements drawn from the scientific data of his time, the Big Bang theory is an astrophysical scientific model with philosophical implications. Certainly, the universe, of which Avicenna is speaking, does not consist simply of material, physical beings, as is assumed in the Big Bang model.

[38] Explanation of the beginning of the universe via the Big Bang theory has become common knowledge. For a well-organized articulation, see Steven Weinberg, *The First Three Minutes: A Modern View of the Origin of the Universe* (New York: Basic Books, 1977) and Joseph Silk, *A Short History of the Universe* (New York: W. H. Freeman & Company, 1997). For an illuminating discussion of the Big Bang theory and creation *ex nihilo* see Stoeger's chapter in the present volume.

[39] William R. Stoeger, 'Contemporary Cosmology and Its Implications for the Science–Religion Dialogue', in Robert John Russell, William R. Stoeger and George V. Coyne (eds.), *Physics, Philosophy and Theology: A Common Quest for Understanding* (Vatican Observatory Publications, 2005), pp. 219–247, esp. pp. 230–232.

Avicenna's conception of creation as the existential relationship between the Creator and the creation is still an important and defensible thesis. Despite its Neoplatonic roots, Avicenna developed and defended it within Islamic culture where the Creator is quite different from the One of Plotinus. His arguments did not produce the necessary results and have not convinced defenders of the idea of creation which assigns a beginning to the universe. However, they were influential enough to secure that beginning to exist may be a secondary issue. Avicenna's metaphysical account of the existence of the universe – i.e., everything other than God – may still be relevant, especially with regard to religious teachings, if one includes in the universe immaterial things, which are not explainable by physical sciences.

CHAPTER 7

Four conceptions of creatio ex nihilo *and the compatibility questions*

Pirooz Fatoorchi

INTRODUCTION

The notion of *creatio ex nihilo* has become a doctrine firmly established in the three Abrahamic religions (i.e., Christianity, Judaism and Islam). Almost all groups of Islamic thinkers accept the truth of the createdness (*creatio*) of the universe, and that it is preceded by its "non-existence" (*ex nihilo*). However, there is a diversity of opinions as to whether the concept of *creatio ex nihilo* is compatible with alternative accounts of the origin of the physical world, and this diversity is particularly marked between Islamic philosophers and *kalam* theologians (*Mutakallimun*). Three major factors, independently or together, play a fundamental role on how Islamic scholars deal with this very issue: (a) their views of the physical world; (b) their approaches to the divine attributes; and (c) their understandings of the teachings of their religion. The aim of this chapter is to investigate whether four different notions of *creatio ex nihilo* espoused by different Islamic thinkers are compatible with seven alternative accounts of the origins of the universe (five philosophical/theological doctrines – first level of compatibility; and two possible interpretations of a modern scientific theory – second level of compatibility).

FOUR CONCEPTIONS OF *CREATIO EX NIHILO* AND THE FIRST LEVEL OF COMPATIBILITY QUESTIONS

To provide an appropriate setting for the debate about *creatio ex nihilo* (hereafter CEN) and to prevent any confusion it might be useful to classify

I would like to express my immense gratitude to the conference organizers and I thank all of the participants for their helpful questions and discussions. I have benefited greatly from the fruitful comments and ideas of Andreas Albrecht, Paul Steinhardt, Neil Tyson, Alexander Vilenkin and David Wands. I am much indebted to Peta Dunstan and Klaas Kraay for their kind help in obtaining some necessary resources. My special appreciation and thanks go to Farshad F. Saniee for his valuable and insightful suggestions and important help in preparing this chapter. I also wish to thank Carlo Cogliati, Daniel Davies and Oliver Soskice for much appreciated editorial assistance.

some of the most important Islamic views on CEN into four conceptions: (a) temporal-historical (TH); (b) essential non-temporal (ENT); (c) objective meta-temporal (OMT); and (d) substantive temporal non-historical (STNH). After a very brief sketch of the main relevant features, I will consider whether each of these conceptions is compatible with five alternative philosophical/theological accounts of the origins of the universe. The first-level compatibility questions I will then answer are the following:

CQ.1 Is CEN compatible with the pre-eternal[1] universe?
CQ.2 Is CEN compatible with the beginningless infinite past events?[2]
CQ.3 Is CEN compatible with the temporal beginning of the universe at an initial instant?
CQ.4 Is CEN compatible with a series of finite past events without a specifiable initial instant?
CQ.5 Is CEN compatible with the eternal divine creative act?

(a.1) Temporal-historical conception (TH) of CEN

The advocates of this position, who are mostly among the early *kalam* theologians, have presented a strictly temporal picture of CEN and have taken the religious scriptures to support their reading of the act of creation. This conception is based on a notion of *temporal origination* which means "coming into existence" out of something that previously did not exist. This implies being preceded by a "temporal non-existence" which is opposed to its "existence" and does not cohabit with it. Metaphysically, this group of early *kalam* theologians holds that the temporal origin of something is the criterion of the need for a cause. In other words, "temporal origination" – and not contingency *per se* – is exactly what makes a "contingent being" require a cause. By taking this criterion seriously, they first try to argue for a temporal beginning of the world[3] and then try to derive the existence of a divine cause.

[1] Pre-eternity (*azal*) is a theological/philosophical term meaning "eternity *a parte ante*," i.e., eternity without beginning as opposite to "eternity *a parte post*," i.e., eternity without end. These two terms represent two aspects or two directions of eternity.

[2] The distinction between CQ.1 and CQ.2 will become clear in our discussion about STNH.

[3] According to the most important proof that could be found in many *kalam* theologians' authoritative books, their argument for the origination of the universe can be briefly presented as follows. The universe is a finite collection of physical bodies, the parts of which, due to their "movement" and "rest," are all temporally originated. So the universe is also a temporally originated entity. See for example Fakhr ad-Din Razi, *al-Matalib al-Aliah*, 9 vols. (Beirut: Dār al-Kitāb al-'Arabī, 1987), vol. IV, pp. 209–210. Also Nasir ad-Din Tusi, *Tajrid al-Itiqad*, with comments by Helli (Qum: Maktab al-I'lām al-Islāmī, 1986), p. 170.

Since (1) creation is the divine origination rather than origination *simpliciter*, and (2) *ex nihilo* implies a *temporal* transition from non-being into being, CEN is therefore God's bringing the universe into existence initially at a point, a finite number of years ago. The *historicity* of creation is then one of the main features of this interpretation.

(a.2) Responses

According to the above position, it seems clear that the TH would favor the temporal beginning of the universe and is not compatible with pre-eternal past events. Therefore the responses to CQ.1 and CQ.2 will be negative but regarding CQ.3 the answer must be affirmative. As to CQ.4 we must note that it has been stressed by many *kalam* theologians who directly or indirectly supported TH that the past temporal finitude of the universe entails an initial instant of origination which is specifiable at the beginning of the physical world. Therefore the adherents of TH should reply to CQ.4 negatively. Concerning CQ.5, it should be noted that the proponents of TH have argued extensively against the eternity of the "divine creative act," mainly because they believe that this kind of agency would imply that God is bereft of free will. Hence their answer to CQ.5 will be negative.

(b.1) Essential non-temporal conception (ENT) of CEN

There is a plausible sense of CEN, held by Avicenna and his followers, that implies an ontological and non-temporal dependence of the universe upon the Creator. In this view, the foundation of CEN is not the "temporal origination" but rather a deeper kind of "coming-into-being," called *essential origination*, which is based on *essential contingency*.

Essential contingency is an analytic concept[4] which means that every existent, except for God, when we consider it in itself, without taking into account anything else, is found not to possess the logical necessity of its existence. This lack of logical necessity means that each thing is inhabited by an essential and innate non-being that is prior to its existence, which is brought to it by an external cause. As Avicenna says: "That which belongs to a thing-in-itself is prior *for the mind*, essentially but not temporally, to that which belongs to it from something else."[5]

[4] In this context, an analytic concept is a concept which is acquired through an analyzing process by our mind when we consider some "thing" or "entity."

[5] Avicenna (Ibn-Sina), *ash-Shifa: Metaphysics*, ed. G.C. Anawati and S. Zayid (Cairo: Organisme Général des Imprimeries Gouvernementales, 1960), p. 266.

This sort of being after "not having been," involving a priority and posteriority in essence, is the meaning of the term "essential origination." This term is applied to everything that gets its "being" from its external cause, after its non-being in itself, even though "after" does not imply time. Thus, every effect, temporal or non-temporal, is originated in this sense.

Contrary to TH, the proponents of ENT believe that what makes a contingent being require a cause is its contingency, not its temporal origination. As Avicenna emphasizes, since it is the contingency of a thing that is the source of the need for a cause, and since the contingent can never shed its contingency while it exists, its need for a cause which bestows existence on it will also continue as long as it exists.[6] Accordingly, extreme longevity will not make a "contingent being" not require a cause; rather the longer its life, the more it will be in need of a cause, even if it lasts forever.

On this basis, proponents of ENT can claim that the universe is eternal without eliminating the need for a divine creator who creates it *ex nihilo*. For this purpose, *creatio ex nihilo* should be understood in line with the concept of essential origination. So, in the phrase "*creatio ex nihilo*," *creatio* (creation) means the divine act of bringing something into existence. The term *ex* (after), having no temporal implications, has to be interpreted in the sense of *essential* posteriority. And *nihilo* must be understood as the inherent non-existence that cohabits with the "created entity" during its existence. Now, since the "essential contingency" and the "essential origination" are applicable to the universe, the creation of the universe *ex nihilo* involves God's bestowing existence upon it after its innate non-being, in terms of essential posteriority.

What is implied by this interpretation of CEN is not that of having been brought into existence at a time finitely distant from the present, but rather an essential and total *ontological* dependence upon God. The advocates of ENT believe that this interpretation by itself suffices to fulfill the criteria of the orthodox religious scriptures on the subject.

(b.2) Responses

Once we appreciate that in ENT there is a non-temporal conception of creation, we can see, as a consequence, the *possibility* of the eternity of "the act of creation" as well as of the eternity of "the created."[7] Hence this

[6] *Ibid.*, p. 263. And Avicenna (Ibn-Sina), *al-Isharat wa at-Tanbihat*, with comments by Tusi, 3 vols. (Tehran: Daftar Nashr al-Kitāb, 1983), vol. III, p. 76.

[7] Accordingly, for the necessity of the eternity of *the creation* and the eternity of *the created* we need a further reason which will be discussed shortly as the "top–down" argument.

conception of CEN would be compatible with "pre-eternal universe," "infinite past events"[8] and "eternal divine agency." Therefore ENT replies positively to CQ.1, CQ.2 and CQ.5.

To examine how the adherents of ENT respond to the two remaining compatibility questions, we should pay attention to a kind of "top–down" argument from the attributes of God, to the eternity of the divine creative action. Avicenna explicates the divine attributes in such a way as to rule out the claim that the acts of God are limited and intermittent. He holds that precisely because of the fact that the divine essence is from all perspectives absolutely necessary, its creative activity is entirely complete. So he argues that the temporal limitation of the world is incompatible with God's immutability and would lead to the nullification of divine generosity as well as the limitation of God's attributes.[9] Tusi (a philosopher and theologian of the thirteenth century) points out that "according to this school of philosophy, the Divine creator is eternal and perfect in activity so that the physical world which is His action must be eternal."[10] Thus ENT describes a world that is both divinely created and temporally unbounded and it will be able to give negative answers to CQ.3 and CQ.4.

(c.1) Objective meta-temporal conception (OMT) of CEN

This conception of CEN is formulated by Mir Damad (a philosopher, theologian and great many-sided Islamic thinker of the sixteenth/seventeenth century). He developed a new notion of "origination" in order to establish a better harmonization between the religious demands and the philosophical thinking regarding the creation of the universe.

In the first chapter of his most significant philosophical work, *Qabasat*, which is devoted to the problems of "origination" and "creation," Mir Damad states that all philosophers unanimously agree that the universe is originated in the essential sense. Also, they all agree on the falsity of the temporal origination of the universe – as we saw in TH.[11] But he holds that the acceptance of the "essential origination" and refutation of TH are not in

[8] The difference between these two terms is based upon Sadra's view of the concept of "universe" which will be explained later in the chapter.

[9] Avicenna (Ibn-Sina), *at-Ta'liqat*, ed. Center of Publication of the Islamic Seminary, 2nd edn. (Qum: The Office of Islamic Propagation of the Islamic Seminary of Qum, 1999), p. 168. See also Avicenna, *ash-Shifa*, pp. 376, 380, and Avicenna, *al-Isharat*, vol. III, pp. 131, 135.

[10] Nasir ad-Din Tusi, *Comments on Avicenna's al-Isharat wa at-Tanbihat*, 3 vols. (Tehran: Daftar Nashr al-Kitāb, 1983), vol. III, p. 82.

[11] Muhammad Baghir Mir Damad, *al-Qabasat*, ed. Mehdi Mohaghegh, Toshihiko Isutsu, A. Musavi Behbahani and Ibrahim Dibaji (Tehran: Institute of Islamic Studies, 1977), p. 29.

themselves sufficient for developing a legitimate conception of creation.[12] Mir Damad considers that, since the essential conception of CEN which is based upon the "essential origination" shows only a kind of analytic, logical or conceptual posteriority to the creation's being, it would be insufficient to represent CEN in its real and objective sense. For the real CEN, we need to develop a real sense of "origination" that, in turn, hinges on an objective sense of non-existence.[13]

In doing so, Mir Damad, inspired by ideas from the writings of Avicenna, pictures a vertical hierarchy of existence. The highest level is the ontological plane of divine presence, God's essence and attributes; no other entity can exist in this domain of pure absolute existence. There is a genuine rupture between God's being, at the superior level, and the physical world with its temporal events, at the inferior level.[14]

This yields a kind of non-existence of the world which is founded on the fact that it is impossible for the world to exist at the transcendent level of God's unique existence. Mir Damad writes: "The macrocosm with all the parts of its whole order is definitely posterior to the rank of God's essence, the Maker, the Active Creator . . . The posteriority of the world is exactly the kind of posteriority that involves a separation or rupture in relation to His being."[15] Thus the existence of the universe would supervene upon an objective, but not temporal, sort of non-existence. This is the meaning of "origination" in Mir Damad's theory. This is the objective meta-temporal (OMT) interpretation of CEN. According to it the accurate conception of *creation* involves a pure meaning of "origination" that is based upon a sheer and categorical sense of "non-existence." Here the *nihilo* means an objective privation and its precedence is neither "essential" nor "temporal," rather *beyond* or *meta-temporal.*

(c.2) Responses

Following Avicenna, Mir Damad puts himself at variance with *kalam* theologians who posit a beginning to God's creative work. He roots God's eternal activity in divine transcendence and perfection and argues that, if there had been a beginning to the divine creative act, then prior to that God would not have been creative, and this implies a change in God's willing or a transition from impotence to power.[16] However, Mir Damad lays great stress on a sharp distinction between the "eternity of creation" and

[12] *Ibid.*, pp. 24–26. [13] *Ibid.*, pp. 87–88. [14] *Ibid.*, p. 7, and pp. 115–116.
[15] *Ibid.*, p. 75. [16] *Ibid.*, pp. 119–120, 250.

the "eternity of the universe." In opposition to ENT, Mir Damad maintains that the eternal divine creation does not entail the pre-eternity of the universe or an infinite chain of past events. In Chapter 6 of *Qabasat* he refutes such infinity and argues against it.[17] Then he concludes that, despite the fact that in OMT God's creativity does not require any sort of limitation, the bestowal of divine emanation depends on the capability and possibility of receiving it. In this view, the physical world does not have the capability for receiving pre-eternal emanation.[18] Therefore, the temporal finitude of the universe must not be considered incompatible with the eternity of the divine creative act. For Mir Damad the universe is temporally finite, but not traceable to a particular moment of beginning.

Thus far, we can conclude that, although OMT replies positively to CQ.5, its response to CQ.1 and CQ.2 is negative. Regarding CQ.3 and CQ.4 we should note that Mir Damad emphasizes that the temporal finitude of the physical world does not mean that there is an actual specifiable initial instant for the existence of the universe. He argues that, just as an initial point is never reached by dividing a line, so the initial instant of a finite time will never be reached in reality. Therefore, the expression "initial instant" is nothing more than a purely imaginary supposition.[19] Therefore, the reply of OMT to CQ.3 would be "no," whereas the reply to CQ.4 would be "yes."

(d.1) Substantive temporal non-historical conception (STNH) of CEN

This is the position taken by the proponents of the *Transcendent Hikmah* – the most recent development in Islamic philosophy (*Hikmah*), founded by Sadra[20] (or Mulla Sadra; a philosopher of the sixteenth/seventeenth century). According to this school the conception of CEN has the following four elements and characteristics:

1 Partial agreement with TH. Although the religious texts allude to the universe being originated and created in time, this should be interpreted in an innovative and non-historical sense.[21]

2 Substantive movement in the physical bodies. The basis for the apparent and accidental movements of physical bodies lies in changes occurring within their substances. Flux and change find their way into the very

[17] *Ibid.*, p. 228. [18] *Ibid.*, pp. 249–250. [19] *Ibid.*, pp. 237, 293–295.

[20] For a detailed discussion of Sadra on creation, see Kalin's chapter in this volume.

[21] Muhammad Sadra (Sadr ad-Din), *Risalah fi-l Huduth-al-Alam*, ed. S. H. Mousawiyan (Tehran: Sadra Islamic Philosophy Research Institute, 1998), p. 16.

substance of physical entities and indeed encompass all aspects of their being. The existence of every physical substance is gradual, passing and constantly renewed.[22]

3 Non-totalistic conception of the universe. The world in its meaning of "a total or collected whole of past and present events" is neither temporally originated nor eternal. This is because a total world that includes past and present can only be a mentally posited concept to which real existence cannot be attributed.[23] In Sadra's words: "Past events cannot be identified as a 'collected total whole' to necessitate the argument of whether or not this whole is preceded by its nonbeing; because what is past does not exist and the *nonexistence* by no means utilizes a whole."[24] Thus Sadra adopts a non-realist interpretation of the totalistic conception of the universe.

4 A novel approach to the temporal conception of creation. According to the doctrine of "substantive movement," everything in the universe moves in its very substance and comes into existence then passes away, so nothing remains the same for two moments. Therefore, every individual event is at *every moment* preceded by a temporal non-existence, i.e., it is temporally originated from moment to moment. Now, since what we call "the universe" is nothing but all the natural entities at each moment, it follows that the universe is also being re-originated and re-created in every instant.[25] This is a temporal conception of CEN which is substantive and continuous, not a *historical* and one-time event residing on the edge of the universe.

(d.2) Responses

The response of STNH to CQ.1 is absolutely negative because, according to Sadra, the term "universe" can be understood in one of the following two ways: (a) as a series of physical objects and events existing at each moment, or (b) as a kind of "total whole" that includes both past and present physical events. In either way it cannot be eternal. The universe, in its first meaning, is being renewed and does not remain the same for two moments, so certainly it could not be eternal. The second concept of "universe" has no *concrete* existence – as indicated before; hence it lacks any kind of attribute such as

[22] See Muhammad Sadra (Sadr ad-Din), *al-Hikmat al-Muta'aliyah fi'l-Asfar Alaqliyyat al-Arba'ah*, 9 vols. (Beirut: Dar Ihya' at-Turath al-'Arabi, 1981), vol. III, Chapters 19 and 26.

[23] Hence, from STNH's point of view, the compatibility of CEN with infinite past events should be asked by an appropriate sort of compatibility question, i.e., CQ.2 not CQ.1. This is why we have proposed CQ.1 and CQ.2 as two distinct questions.

[24] Sadra, *al-Hikmat al-Muta'aliyah*, vol. VII, p. 311.

[25] *Ibid.*, p. 298 and Sadra, *Risalah*, pp. 112–113.

eternity.[26] Sadra and other advocates of STNH agree with ENT on the infinity of past events, and they also accept ENT's arguments for the eternity of the divine generous action. Therefore, STNH does agree with ENT on responding positively to both CQ.2 and CQ.5; and consequently STNH should reply negatively to CQ.4. However, contrary to ENT, the proponents of STNH, mainly because of their non-realist approach to the totalistic conception of "universe," believe that we should not conclude from the infinity of past events the pre-eternity of the universe. Rather this kind of infinity merely means the continuous and limitless creative act by God.[27] The answer to CQ.3 would be affirmative *and* negative, depending on two distinct (historical and non-historical) interpretations of the phrase "temporal beginning of the universe." On the one hand, we saw that STNH provides a novel temporal interpretation of the theme "beginning of the universe" which does not involve the historicity of CEN, and this would enable us to provide a non-historical reading of CQ.3. Then, we can definitely say that STNH replies to CQ.3 positively since, according to STNH, the universe is temporally (though not historically) created from moment to moment and thus it has a "beginning" at every instant. On the other hand, if we consider CQ.3 as a question about the "temporal beginning of the universe," in a historical reading of the phrase, there will be no room for receiving a positive reply from STNH.

CEN AND THE IMPLICATIONS OF BIG BANG COSMOLOGY

Let us now turn to a second level of compatibility questions: whether the four accounts of *creatio ex nihilo* illustrated in the previous section are compatible with two possible interpretations of a modern scientific theory which aims to explain the origins of the physical universe. The need for this level of discussion is evident if we believe that we cannot satisfactorily speak about the doctrine of creation without taking account of what scientific theories have to say about the actual nature of the universe and reflecting on their philosophical and theological implications. Here, I confine myself to considering the compatibility or incompatibility of CEN with the implications of the standard Big Bang model in modern cosmology.[28]

The Big Bang model provides a mathematical description for the evolution of the cosmos, according to which the universe started from an infinite

[26] Sadra holds that the phrase "pre-eternity of the universe" does rest on a batch of mistakes and fallacies. Some of these mistakes are similar to what Gilbert Ryle called the "category mistake." For reference see Gilbert Ryle, *The Concept of Mind* (London: Hutchinson, 1949), pp. 16–17.

[27] Sadra, *al-Hikmat al-Muta'aliyah*, vol. VII, pp. 298–300.

[28] See also W. Stoeger's chapter in this volume.

density and very high temperature, and has been expanding and cooling over the last 14 billion years. Strong evidence in support of the Big Bang, which is called also the concordance model, began with the first observations of the cosmic microwave background in the 1960s. Subsequent measurements of this background with higher sensitivities and greater resolution further confirmed the predictions drawn from the Big Bang model. The primary satellite involved here is COBE, and some of the most recent big data sets are the Wilkinson Anisotropy Probe (WMAP) and the Sloan Digital Sky Survey (SDSS). At the moment, most cosmologists believe that the Big Bang is still the best theoretical model for cosmology, and it is even claimed by some that this model has achieved consensus.[29]

The general theory of relativity is the basis of Big Bang cosmology. One of the essential features of "general relativity" is that it correlates matter with space and time. As predicted by Friedmann and Lemaître, moving backward in time, the galaxies get closer and closer together until they merge. Then the galactic material gets squeezed more and more until in the finite past a singular point of enormous density is reached. At this initial "singularity," the gravitational force and the density of matter are infinite. Since there is a mutual relationship between space and matter, the infinite compression of matter involves the infinite shrinkage of space. And the correlation of matter, space and time further implies that "time" must disappear too. Thus the material singularity is also a space–time singularity.[30] This "singularity," in the equations of many cosmological models, is shown by "t=0."[31]

This invites a new kind of discussion about the compatibility of CEN with standard Big Bang cosmology. Before asking the relevant compatibility questions we should note that there are two principal views on the implications of the Big Bang model as far as *the problem of the beginning of the universe* is concerned: the strong and the weak interpretation.

(a) Strong interpretation of the Big Bang (SIB)

For some, the Big Bang implies an actual coming-into-being of space and time after nothing. They see the Big Bang cosmogony as a positive interpretation or a confirmation of *creatio ex nihilo*. Here are some examples:

29 Neil Tyson, in a private correspondence.

30 Paul Davies, *The Mind of God* (New York: Touchstone, 1992), pp. 48–50.

31 William R. Stoeger, "Contemporary Cosmology and Its Implications for the Science–Religion Dialogue" in R. J. Russell, W. R. Stoeger and G. Coyne (eds.), *Physics, Philosophy and Theology: A Common Quest for Understanding* (Vatican Observatory Publications, 1998), pp. 219–247, at p. 222.

1 Pope Pius XII in an address to the Pontifical Academy of Science (1951) praised cosmologists for disclosing astrophysical evidence which is entirely compatible with Christian theological convictions about divine creation. As George Coyne points out, "Pius XII attempted to claim that with Big Bang cosmologies scientists were coming to discover what had already been known from the Book of Genesis, namely that the universe had a beginning in God's creative action."[32] Pius XII observes:

> Contemporary science with one sweep back across the centuries has succeeded in bearing witness to the august instant of the primordial *fiat lux*, when along with matter there burst forth from nothing a sea of light and radiation . . . Thus . . . modern science has confirmed the contingency of the Universe and also the well-founded deduction to the epoch when the world came forth from the hands of the Creator.[33]

2 The physicist Edmund Whittaker writes concerning the initial instant of the Big Bang in the following terms: "For what could have determined this instant rather than all the other instants of past eternity? It is simpler to postulate a creation *ex nihilo*, an operation of the Divine will to constitute Nature from nothingness."[34]

3 Ted Peters, a theologian, asserts explicitly that the Big Bang singularity is the event at which space and time were created. He believes that the content of "singularity" in the Big Bang cosmology interprets the meaning of "creation" and "the dependence of the universe on God," so that this dependence would not be well understood if one ignores the consequences of the Big Bang theory.[35]

4 Lenn Evan Goodman, a scholar in the field of Jewish and Islamic philosophy, in his discussion of the meaning of creation, points to the achievements of the Big Bang cosmology and says that: "Evidence is mounting that would tend to support the thesis that the world is originated."[36]

5 Frank Tipler and John Barrow in their seminal book on the anthropic principle emphasize: "At this singularity, space and time came into

[32] George Coyne, "The Sacred Cows of Religion and Science Meet" in C. Impey and C. Petry (eds.), *Science and Theology: Ruminations on the Cosmos* (Vatican Observatory, 2003), pp. 19–34, at pp. 25–26.

[33] *Ibid.*, p. 26.

[34] Mark W. Worthing, *God, Creation, and Contemporary Physics* (Minneapolis, MN: Fortress Press, 1996), p. 86.

[35] Ted Peters, "On Creating the Cosmos" in R. J. Russell, W. R. Stoeger and G. Coyne (eds.), *Physics, Philosophy and Theology: A Common Quest for Understanding* (Vatican Observatory Publications, 1988), pp. 273–292, at p. 288.

[36] Lenn E. Goodman, "Three Meanings of the Idea of Creation" in D. Burrell and B. McGinn (eds.), *God and Creation: An Ecumenical Symposium* (University of Notre Dame Press, 1990), pp. 85–113, at p. 85.

existence; literally nothing existed before the singularity, so, if the Universe originated at such a singularity, we would truly have a creation *ex nihilo*."[37]

6 The philosopher and theologian William Lane Craig claims that "the standard Big Bang model describes a universe which is not eternal in the past, but which came into being a finite time ago. Moreover, the origin it posits is an absolute origin *ex nihilo* . . . On such a model the universe originates *ex nihilo*."[38] Hence he observes that the Big Bang model does constitute a powerful argument for the existence of a Creator of the universe.[39]

Thus the adherents of SIB accept two significant points: (1) the initial singularity (t=0) is literally the beginning instant of the universe, and (2) its coming-into-being supervenes upon a true "nothingness" in the strict sense of the word.

(b) *Weak interpretation of the Big Bang (WIB)*

Contrary to SIB, there are many scholars who interpret the possible implications of the Big Bang model in a weaker sense. They do not believe that the Big Bang theory implies an actual beginning of the universe and deny that one may speak of a strict nothingness before the initial singularity (t=0). The following are some instances of this position:

1 The distinguished cosmologist Andreas Albrecht tends to view the singularity as a statement of a breakdown within the standard Big Bang theory. He thus believes that the singularity will someday be "resolved" by discovering corrections to our equations (probably due to a more adequate theory of quantum gravity) which will give some behavior other than a singularity once we extrapolate back to the very early universe. Regarding the notion of "nothingness" in the context of modern physical cosmology he says:

> The main message from current physics is that "absolute nothing" does not mean very much in the physical world. There is pretty much always something. Particle physicists make a lot of use of the concept of the "vacuum", but that is really just another state of matter. And it is not clear that the idea of the

[37] J. Barrow and F. Tipler, *The Anthropic Cosmological Principle* (Oxford: Clarendon Press, 1986), p. 442.

[38] P. Copan and W. L. Craig, *Creation out of Nothing: A Biblical, Philosophical and Scientific Exploration* (Grand Rapids, MI: Baker Academic, 2004), p. 223.

[39] W. L. Craig, "A Criticism of the Cosmological Argument for God's Non-existence" in W. L. Craig and Q. Smith (eds.), *Theism, Atheism and Big Bang Cosmology* (Oxford University Press, 1995), pp. 256–276, at p. 276.

"vacuum" can even be extended to the whole universe at all. However people sometimes call the vacuum state "nothing", and even write papers about the "creation of the universe from nothing", but I don't really approve of using "nothing" in that way.[40]

2 David Wands, a cosmologist at the University of Portsmouth, maintains that a singular point is the limit of a scientific model. So the singularity of the Big Bang is just a limitation of the Big Bang model based on general relativity. He hopes that one day we will find a scientific theory that can describe what we now call the Big Bang singularity. He holds that absolute nothingness cannot be explained by current scientific knowledge.[41]

3 The eminent cosmologist Alexander Vilenkin explicitly asserts that: "Singularity is where the equations of the theory break down. This indicates limits of the Big Bang theory, not of the universe." In a letter to me he wrote about the concept of "nothingness" in modern cosmology as follows: "When we say the universe could originate from nothing, this means from a state with no space or time. But this process of nucleation of the universe is described by equations of quantum cosmology. I don't think you can say it is absolute nothingness, because it is assumed that the equations are 'there'."[42]

4 Another cosmologist, Paul Steinhardt, observes that the initial singularity is literally a mathematical breakdown of general relativity – a sign that we have extrapolated the equations to a regime where they cannot be trusted. Regarding the concept of "nothingness" in modern cosmology he points out that:

> We know space itself can have energy even when it is empty. We know that it can undergo quantum fluctuations. We know that it can gravitate, etc. You might argue that this is not "nothing." Einstein (and I) would agree with you. Einstein taught us that space is not an inert background in which things move. Rather, space itself is a dynamical elastic entity. It can stretch, contract, wiggle and vibrate.[43]

5 The philosopher Milton Munitz in his excellent book *Cosmic Understanding* emphasizes that the initial cosmological singularity is a property of a cosmological model – a sign of a model's breakdown in making the universe intelligible – not a property of the universe it would describe. Every cosmological model attempts to interpret the universe

[40] Private correspondence. [41] Private correspondence.
[42] Private correspondence. [43] Private correspondence.

within its conceptual framework and to push back the boundaries of intelligibility of the universe. Yet every model has its own limitations and is unable to answer some questions. Munitz calls these limitations the conceptual horizons.[44] He writes:

> I wish to suggest that the cosmologist's use of the expression "the origin of the universe" is best understood if taken as a description of the bounds of a conceptual scheme. It defines the horizon of the *intelligible universe*, that is, the universe as *conceived* in terms of a particular model or class of models. It should not be taken as referring to an inherent property of an objectively and independently existing entity – the universe "in itself".[45]

6 William Stoeger, a cosmologist and scholar in the field of "science and theology" (and a co-editor as well as a contributor to this volume), maintains that "t=0" can only be considered a "beginning" within the Big Bang model itself. It is a limit that falls outside the model in the sense that the model itself cannot adequately deal with it or interpret it. Thus he believes that "the Big Bang, however we describe it within the framework of cosmology, should not be considered as a beginning either of the universe or of time in any specific or definite sense, much less of creation in the theological sense of that word."[46]

7 Michael Heller, another cosmologist who has contributed to the "science and theology" debates (and 2008 Templeton Prize Laureate), argues that it would be premature to claim that the singularity theorems prove the beginning of the universe, let alone its creation. He warns us about the confusion between philosophical/theological and modern cosmological conceptions of *nothingness*. Here are Heller's words:

> Strong reasons also prevent one from identifying the initial singularity with the "moment of creation." The nothingness out of which the histories of particles or observers emerge has nothing in common with the "metaphysical nonbeing" of philosophers and theologians. The singularity theorems have been proven within the conceptual environment of the precisely defined model of space-time and saying that some histories suddenly end at the final singularity only means that the curves representing these histories have reached the edges of the model. It is true that, in the case of the initial singularity, these histories emerge out of nothingness, but it is nothingness

[44] Milton K. Munitz, *Cosmic Understanding: Philosophy and Science of the Universe* (Princeton University Press, 1986), pp. 167, 175.

[45] *Ibid.*, pp. 171–172.

[46] William R. Stoeger, "Key Developments in Physics Challenging Philosophy and Theology" in W. M. Richardson and W. J. Wildman (eds.), *Religion and Science: History, Method, Dialogue* (London: Routledge, 1996), pp. 183–200, at p. 193.

> from the point of view of the model. The *nothingness*, in this sense, is only what the model *says nothing* about. What is outside the model, the model itself does not specify.[47]

In light of the above evidences, we can conclude that, in WIB, such terms as "initial singularity," "origin," "beginning of time" and "nothingness," which are crucial to any serious debate about the relationship between CEN and modern scientific theory concerning the origins of the physical universe, cannot straightforwardly be taken in their strict sense without more ado. Rather, such terms signify the explanatory or epistemic limitations of each model, and not an objective and real boundedness or beginning of the universe. For this reason, it is not befitting to expect the Big Bang model to prove, confirm or interpret something like the "origination of the universe from an absolute nothingness" which stands outside its horizon. Hence, as many scholars in the field of "science and theology" indicate, any attempt to build a doctrine of CEN on the Big Bang theory will encounter serious challenges.

Having clarified two possible interpretations of Big Bang cosmology (SIB and WIB), we can now answer the second level of compatibility questions.

CQ.6: Is CEN compatible with the implications of SIB?
CQ.7: Is CEN compatible with the implications of WIB?

It is clear that, because of the historical element in TH, this conception of CEN would favor SIB. So not only does TH reply to CQ.6 positively but also, *within this framework*, it seems justifiable that the content of "t=0" in the Big Bang cosmology confirms and interprets CEN. However, in the light of the foregoing, since all other conceptions of CEN (i.e., ENT, OMT and STNH) do not envisage an initial instant in the past history of the universe, they should respond negatively to CQ.6.

Concerning CQ.7, since WIB is neutral about the initial moment of the universe, it can be consonant with various conceptions of CEN. Hence all the four alternative accounts of *creatio ex nihilo* presented in this chapter can reply to CQ.7 positively. In this connection, we can at least say that those who believe in the doctrine of *creatio ex nihilo* will not find themselves contradicted by the standard Big Bang cosmology.

[47] Michael Heller, "Cosmological Singularity and the Creation of the Universe," *Zygon: Journal of Religion and Science* 35:3 (2000), pp. 665–685, at p. 670.

CONCLUSION

In this chapter I have investigated whether four different conceptions of *creatio ex nihilo* espoused by different groups of Islamic philosophers and theologians are compatible with seven alternative accounts of the origins of the universe. The findings of this investigation are summarized in Table 1.

Table 1 *Responses to the compatibility questions*

Conceptions of CEN \ Compatibility questions	CQ.1	CQ.2	CQ.3	CQ.4	CQ.5	CQ.6	CQ.7
TH	No	No	Yes	No	No	Yes	Yes
ENT	Yes	Yes	No	No	Yes	No	Yes
OMT	No	No	No	Yes	Yes	No	Yes
STNH	No	Yes	Yes/No	No	Yes	No	Yes

CHAPTER 8

Will, necessity and creation as monistic theophany in the Islamic philosophical tradition

Ibrahim Kalin

INTRODUCTION

Two interrelated questions present creation as a problem in the theistic traditions of Judaism, Christianity and Islam. The first is why a perfect God would create anything at all. The second is how He does it. While the first is a question of origination, the second is one of conservation. These questions become especially poignant when we consider another theistic tenet that creation adds to or extracts nothing from the infinite perfection of God. For medieval philosophers, these questions were not only theological but also strictly philosophical and methodical because, with Aristotle, they believed that to know something fully is to know its cause and origin. A proper understanding of the world is not possible without knowing who created it and why.

This is where the first paradox of creation arises: while we can know God through His creation, we are also urged to know the world through Him, i.e., as His creation. The world is something intelligible when seen as created, shaped and formed by the Supreme Artisan. Yet the arguments of contingency and creation-in-time are about the world, not God. This is natural theology at its best whereby we move from the radical contingency of the world to the supreme power of God. It was al-Kindi who first formulated an argument of creation in such clear and simple terms. Having established that the world is finite because it is composed of parts that are finite and conjoined to one another, he states that the world "must therefore be generated [*muhdath*] of necessity. Now what is generated is generated by a generator [*muhdith*] since generator and generated are correlative terms. The world as a whole must be generated out of nothing."[1]

[1] Abu Rida, *Rasa'il*, 1, p. 214, quoted in Majid Fakhry, *A History of Islamic Philosophy* (New York: Columbia University Press, 1983), p. 76.

In purely logical terms, we move from premise one ("the world exists as a finite being") to premise two ("God exists as an infinite being") and then to the conclusion ("the world must be created"). But in ontological terms, we are trying to prove something infinitely supreme and omnipotent with something finite and weak. Theologically speaking, God cannot be seen as in need of a proof, otherwise He would not be self-sufficient. Ibn Sina considers all proofs for the existence of God to be eventually futile since "there is no argument to prove Him; rather, He is the proof for everything."[2]

In his seminal work *al-Asfar*, Sadr al-Din al-Shirazi, better known as Mulla Sadra (d. 1640), reiterates the same point:

> the Necessary Being has no proof, no definition and therefore no reason from a number of different points of view. It has no reason for existence like an active [agent] and ultimate goal, no reason for constitution [*al-qiwam*] like matter and form and no reason for quiddity like genus and differentia. In spite of this, nothing is hidden from Him; He is the proof of everything and closest to everything as He the Exalted said: "And We are closer to you than your jugular vein". And He said: "And He is with you wherever you are". And He is the proof of His own Essence as He said: "God testifies that there is no god but He". He also said: "Is your Lord not sufficient [as a proof] that He is a witness to all things" and "Say: What is greater as witness? Say: God."[3]

As the only source and ground of existence, God is supremely transcendent and thus above all association and comparison. But a transcendent God is not the most supreme being among others. No matter how majestic, powerful or supreme God is described to be, His transcendence cannot be conceived in terms of having a bigger and better share of certain qualities. His existence and qualities must belong to another order of reality essentially different from everything else.

To stress the radical contingency of the world, a major distinction has been made between the Creator and creatures or, in the language of the philosophers, between what is "created-in-time" (*hadith*) and what is eternal (*qadim*). The theistic philosopher's interest lies not only in stating the difference between God and His creation but also in demonstrating the utter contingency and dependence of the world upon God. Departing from the moderate Aristotelian idea that things could be different from what they actually are, the radical distinction between *hadith* and *qadim* entails an

[2] *Kitab al-Shifa'*, 10 vols. (Cairo: al-Hay'ah al-'Āmmah li-Shu'ūn al-Maṭābi' al-Amīrīyah, 1960), vol. II, p. 354.

[3] *Al-Hikmat al-muta'aliyah fi'l-asfar al-'aqliyyah al-arba'ah* (cited hereafter as *Asfar*), 3rd edn. (Beirut: Dar Ihya' al-Turath al-'Arabi, 1981), I.3, pp. 399–400.

ontology which grows out of a robust metaphysics of creation.[4] Creation as *distinction* is couched in the language of, to use Schleiermacher's term, "absolute dependence."[5] For a philosopher like al-Ghazali, the matter at hand is always more than stating a scholastic truth. It is at the same time intimately personal and experiential: only the God of Abraham can put such a distinction between Himself and what He creates.[6] This explains to a certain extent al-Ghazali's ruthless attack on the philosophers' weak notion of creation. The problem is not simply a matter of logical error in the philosophers' notion of the eternity of the world. It is also a metaphysical sin, for it makes God less than what He is and the world more than what it is.

Like the Hebrew Bible and the New Testament, the Qur'an does not have an explicit statement of *creatio ex nihilo*. What we have instead is a heavy emphasis on God as the creator and sustainer of things. The emphasis is important because accepting God as the sole creator of the world is foundational to the (mono)theistic idea of God. God's unity is inseparable from the fact that He is the only agent of creation with no pre-existing matter, eternal order or anything else that may put into question His uniqueness and absolute power. The vocabulary of *creatio ex nihilo* is meant to bring out this distinctive feature of God's creative act: *ex nihilo* or *min ʿadam* means with nothing, no precedent, no pre-existing pattern, matter or form. It is not the case that there is something called "nothing" out of which God creates. It is a basic mistake of language to conceive "out of nothing" as something with which God works in creating things. As we will see below, an attempt has been made to reduce all such possibilities to the intrinsic qualities of God, thus freeing Him from being bound by anything external to Himself. But even this model of explanation falls short of stressing the radical contingency of the world because it can somehow make the world necessary through Divine nature. *Ex nihilo* has not only ontological but also axiological overtones: God creates with no motive, no goal, no purpose, no expectation, no desire extrinsic to Himself.[7] Other

[4] A masterly analysis of "the distinction" argument is given in David Burrell, *Faith and Freedom: An Interfaith Perspective* (Malden, MA: Blackwell Publishing, 2004).

[5] Friedrich Schleiermacher, in H. R. Mackintosh and J. S. Stewart (eds.), *The Christian Faith* (Edinburgh: T&T Clark, 1928), p. 12.

[6] For this aspect of al-Ghazali's thought, which is often overlooked, see Eric L. Ormsby, "Creation in Time in Islamic Thought with Special Reference to al-Ghazali" in David B. Burrell and Bernard McGinn (eds.), *God and Creation: An Ecumenical Symposium* (University of Notre Dame Press, 1990), pp. 246–264.

[7] For an overview of this point in Ibn Sina, see Rahim Acar, *Talking about God and Talking about Creation: Avicenna's and Thomas Aquinas' Positions* (Leiden: Brill, 2005). See also his chapter in the present volume.

agents do things that resemble creation but cannot really do what God does, for they carry out actions for extrinsic reasons, i.e., to fulfill a desire, to reach a goal, to satisfy a need and so on. God acts with a set of principles radically different from ours. In this sense, only God can be said to create. Hence the uneasiness of using the verb "to create" for human actions in practically all Islamic languages.

The createdness of the world also has important eschatological consequences. If we can establish that the world has been created, then we can also say that it will have an end. After all, the "purpose of the creation of the world is not itself but something more noble than it. The purpose of the creation of the heavens and earth and what is in them is to deliver things back to their essential purpose and fundamental goodness."[8] This brings everything back to where it all begins: God alone without anything with, before, after or besides Him. Proof of creation leads to a proof of faith in one God. The Qur'an establishes an inalienable link between creation and faith, moving from the fact of creation to the act of faith (Al-Baqara 2:21–22):

> O People! Worship your Lord who has created you and those before you so that you may be God-fearing. [He] who has made the earth a resting place for you and the sky a canopy, and sent down water from the sky and thereby brought forth fruits for your sustenance. Do not then set up rivals for God when you know [that He is the only one to be worshipped].

Al-Baqara 2:28 continues the same theme: "How can you deny God seeing that you were dead and He gave you life, and that He will cause you to die and then will bring you to life again, whereupon you will be brought back to Him?"

What is at stake here is the core of all religious faith: giving oneself to God, which in the language of formal theology is called "worship" (*'ibadah*). Fakhr al-Din al-Razi is aware of the link between believing in creation and worshipping God when he says "that God the Exalted ordered the worship of Himself. But this order of worship is dependent upon knowing His existence. Since the knowledge of His existence is not necessary (*daruri*) but inferential (*istidlali*), [only] what proves His existence is mentioned here."[9] The argument from creation to faith and then to worship is thus clearly articulated. But al-Razi adds: "We have explained in our philosophical books that the way to prove Him the Exalted is through contingency [*imkan*] and creation-in-time [*huduth*]."

[8] Sadra, *al-Mazahir al-ilahiyyah fi asrar al-'ulum al-kamaliyyah*, ed. S. M. Khamanei (Tehran: Bunyad-i Hikmat-i Islami-yi Sadra [SIPRIN], AH 1378), p. 64.

[9] *al-Tafsir al-Kabir*, 11 vols. (Beirut: Dar Ihya al-Turath al-Arabi, 2001), 2:97, vol. 1, p. 332.

The Qur'an spends a good amount of time confronting the Meccan polytheists on this issue. How can you acknowledge God as creator and still worship other deities? Numerous verses refer to the fallacy of their logic (Qur'an Luqman 25; al-Mu'minun 86–87).[10] In essence, the problem is not disbelief, i.e., denying the existence of God, but polytheism, i.e., taking partners unto God and making Him not the sole master but one of the agents of the universe.[11] Ibn Qayyim interprets "when you know" (al-Baqara 2:22) as referring to the fact that the Meccan polytheists did believe in God as the one who created the heaven, brought down water and so on.[12] Ibn Kathir concurs: since God is the sole creator of everything, He alone deserves to be worshipped.[13]

Coming back to the question of why God creates in the first place, we can group the theories of creation in classical Islamic thought, which extends to medieval Jewish and Christian thought, under two models. Following Kretzmann,[14] I will identify them as the "necessitarian" and "libertarian" views of creation. While the two at first appear to be diametrically opposed to one another, I will argue that a closer look reveals a number of convergences. Furthermore, as I shall discuss below, Mulla Sadra's elaborate scheme of the "temporal origination of the world" (*huduth al-'alam*) interprets creation in terms of monistic theophany and theistic ontology, and such a scheme purports to take us beyond the volition-versus-necessity framework.

VOLITION VERSUS NECESSITY

In the necessitarian model, God creates out of necessity in the sense that a perfect and infinitely good being cannot be conceived of existing only by

10 Deuteronomy 4:19 reiterates the same point: "And beware not to lift up your eyes to heaven and see the sun and the moon and the stars, all the host of heaven, and be drawn away and worship them and serve them, those which the LORD your God has allotted to all the peoples under the whole heaven."

11 The contradiction between believing in God and worshipping other deities has led to a distinction between two types of Divine unity: "oneness of lordship" (*tawhid al-rububiyyah*) and "oneness of divinity" (*tawhid al-uluhiyyah*). While the former refers to believing in God as the creator and sustainer of the world, the latter refers to the more specific act of worshipping Him as the only deity. Ibn Taymiyyah seems to be the first to introduce this distinction in his *Minhaj al-Sunnah*. In addition to the two types above, he adds the "oneness of divine names and qualities" (*tawhid al-asma wa'l-sifat*) to assert that God has only one set of names and qualities (i.e., no two creators, hearers, speakers and so on), and that they do not contradict one another.

12 Ibn Qayyim al-Jawziyyah, *Zad al-Masir fi 'ilm al-tafsir* (Beirut: al-Maktab al-Islami, 2002), p. 48.

13 Ibn Kathir, *Tafsir al-Qur'an al-'Azim* (Beirut: Dar al-Ma'rifah, 2006), p. 49.

14 Norman Kretzmann, "A General Problem of Creation: Why Would God Create Anything at All?" in Scott MacDonald (ed.), *Being and Goodness: The Concept of the Good in Metaphysics and Philosophical Theology* (Ithaca, NY: Cornell University Press, 1999), pp. 202–228, at p. 208.

and for itself. In the language of Plato and later St. Augustine, the good cannot not give of itself. *Timaeus* 29–30 lays the foundations of the necessitarian paradigm of creation:

> Let me tell you then why the creator made this world of generation. He was good, and the good can never have any jealousy of anything. And being free from jealousy, he desired that all things should be as like himself as they could be. This is in the truest sense the origin of creation and of the world . . . the deeds of the best could never be or have been other than the fairest.

In the language of Neoplatonic emanationism, which the Muslim philosophers accepted wholeheartedly, we cannot conceive a state of affairs in which the infinitely good will be jealous not to manifest itself and create its own other. Being all-good and gracious, God cannot be so envious as not to allow anything else besides him to exist. The necessitarian view thus limits God in His choice of creation and argues that God had to create in the first place out of His infinite perfection and goodness. (We shall ask later if this self-imposed goodness and "generosity" (*jud*) of the Divine constitutes "necessity" as it applies to voluntary choices.) God cannot go against His own nature which forces Him to give of Himself. Even though this appears to jeopardize God's omnipotence and will, it at least preempts the possibility of a wishful deity and secures the essential intelligibility of the order of existence which God has created. Contrary to the conventional understanding, necessitarianism does not automatically lead to the eternity of the world because God always precedes what He creates despite the fact that the universe comes into being through some sort of a necessity.

The proponents of this view argue for a kind of Divine determinism whereby God does not have the choice not to create. As practically all medieval philosophers insist, however, this is not a necessity imposed upon God from outside. Creation as "emanation" or "gushing forth" is not a material or natural necessity whereby God is forced to act by an agent or set of conditions outside Himself. Rather, this is an internal necessity, an intrinsic determinism that can be accounted for only within the purview of the Divine itself. It is the Divine nature that generates this necessity, and His nature is such that it cannot be overruled by His will. Self-necessity is not necessity in the ordinary sense of the term.

Even though denounced as a radical necessitarian and as holding a minimalist view of God, Ibn Sina insists on God's freedom to create. While God's will is eternal and necessary just like His essence, this does not make Him subject to the set of conditions which in our vocabulary correspond to what we call necessity. It is simply bad logic to call God limited because of the fact that He *necessarily* exists. This is like calling mathematics imperfect because it is governed by strict rules. God is free to create through the necessity of His existence, which is the source of His will, not through a necessity imposed upon Him from outside. A certain concept of order and some degree of determinism are required to call anything free.[15] Ibn Sina refers to two orders of human and Divine volition to flesh out the difference between what constitutes necessity in the case of imperfect human will and the "purely intellectual volition." While the human volition is based on satisfying a need or reaching a goal, the Divine volition involves no such conditions. Ibn Sina sums it up as follows:

> the object of volition [*murad*] of the First is not in the manner of our object of volition [*muradina*], such that he would have an aim [*gharad*] in what comes to be [*yakun*] because of him [*'anhu*] ... he is the willer [*murid*] of his essence [*li dhatihi*]. This kind of pure intellectual [*'aqliyyah*] volition [*irada*] and this life of his, similarly, are identical to him [*bi 'aynihi*].[16]

While the necessitarian school insists on the self-binding condition of God's nature, the libertarian or voluntaristic[17] view of creation conceives creation as a free and voluntary act of God with no necessities involved. God creates because He chooses to, and there is no further explanation to be offered. The principle applies not only to the fact that God creates but also to the way(s) in which He creates. This view, which may sound quaint today, made perfect sense within the framework of traditional metaphysics because medieval philosophers believed, on the basis of an authority no less than Aristotle and centuries before Wittgenstein, that all explanations (must) eventually come to an end. Furthermore, as St. Augustine says, if everything is explainable in terms of its cause, then the world can be explained in terms of God alone.[18] And since God is the cause of all causes beyond which there is no more, then God's will to create must be accepted as the final answer to the question of "why?" God's will is the efficient and final cause of everything. All explanations end in God. God's will triumphs over everything else.

[15] In terms of voluntary and free human action, one needs to follow certain rules and thus be subject to certain limitations to be entitled to freedom. For an engaging discussion of this point in a modern context, see *The Chomsky–Foucault Debate*.

[16] Ibn Sina, *Shifa*, *Metaphysics* VIII.7, p. 366.8–13 quoted in Acar, *Talking about God and Talking about Creation*, p. 137.

[17] I use the term voluntarism as reducing all reasons and explanations to an agent's will and in our case to God's free will beyond which there is no further explanation.

[18] See the references in Kretzmann, "A General Problem of Creation," p. 210.

It might be objected that such a dichotomous view of creation does not hold up. Will, let alone God's will, is not devoid of wisdom and intelligence, for willing something is predicated upon certain conditions. An agent that wills must know what he is willing and anticipate its consequences. He must have an understanding of what he wants. He must see what his will means for others. He must make a decision to want one thing rather than something else, and so on. Furthermore, willing is never willing as such but willing a particular thing, i.e., to eat something, to see a friend, to read a book and so on. In the case of God, this, among other things, is the creation of the world. Therefore, God must have known what He had willed when he decided to create. Still, God must have known the scope of His will as he created the world the way it is rather than some other way. While there are fundamental differences between Divine will and human volition, it is clear that God wills through knowledge and wisdom.

Therefore it is not so easy to accuse the voluntarist of stripping God of intelligent and purposeful creation. As a matter of fact the radical voluntarists, like Fakhr al-Din al-Razi among the prominent Asharites, rejected any explanation other than God because they were genuinely concerned about the possibility of the human mind overriding the Divine command. No one denies that God acts with a purpose and wants the best for His creation. The problem arises when we propose an explanatory model in which God's doing so and so is projected to be dependent upon the presence of certain conditions. But who decides on these conditions? Can the human mind be allowed to make such a claim?

Yet there are questions the Asharite voluntarism cannot answer: if God willed to create and He did it with a certain plan in mind, why did He will it in the first place? Was there any particular reason or set of reasons for Him to do so? If it was His will and nothing else, then why did he create an imperfect world? Lastly, what does the existence of the world mean to Him *now*? This is where the two models of creation diverge again. While the school of necessity claims to have an answer by invoking God's nature, the libertarian school simply refuses to answer for it considers such questions to be beyond the limits of human inquiry. Furthermore, any attempt to explain away hard metaphysical questions runs the risk of eliminating the mystery of God's creation.

The proponents of the libertarian view in the Islamic tradition came to advocate *creatio ex nihilo* as the primary form of creation even though there is no direct link between the two. A voluntarist should in principle be able to adopt a model of creation other than *creatio ex nihilo* because the *why question* of creation is in some ways separable from the *how question*. We should be able to explain how something happens without necessarily knowing why it happens – after all, this is what the natural sciences do all the time.

Historically speaking, however, this has not been the case. The libertarian model has been almost invariably tied up with *creatio ex nihilo* and for a good reason: God creates out of nothing, with nothing and with no apparent reason other than His own will. Here "nothing" means both "out of" and "with" nothing: God creates without any pre-existing matter but also without any pre-existing design, pattern, idea or model. In the end, the theologians give the power of creation not to nothingness but to God.[19] To assume something other than nothing as a point of reference in God's creation would bring up a host of cosmological and theological problems including a pre-existing agent or order of being prior to or coterminous with God out of which He creates the world. Why bother with such theological clumsiness? Keep it simple and safe!

Appeal for this kind of simplicity is a good strategy if you are a theologian responsible for the orthodox faith of the common believer. Yet not all souls are satisfied with such populist strategies. Now, if we cannot search for an answer beyond God, we can perhaps try to find one within Him. Given that we accept God's will to create as the ultimate explanation, we can still try to understand God's reasons to choose to create. This, however, is an obviously dangerous enterprise, because it lands us in a search for the mind of God – a terrain theologians and doctors of law would dread stepping into. But this is precisely what some thinkers, certainly the Sufis among them, did in the Islamic tradition. Instead of relegating creation to emanation-by-necessity or to an unconditional will, they sought to understand the Divine logic in choosing to create the world by subscribing to a form of "creation in God." Their proposed solution does not add up to a third alternative view of creation but rather emerges as a synthesis of the necessitarian and libertarian views. Yet, as Mulla Sadra's thought shows, the concept of creation as theophany is in need of serious revision to expound the ontological structures and logical relations that underlie the created order.

The two views of creation that I have been discussing also represent two theological positions, not only with regard to why the world was created, but also with regard to the way it is. This we see best outlined in the debate between the Mutazilites and the Asharites. Combined with a radical form of occasionalism, the Asharite voluntarism conceived the world order to be

[19] Lenn Goodman, *Jewish and Islamic Philosophy: Crosspolinations in the Classic Age* (New Brunswick, NJ: Rutgers University Press, 1999), p. 93.

dependent solely on the mercy of God and His gracious decision to sustain the world the way it is. The Asharites took this view to its logical end and formulated a voluntaristic ethics of a radical kind. God, they said, can be unjust if He wills so because He has power over all things. If He wishes so, God can contradict Himself and the world order which He has created. If this is His creation, then he can remake the rules, and establish, for instance, that 2+2 equals 5 instead of 4.[20]

The Mutazilites rejected the Asharite voluntarism even before al-Ashari had a chance to formulate it fully, because the Mutazilites from the time of al-Jahiz (d. 868) onwards were aware of the implications of that position held by the Murjia, the Hanbalites and the Jabriyyah. Unlike the Asharites, the Mutazilites sought to understand God's will through His nature on the one hand, and His names and qualities on the other. They maintained God's wisdom and justice as a standing condition of creation without which the created order could not have any meaning and continuity. Yet, just like the Asharites, they ended up settling with a form of *creatio ex nihilo* to protect God's transcendence.

A few centuries later, this very debate took a new turn when Ibn Rushd took it upon himself to safeguard philosophy against what he considered to be an increasingly dogmatic theology proposed by Ashari, developed by his students, and made insurmountable by the great Ghazali. Ibn Rushd's rebuttal in the *Tahafut al-Tahafut* is a response not only to Ghazali but also to the entire Asharite tradition, and a warning against making (Asharite) theology the arbiter of philosophy, metaphysics and science all at once. Ibn Rushd's cry is that of a believing "rationalist" who thought it to be an insult against God to describe Him as capable of contradicting Himself, disregarding His own creation and servants, and judging them at will and almost whimsically. For him, this makes justice and accountability, the two tenets of the Islamic faith, practically meaningless, and creates a metaphysical chaos where nobody can know anything for sure. To save philosophy from the Asharites and to save Aristotle from mystical Avicennism, Ibn Rushd questions Ibn Sina's notion of contingency (*imkan*) and rejects the premise that one can easily write off the current

[20] An omnipotent God can certainly do that but such a radical reordering of things would be meaningful only in a different world order, which brings up the question of God's power versus wisdom. This is part of the celebrated debate about the "best of all possible worlds" (*ahsan al-nizam*) in the Islamic philosophical tradition. For a comprehensive overview, see Eric L. Ormsby, *Theodicy in Islamic Thought: The Dispute over al-Ghazali's "Best of All Possible Worlds"* (Princeton University Press, 1984). For Mulla Sadra's ontological defense of the argument, see my "Mulla Sadra on Theodicy and the Best of All Possible Worlds," *Oxford Journal of Islamic Studies* 18:2 (2007), pp. 183–201.

world order as it is. Otherwise, Ibn Rushd thought, we would be questioning God's wisdom and eventually abandoning it. "For wisdom," Ibn Rushd said in the *Tahafut*, "is nothing more than the knowledge of the causes of things. If things did not have any necessary causes determining their existence in the manner in which they are what they are, then there would really be no knowledge proper to the Wise Creator or anyone else."[21]

The grave consequences of voluntarism combined with atomistic occasionalism do not stop at theology. They spill over to the natural and mathematical sciences. For a loyal follower of Aristotle like Ibn Rushd, it is no less an affront to God's wisdom and providence to jettison the firmly established world order and replace it with a whimsical theology of direct causality than to call God unjust *in potentia*.[22]

THE PARADOX OF CREATION

The paradox of creation is that, while it establishes the world as utterly different from God as the creator, it also inserts an inalienable link between the two. The world is what it is insofar as it is different from God: in the language of classical Muslim thinkers, the world is "that which is other than God" (*ma siwallah*).[23] But the world is also what it is insofar as it is a manifestation and self-disclosure of God. No theistic tradition would allow the separation of creation from conservation, for God has not only created the world but also conserves and sustains it in existence. The problem of substantial continuity and discontinuity between God and His creation is an essential part of any metaphysics of creation, and no serious theologian can afford to ignore it.

This brings us to another related issue, that is, the question of transcendence (*tanzih*) and immanence (*tashbih*). Insofar as God is transcendent and utterly different from everything else, there is an essential discontinuity between Him and His creation. To stress His otherness, the Muslim Peripatetics seem to have argued that God has created the world order in such a way that He is absolved of the *need* to know all of its details and

[21] Quoted in Majid Fakhry, *Averroes* (Oxford: Oneworld, 2001), p. 76.

[22] On Ghazali's objection that eternalism as held by the philosophers is self-contradictory and incompatible with theism, see Lenn Goodman, "Ghazali's Argument from Creation," *International Journal of Middle East Studies* 2 (1971), pp. 67–85 and pp. 168–188.

[23] 'Ala' al-Din al-Tusi (d. 1482), who wrote his *al-Zakhirah fi'l-muhakama bayn al-ghazali wa'l-hukama* upon the request of the Ottoman Sultan Mehmed the Conqueror to assess the arguments of the two *Tahafut*s of Ghazali and Ibn Rushd, adds that "the whole universe, which is other than God's essence and His attributes, . . . is created in time [*hadith*], i.e., existing after it did not." 'Ala' al-Din al-Tusi, *Tahafut al-Falasifa* (Beirut: Dar al-Kutub al-'Ilmiyyah, 2004), p. 15.

intervene through secondary causes. While seeking to protect God's transcendence, this view runs the risk of conceiving of the world as a self-subsisting system.

Yet there is also continuity between God and His creation insofar as He is immanent. The Qur'an describes God as "closer to you than your jugular vein." If God is not only the original creator but also the sustainer, i.e., the continuous creator of the world, then He cannot be totally separate from the world. Furthermore, God's creating is not a mechanical process by which things simply come into some sort of an existence of their own. Rather, it is a continuous act of self-disclosure whereby He bestows existence upon things as an execution of His mercy and, to use an Avicennian metaphor, tips the ontological balance towards existence rather than non-existence. This creates a relationship of intimacy between the Creator and the created – a relationship that cannot be maintained in a model of creation which assumes that creation has happened once and for all.

But we cannot push either of these arguments too far as they lead either to a world independent of God or to a God completely caught up in His own creation. It is true that there is something of the painter in the painting, something of the builder in the building and something of the speaker in the speech. The Qur'an refers to this subtle point when God says "when I fashioned him and breathed into him from my spirit" (Al-Hijr 15:29). The great Andalusian exegete al-Qurtubi explains the reference to "my spirit" as "the link between creation and the Creator."[24] Given the ontological disparity between what is necessary and what is contingent, however, we should perhaps remember Ibn al-'Arabi's "perfect believer with two eyes": with one eye he sees the pole of transcendence and with the other eye the pole of immanence. While we see through two eyes, what we see is not two things but one.

In broaching the subject of how the creator and the created are related to one another, Mulla Sadra turns to history and expresses his confidence in the consensus of the major philosophers from the Greeks through the Islamic period on the premise that the world has been created not only temporally but also essentially. Sadra calls them "the people of truth and certainty" and sees them in perfect harmony with "saints and those who are deep in knowledge and who take their light from the niche of the prophecy of the perfect prophets."[25] Sadra believes that the createdness or temporal

[24] Al-Qurtubi, *Tafsir al-jami' li-ahkam al-qur'an*, at www.altafsir.com.

[25] *Risalah fi'l-huduth (Huduth al-'alam)* (cited hereafter as *Huduth*), ed. S. H. Musawiyan (Tehran: Bunyad-i Hikmat-i Islami-yi Sadra, AH 1378), p. 18.

origination of the world is the key belief of Jews, Christians and Muslims in the sense that

> the world as that which is other than God, His Names and Qualities is temporally originated, i.e., it is an existent after having been non-existent. This "after-ness" is a real after-ness and real temporality, not just essential [*dhati*] posteriority. The world is in need of something prior to it in its own essence as this is the case for everything contingent from the point of view of its essential origination [*huduth dhati*]. [Such a being] substantiates neither existence nor non-existence by itself.[26]

There are philosophical schools that uphold the eternity of the world as a logical premise and cannot prove its temporal origination unless another set of arguments is introduced. Sadra believes that the idea of the eternity of the world began after Aristotle and this was a major breach of the tradition of the Greeks themselves. It was also against the belief of the three Abrahamic faiths. Sadra calls this an "average philosophy based on conjecture ... in which truth and falsehood are mixed together."[27] But "faith is different from certainty" and, as a light from God, the "path to certainty is either through demonstration [*burhan*] or intuition through inspiration [*al-hads bi'l-ilham*]."[28] No matter how sound it is, however, philosophical demonstration alone is not enough to yield certainty in such a matter as the creation of the world; one needs the guidance of revelation and the light of prophecy. In his introduction to *Huduth al-'alam*, it is clear that Sadra is directly engaging the Muslim Peripatetics and wants to show how their ontology and cosmology had inevitably led them to believing in the temporal origination of the world while maintaining its eternal co-existence with God.

The reason why Sadra insists on the essential origination (*huduth al-dhati*) of the world as opposed to its mere temporal origination (*huduth al-zamani*) is that, while the former makes the world absolutely contingent and originated, the latter does this only partially and leaves too much independence for the world. Sadra's goal is to move from *time* to *essence* to prove the utter dependence of the world on its creator. To that effect, he develops an elaborate vocabulary of relation and dependence.

> The meaning of contingency [*imkan*] in particular beings, which radiate [*al-faidah*] from the True One, goes back to their deficiency and essential poverty and their being essentially related [to the creator] whereby their origination is impossible

[26] Sadra, *Huduth*, p. 16. Towards the end of his detailed analysis, Sadra says that the differences in religious explanations of creation are related to "different actions and politics of different times" (*Huduth*, p. 148).

[27] *Huduth*, p. 14. [28] *Huduth*, p. 9.

without their self-sufficient maker. They have no essence in themselves except that they are related to the First Truth and dependent on It as God the Exalted said "God is rich and you are poor."[29]

Put in simple terms, "origination" signifies an essential quality of created things whereby they are always preceded by non-existence. "The essential origination is that the existence of something is not dependent upon itself by itself but upon something else whether this dependence is specific to a particular time, continuous in all times or above the horizon of time and motion."[30] But the essential and temporal origination of things is not something added to their identities *a posteriori*. It is in the very nature of things to be "originated" (*muhdath*) once they exist as individual beings. This applies to all corporeal beings because "that which is not individualized cannot exist."[31] Conversely, all things exist as individual beings, and this makes them part of the continuum of motion and time: "Origination is part of time and motion, both of which have a weak existence whereby the passing of one of its parts requires the passing of another part."[32] In this generic sense, Sadra seems to agree with the Mutazilite Qadi Abd al-Jabbar that the best definition we can give of the universe is that it is a created or an "originated existent" (*mawjud muhdath*).[33] If existence (*wujud*) is the most fundamental and universal quality of all existing beings, then the question is how things come to exist after being non-existent. This explains to a certain extent the reason why Sadra uses the word *huduth* and its derivatives rather than *khalq* and its derivatives to avoid the conceptual difficulties of *khalq min 'adam* and skip the whole *kalam* controversy.

TWO MEANINGS OF CONTINGENCY

Following Sadra and much of the post-Avicennian philosophical tradition, we have to make a distinction between two orders of contingency. The first is the order of existence and non-existence, i.e., the level of *absolute contingency* where things may or may not exist. Things are *essentially* contingent in regard to existence and non-existence, not in regard to certain attributes and qualities. The second is the order of *relative contingency* or contingency as capacity (*isti'dad*) and potency (*quwwah*) where things, by virtue of their existing as a certain substance or entity, have certain

[29] *Huduth*, pp. 28–29, with ending quote from Qur'an 47:38. See also *Asfar* 1.1, p. 181.

[30] *Asfar* 1.3, p. 249. [31] *Asfar* 1.3, p. 253. [32] *Asfar* 1.3, p. 255.

[33] J. R. T. M. Peters, *God's Created Speech: A Study in the Speculative Theology of the Mutazili Qad'l-Qudat Abu'l-Hasan 'Abd al-Jabbar ibn Ahmad al-Hamadhani* (Leiden: Brill, 1976), p. 106.

properties and possibilities. A seed has the capacity to become a tree, a cold object has the capacity to become hot, a baby has the capacity to walk and so on. This second contingency is further divided into two: "proximate contingency" (*al-imkan al-qarib*) is called "capacity" (*isti'dad*) and "distant contingency" (*al-imkan al-ba'id*) is called "potency" (*quwwah*).[34] While potency is more generic, capacity is specific and applies to a limited range of possibilities. That is why the prime matter or the hyle has the "*potency* of being all things" because it can be qualified and actualized by any specific form (*al-surah*). But we cannot say the hyle has the *capacity* to become all things, for this would make it a specific substance before it is conjoined with a form.[35]

If the world is contingent both essentially and temporally, then it is always hung between existence and non-existence. But since the world exists in actuality, it must be something specific. As Sadra says in the *Asfar*, "something exists by necessity [*wajib al-wujud*] when considered from the point of its actual existence and it is non-existent by necessity [*wajib al-'adam*] when considered from the point of view of its non-existence. This is a kind of essential necessity ... temporal origination [*huduth*] is a combination of these two states (of existence)."[36] This brings us back to the two meanings of contingency. On the one hand, the world may not have existed at all. This is what we called absolute contingency. On the other hand, the world exists in a certain way and this grants it certain possibilities. We may call this specific contingency whereby things have certain capacities and potentialities to be realized when appropriate circumstances obtain. In both cases, the world needs an agent, a "doer" (*fa'il*), an agent that "prefers" or "chooses" (*murajjih*) existence rather than non-existence because "an originated [being], after having been non-existent, must have a *murajjih* because nothing happens without a reason."[37] Such an agent is also needed to specify the non-definite and absolute order of things because the world, while conceivable as a whole, exists *also* as an aggregate of particular beings. This means that God's agency must be dual at all times: first, for creating and sustaining things in existence and, second, for making them specific things belonging to an order, a species, genus, class, etc.

To realize both kinds of contingency, we need an agent that acts with a reason (i.e., wisdom) and brings things out of pure potentiality into a specific form of existence. Sadra takes up the two issues together and calls them "agency of existence" (*mabda' al-wujud*) and "agency of change"

[34] *Huduth*, p. 28. [35] *Huduth*, p. 34. [36] *Asfar* I.2, p. 389. [37] Sadra, *Mazahir*, p. 65.

(*mabda' al-harakah*).[38] God is the only being that deserves to be called the agent of both acts for He gives existence to all things in comparison to which all other forms of agency are secondary and derivative. Other agents can only be called "preparatory agents" (*al-mu'iddat*)[39] for they act as secondary causes: "His act is the radiance of existence and the giving of goodness in an unconditional manner to all things that may possibly exist."[40] This "existential priority" is of a different order from the other five types of priority which are "priority by causality, nature, nobility, rank and time" for these are also derivative from the creative act of God as giving existence to things. In this sense, "the proximate cause of the actual happening of events [*ḥudūth al-hawadith*] is something passing and renewing in a continuous manner, not composed of indivisible instantaneous things [i.e., moments] . . . the temporal origination of an event is possible when it is preceded by another temporally originated entity. But this cannot go on *ad infinitum*."[41]

If God is the direct agent of existentiation (*al-mu'ti li'l-wujud*),[42] then every happening can be attributed *directly* to God. But God acts through agents and this suggests that there must be a hierarchy of agencies. Sadra's cosmology is an elaborate statement of how this hierarchy is set up and how the present world order is maintained by it. The challenge is therefore to explain how one moves from God as the highest point of the arc of existence to hyle or prime matter as the lowest point of existence while still maintaining the substantial discontinuity between the creator and the created.[43]

But there is another question Sadra ought to answer: how does such an absolutely contingent world maintain its order? This is a crucial question, a question Ibn Rushd had put to the Asharites. If the present world order is totally non-substantial and contingent, then it cannot be said to have any order, design, pattern and intelligibility. Both philosophical and scriptural evidence, however, suggest that the world of creation has an enduring identity. Sadra's answer to this key question comes from his natural philosophy and cosmology. The proximate cause of change is nature "whose essence is continuously changing and whose reality is constantly renewing."[44] If nature is the cause of change in all things, then there must be an agent to make nature change constantly. Who can be this agent other than God? If God is the proximate agent of nature as the principle of change, then the chain of change must go up all the way to God himself. Sadra's answer to this question is usually very detailed and substantial. In the *Huduth*, however, he gives only a short answer. It is true that nature

[38] *Huduth*, p. 35. [39] *Huduth*, p. 39. [40] *Huduth*, p. 36. [41] *Asfar* I.2, p. 134; also p. 393.
[42] *Huduth*, p. 39. [43] *Huduth*, p. 42. [44] *Huduth*, pp. 46–47.

needs an agent to create it as constantly changing and renewing. For nature to be the principle of change, however, it suffices for its agent to create it. It does not need to create it and then make it change at the same time because, once created, nature exists as what it is, i.e., the principle of change. Therefore, change in nature does not mean change in the creator, for the creator does not create change but creates an enduring substance whose nature is change.[45] This is how Sadra links the creator as beyond change with the world as change: insofar as it is related to the creator, nature is unchanging; insofar as it is related to corporeal beings, it is constantly changing.

MULLA SADRA'S FLUID WORLD ORDER

Sadra is aware of the fact that the function that he assigns to nature has been traditionally attributed to time and motion (*harakah*) and that no one has called nature the principle of change. This is an "innovation" and, like all innovations in traditional philosophy, calls for an explanation. Sadra's response is that motion cannot function as principle of change for it does not define change itself but only the process of something changing from one state of being to another. Motion can only be an incident of change, not change itself. In simple terms, "the fact of changing from potentiality to actuality" is motion but "that by which change takes place" is nature.[46] This makes the present world order continuously changing and replaces the Aristotelian universe of fixed substances with processes of change and renewal. Sadra's concept of substantial change (*al-harakat al-jawhariyyah*) offers a new world order based on patterns of essential change and continuity through renewal and repetition.[47]

All of this is underlined by the dynamic nature of "expanding existence" (*al-wujud al-munbasit*) which constantly seeks to return to its point of origin. The ultimate agent of change is existence but, since existence is the principle of *both* change and permanence, the universe displays them without contradiction. Thus "the existence of substance is substance just as the existence of accident is accident."[48] This model may explain why there is permanence-in-change. But it fails to answer the question of why the essential nature of things remains the same. For Sadra, the answer comes from the doctrine of Platonic forms according to which the "intellective existence of things and their separate Platonic forms are eternally the same

[45] *Huduth*, p. 51. [46] *Huduth*, p. 53. [47] See *Asfar* 1.3, pp. 128ff. [48] *Huduth*, p. 57.

in God's knowledge."[49] Combining the language of temporal and ontological causality, he further adds that

> Both demonstrative proof and the Qur'an establish that this corporeal world as a whole is originated and preceded by temporal non-existence. Natural entities have no enduring subsistence [*baqa'*] because they are never devoid of temporal origination; and whatever is not devoid of temporal origination has an identity that is originated with a gradual essence [*tadriji al-dhat*] and changing constitution [*kawn*]. But the truth of the species has an unchanging existence in God's knowledge.[50]

Sadra's defense of change as an essential nature of things lies at the heart of his attempt to relate the "temporally originated" to the "eternal" (*rabt al-hadith bi'l-qadim*). Sadra tries to link the two orders of reality in a way that would not harm the eternal unity and permanence of the creator. As he puts it, "there is no harm in assuming that from God's making [*sun' Allah*] comes the existence of a substance by which happenings and renewals emanate from God the Exalted who is above any change. Accordingly, this substance must have infinite potency [*quwwah*] in actual effects [*infi'al*] in a continuous manner."[51] Sadra's goal is to establish change as the essence of *all* things so that he can account for change in the world of creation without having this change reflect upon the Creator. Clearly, this argument purports to respond to the Muslim Peripatetics. But it is also obvious that Sadra essentially accepts the Avicennian claim that change in the content of God's knowledge leads to change in God himself. Hence God's inability to know the particulars. But, since this foregone conclusion would theologically jeopardize God's unity and transcendence, Sadra rejects the premise. While accepting Ibn Sina's syllogism, he instead offers a new premise based on his "substantial motion."

Substantial motion as developed by Sadra breaks away from the Aristotelian metaphysics of fixed substances and turns the present world order into a constant state of flow. But he rejects the charge that this is a philosophical innovation. The first to speak of it, Sadra says, is God's revealed book itself.[52] After the Qur'an, Sadra quotes from the

[49] *Huduth*, p. 58.

[50] Sadra, *Mazahir*, p. 67. See also *Asfar* I.3, p. 131 and p. 137. Sadra adds that "His knowledge of things is unchanging whereas the content of His knowledge [*ma'lumat*] is changing. This is just like His power being eternal whereas the subjects of His power [*maqdurat*] are changing." This is a reference to the celebrated debate about God's knowledge of particulars.

[51] *Asfar* III.2, p. 121.

[52] Sadra quotes a number of verses including Al-Naml 27:88, Al-Qaf 50:15, Al-Furqan 25:59 and Al-Sajdah 32:4. *Huduth*, pp. 59–60.

Uthulujiyya, the "great" Zeno,[53] Ibn al-'Arabi as well as Bahmanyar, Ibn Sina's famous student and the author of *Kitab al-Tahsil*, to establish substantial motion as an integral part of the history of philosophy from Greeks to Muslims. With his history on his side, Sadra states that "motion is the emergence [*khuruj*] of something from potentiality to actuality, not something with which it moves from the former to the latter."[54] The crucial point is the distinction between the *act* of motion and the *principle* of motion. A substance changing from one thing to another, for instance a green apple becoming red, explains only the process of motion, not the principle by which it changes. The ancient philosophers as well as Ibn Sina and Suhrawardi were mistaken to take the act of motion for the principle of change.

Why is this so important? Because Sadra wants to reduce both change and permanence to one single principle: existence. As was pointed out, however, this is not existence in the generic sense but "existence in expansion" (*al-wujud al-munbasit*) taking up various modalities and different states. Sadra wants to establish that things change but also remain the same, i.e., preserve their essential identity in a continuum. To illustrate how this change-in-continuity happens, he refers to the difference between the soul (*al-nafs*) and the character (*al-mizaj*). While the soul remains the same, the character is "something in constant flow and renewal." The totality of the two, however, gives us a unified entity called the human person: "Everyone feels himself to be one single person without change even though it is one through the conjunction (of successive states) throughout the lapse of one's life."[55]

At this juncture, Sadra finds the Peripatetics' explanation of quantitative change unsatisfactory because it fails to account for the continuously successive stages of change. The Peripatetics subscribe to a softened version of the generation (*kawn*) and corruption (*fasad*) argument, which accounts for radical change rather than gradual transformation. As a matter of fact, it was this confusion that had led Suhrawardi to reject quantitative change altogether.[56] Why? Because their ontology was too opaque to explain the internal dynamism of existence and its modalities. Following the

[53] *Huduth*, p. 76. [54] *Huduth*, p. 68. [55] *Huduth*, p. 69.

[56] *Huduth*, p. 77. Ibn Sina, too, was frustrated with the whole issue of quantitative change. After spending a good amount of time on change in the *Shifa*, he admits that the issue is far from being resolved: "We cannot say anything comprehensive about the attribution of these matters to one another. This is a disputed issue without precision. Whoever wishes to encapsulate the whole matter would run into difficulty. What we have heard about it has not convinced us and we have not understood the matter fully. Let us hope someone other than us understands it as it [should be understood]" (*Shifa' Tabi'iyyat*, vol. IV, p. 95).

Peripatetics, Suhrawardi had taken substances to be solid objects that can accept only accidents without themselves being amenable to change.[57] But this gives us a one-dimensional ontology and a static world order, which follows the Aristotelian notion that only the unchanging substances can account for the order and structure of the physical world.

Sadra rejects this static ontology of substances on the ground that it fails to provide a philosophically cogent and theologically appropriate explanation of how the created is related to the creator without harming God's absolute oneness. In addition to several general arguments, Sadra gives the example of substances with certain accidents. When we look at a black object, for instance, what we have is something black "which is a single identity through a single conjunction [*wahdah ittisaliyyah*] from the first state of its intensification to its ultimate point."[58] Sadra takes this to be a generic property of existence qualified by such modalities as "blackness." In this strongly ontological view, not only substances but also accidents become modalities of existence. Instead of saying that "a black object exists," Sadra would have us say that "existence-as-black" has such and such qualities. Existence qualified as such is

> by itself an existence and is renewed continuously and divided into antecedent, subsequent, deficient and complete. It has parts and individuals some of which vanish, some emerge and some are yet to come . . . this single and continuous existence is also a conjoined and changing existence. This is also true for all of its parts. Thus it has oneness that expands to (its) numbers for it is oneness that comprises (all of its parts). Therefore if we say "it is one", we would be right. If we say "it is many", we would be right. If we say "it is the same from the beginning of change to the end", we would be right. If we say "it is changing at every moment", we would be right. If we say "it is existent with all of its components", we would be right. And if we say "it is non-existent", we would be right.[59]

On such occasions, Sadra never misses the opportunity to put on his mantle of the mystic philosopher. His discussion of the modalities of existence is a good example. For him, most people are ignorant about the "continuous renewal of existence . . . for perceiving it requires a pure disposition and an illuminating vision through the light of which one sees what is permanent and what is changing all at once."[60] The gist of Sadra's argument is that existence is the only "ground" (*asl*) of things and underlies all beings through gradation (*tashkik*). Thus "a single being can have many states

[57] Compare *Asfar* 1.3, pp. 89–90.
[58] *Huduth*, p. 69. See also Sadra's more detailed discussion of this point in *Asfar* 1.3, pp. 128–137.
[59] *Huduth*, pp. 70–71. [60] *Huduth*, p. 71.

and modalities as it may have both perfection and imperfection; that which is one through conjunction is one through individuation and existence."[61] Whether terrestrial and celestial, all things are subject to substantial change for it is a "virtue of existence" that things contain simultaneously the principles of change and permanence in them without a need for an external agent. In other words, all beings have two aspects: "conjunctive unity" (*wahdah ittisaliyyah*), i.e., unity established through conjunction, and "renewing multiplicity" (*kathrah tajaddudiyyah*), i.e., multiplicity established through renewal.[62]

In a clearly Platonic fashion, entities retain their essential identities through their eternal forms in God. Things as particular beings never remain the same; they seek to attain their "final differentia" (*al-fasl al-akhir*) in the great circle of being. But their intellective substance (i.e., Platonic form) is permanently the same in God's knowledge: "These intellective substances are like the rays and glimpses of the First Single Light for they are the forms of what is in God's knowledge. They do not have an existence independent of God; they are beings whose essences are intimately related to the First Reality."[63]

What we have here is the convergence of the two axes of agency whereby the horizontal agency of natural causes is incorporated into the vertical agency of Divine causation. Created beings seek to attain their final differentia and the perfection of their species throughout their life span. As the ultimate agent of all acts, God secures their essential identity and protects them from total chaos and destruction. All God needs to do to ensure this order is to remain unchanging in His essence and knowledge. Through the first act of creation, God has already set the limits of what the present world order can grow or decay into. He has created things in such a way that once the smell of corporeal existence reaches them, they possess the qualities of change and permanence at the same time. Now, this obviously is not the Aristotelian clock-maker since Sadra's scheme of creation gives ultimate agency always to God. Sadra has no qualms about God's continuous creation. As a matter of fact, God's act of creation and preservation is what keeps things in existence, not some set of eternal substances.

It will be noted that the hierarchy of agents Sadra sets up in order to explain the degrees of existence is a key component of his argument. The sharp distinction he draws between motion as the process of change and nature as the principle of change leads us to the agency of existence that generates both forms of change. As the proximate agent of the various kinds

[61] *Huduth*, p. 71. [62] *Huduth*, p. 95; also p. 102. [63] *Huduth*, p. 81.

of corporeal motion, nature acts like the "spirit of a person." Compared to existence, however, nature is like "a ray from the sun" by which entities become particularized.[64] Furthermore, existence particularizes itself by itself without needing an external agent such as an essence or differentia. This also means that existence as the ultimate agent of all particular beings contains in itself the principles of self-renewal and preservation at the same time. When corporeal beings change, they basically serve as a stage for existence to disclose itself in different modalities. It is through the direct agency of existence that God develops an intimate relationship with His creation.

As the face of God turned to the world of creation, existence serves as the ultimate link between the absolutely unchanging God and the continuously changing world. In Ibn al-'Arabi's words, "existence [*al-wujud*] ... is finding the Truth [*wijdan al-haqq*] in ecstasy [*al-wajd*]." Existence is crucial for both cosmology and metaphysics because "the existence of the Truth in ecstasy is commensurate with the Divine Name, which it contemplates, and the Divine Names ultimately belong to the Truth itself."[65] It is in reference to this "secret" (*al-sirr*) that Sadra says that

> the particular existence for everything is its principle [*al-asl*]; and it is particularized by itself. While remaining one, it may possess various states and degrees. In each state and degree, it has universal and essential properties. While maintaining its oneness, it possesses different meanings abstracted from it and united with it through the kind of unification that comes about because of its change in various states of transformation.[66]

Not surprisingly, Sadra ends his discussion by saying that one can attain this state of understanding only through a "second nature" (*fitrah thaniyah*).[67]

[64] *Huduth*, p. 85.

[65] Ibn al-'Arabi, *al-Futuhat al-Makkiyyah*, 4 vols. (Beirut: Dar al-Ihya al-Turath al-Arabi, 1997), vol. III, Chapter 237, p. 527.

[66] *Huduth*, p. 83.

[67] The concept of "second nature," usually attributed to Aristotle, refers in Sadra's vocabulary to a higher level of intellection where the divine forms of knowledge are perceived and the unification of the intellect (*al-'aqil*) and the intelligible (*al-ma'qul*) is realized. Compare Mulla Sadra, in M. Zabihi and J. Shah-Nazari (eds.), *al-Mabda' wa'l-ma'ad fi'l-hikmat al-muta'aliyah*, 2 vols. (Tehran: Bunyad-i Hikmat-i Islami-yi Sadra, AH 1381), vol. I, p. 9. There is an indirect reference to it in Plato (*Republic* III.395) but with a different meaning. What Aristotle means by first nature is what we roughly call "instincts" today, i.e., the first and primary forms of perception. What he means by second nature refers to a higher form of perception where we perceive the intellectual forms of things. But second nature also refers to something like a habit or custom, something we make a *second nature to ourselves* through repetition and habituation. These two kinds of perception would normally correspond to sensual and intellectual knowledge. But Sadra adds a metaphysical content to "second nature" and seems to read more into it than Aristotle intended.

What does this nature tell us? Essentially, it asks us to see God as both the proximate and the distant agent of all change.[68] Sadra further suggests that a proper account of creation cannot separate the question of why God creates in the first place from the question of how He preserves things in existence. God uses intermediary agents to create, form, generate and do a host of other things.[69] This does not prevent God from exercising His absolute power, nor does it prevent other agents from using their relative power. In his discussion of time, Sadra presents God as the agent behind all other relative agents:

Even though all these things are constantly renewed, their primary cause must be something eternal, unchanging in its essence and outside the series of time and space. This is God, may He be exalted, through His one essence, or from the point of view of some of His qualities of eternity, or still from the point of view of the world of His command by which, when He says to something to "be", it is.[70]

Time is preceded by "God, His will, power and command, which is sometimes called God's 'detailed knowledge'. Some people call it 'qualities', others 'intellective angels' [*al-mala'ikat al-'aqliyyah*]. In this [discussion], people love to have different schools of thought [*madhahib*]."[71]

The way God is related to the world is similar to the way existence is related to its various modalities. In Sadra's cosmo-temporal language, this denotes three types of temporality and three levels of existence:

In the language of the pillars of wisdom,[72] the relation of the unchanging to the unchanging is *sarmad* [perpetuity], unchanging to the changing is *dahr* [eternity], and the changing to the changing is *zaman* [time]. What they mean by the first is the relation of God to His names, qualities and knowledge. By the second, they mean the relation of His unchanging knowledge [*'ilmihi*] to His continuously renewing contents of knowledge [*ma'lumatihi*], which are the existents of this world through an existential togetherness. By the third, they mean the relation of some of the continuously renewing contents of His knowledge to some others

[68] See *Huduth*, pp. 137–138 for Sadra's explanation of this point in his heavily ontological language.

[69] David Burrell mentions eight Divine names that describe the multiple modalities of creating: *al-Badi'* (Absolute Cause), *al-Bari'* (Producer), *al-Khaliq* (Creator), *al-Mubdi'* (Beginner), *al-Muqtadir* (All-Determiner), *al-Musawwir* (Fashioner), *al-Qadir* (All-Powerful) and *al-Qahhar* (Dominator). See his "Creation" in Tim Winter (ed.), *The Cambridge Companion to Classical Islamic Theology* (Cambridge University Press, 2008), pp. 141–160, at p. 141.

[70] *Huduth*, p. 103.

[71] *Huduth*, p. 105. As I have discussed elsewhere, Sadra rejects the Peripatetic view of the circular movement of celestial spheres as the source of time on the grounds that it gives time or eternity a semi-divine role, which should be reserved solely for God. See my "From the Temporal Time to the Eternal Now: Ibn al-'Arabi and Mulla Sadra on Time," *Journal of the Muhyiddin ibn 'Arabi Society* 41 (2007), pp. 31–62.

[72] Among other things, this is a reference to Plato. Compare *Asfar* 1.3, p. 144.

through temporal togetherness, which is itself the temporal antecedence and precedence. Ponder over this![73]

The problem of creation and preservation comes back at the end of Sadra's analysis, and for good reason: Creation is not something God "does" like a mechanical or disinterested agent. God acts with wisdom and purpose but also with love and affection for what He creates. This is where the utterly transcendent God once again discloses Himself through a loving act of creation. The intellective forms of things, which Plato and his followers have called the "divine similes" (*al-muthul al-ilahiyyah*),[74] thus form an intimate relationship between God and His creation. What makes creation meaningful is not its ontic qualities such as quantity, quality, position and so on but its intelligible substance because "these intellective forms, illuminative similes and divine forms of knowledge are eternally tied to their agent; and their purpose is to contemplate the beauty of their source and creator."[75] The *mysterium tremendum* is revealed in both love and knowledge because "no one can deny the existence of Divine love and affection in these separate forms since, as we have explained, the love of that which is higher is embedded firmly in that which is lower."[76]

CONCLUSION: CREATION AS MONISTIC THEOPHANY

It is clear that for Sadra, creation is a theophany of God's creative act. But is it simply something "out there," a phenomenon separate from God? As a follower of Ibn al-'Arabi on the mystery of creation, Sadra is not satisfied with the position of the Mutakallimun and the Peripatetics when they talk about God and creation as two "things." He is even critical of their attempt to establish a "relationship" between the two because relationship, even when it is strictly hierarchical, is still a term of duality and imparts some kind of an independent existence to the world. All relational terms imply duality, whereas "relationality [*al-idafah*] by itself is not one of the sound goals because it has no existence of itself especially in the transcendent

[73] *Huduth*, p. 130. See also *Asfar* 1.3, pp. 145–148 and 182–183. Sadra refers to three questions which he says have been asked of Plato in the *Timaeus*. The three levels or kinds of existence that come up in the answers roughly correspond to the three states of time. The questions are: "What is that for which there is no origination [*huduth*]? What is the originated thing with no permanence? And what is that which exists in actuality and is eternally the same?" Sadra quotes Plato as answering these questions as follows: "By the first, he means God's existence, by second the existence of temporal events which never remain the same, and by third the existence of intellective principles, divine forms, the lights of the world of dominion [*al-jabarrut*] and the knowledge of destiny which never changes" (*Huduth*, pp. 184–185).

[74] *Huduth*, p. 139. [75] *Huduth*, p. 140. [76] *Huduth*, p. 141.

essences."[77] To relate the world to God is to accept its separate existence in the first place and this, for Sadra, comes close to committing another metaphysical error because "there is nothing in existence [*mawjud*] . . . except God the exalted."[78]

This, however, is not pantheism whereby God drowns in His own creation. It is more appropriate to say that God reveals himself in *His* creation through the degrees and stages of descent. God creates both *things* and the *principles* by which they exist. What we call existence (*al-wujud*) contains the principles of created beings, whereas what we call the world of creation (*al-khalq*) contains the things themselves. Sadra sums up this point with a historical overview:

> The Divine Essence has rays, lights, glimpses and effects. Existence is nothing but a dawning of His light and a ray of His manifestation. The majority of the philosophers have called these rays and lights "active intellects". The Peripatetics, who are the followers of the First Teacher, call them "forms of knowledge" which subsist with His Essence. Plato and his followers call them "illuminative similes". The majority of the Mutakallimun call them "states" [*al-ahwal*] and the Sufis sometimes call them "names" and sometimes "fixed essences" [*al-a'yan al-thabitah*].[79]

These illuminative substances are essential to explaining why the world has meaning. To put it bluntly, the world of creation is meaningful because God has created it, and God, the Qur'an says, does not do anything in vain (Al-i Imran 3:191). But the world is also meaningful because it moves towards a higher purpose, a *telos*, which relates all of its discrete parts to one another. The intrinsic meaning and intelligibility which Sadra attributes to the world of creation is not something superadded to it *a posteriori*. Rather, it is ingrained in the way things exist. Thus the world is meaningful for a third reason: Its intrinsic structures and internal relations themselves are structures of meaning. By establishing a strong axiological link between creation and existence, Sadra thus advocates a radical version of axiarchism and makes philosophy an ultimate footnote to the ontology of meaning:

> The house of your heart has now been enlightened by the light of the sun of the truth from the firmament of the sacred intellect. You also believe that the purpose of the will of the spheres, the movement of the celestial bodies and the flow of the universe as it is is that all of this be good and blissful. The source of creation is the existence of God and His effulgence. The soul's attainment of the degree of the intellect is its repose and its final stage whereby there is continuous restfulness and perfect satisfaction.

[77] *Huduth*, p. 142. [78] This is obviously from Ibn al-'Arabi. See *Futuhat*, vol. II, Chapter 222, p. 505.
[79] *Huduth*, p. 144.

> This is the final goal of the making of the universe, the rule of the spheres, the movement of the celestial spheres, the coming of the prophets and messengers, and the descent of angels from the heavens with revelation and messages. The purpose of all of this is such that the whole universe will be good; evil and imperfection will cease in it; it will return to where it began and will be (re)attached with it; wisdom will be completed and creation will be perfected; the world of generation and corruption will come to an end; the world will be extinguished; the great day of reckoning will arrive; evil and its people will be effaced; disbelief and its party will perish; falsehood will become null and void; and the Truth will be realized through Its words and signs. This is the ultimate goal and the supreme knowledge.[80]

By going back to existence (*al-wujud*) as the proper term of creation and conservation, Mulla Sadra seeks to overcome the dichotomous framework of necessity versus volition in Divine creation. God does create with free will but this volition is conditioned by Divine nature. He may have chosen not to create the world. But He *has* and this is what matters *now*. Once God wills the world of creation, this new order of existence exists as subject to strict rules and principles. From this point onward, a highly sophisticated and structured ontology is needed to explain the internal workings of the present world order. This is the main task of Sadra's ontology, and it is through this ontology that Sadra develops his concept of creation as monistic theophany, i.e., an ontology of creation that begins with existence and ends with it.

80 *Huduth*, pp. 145–146.

CHAPTER 9

Trinity, motion and creation ex nihilo

Simon Oliver

INTRODUCTION

The doctrine of creation *ex nihilo* apparently distinguishes theological cosmology from ancient Greek conceptions of a universe which has no temporal beginning (as in Aristotle) or a cosmos which is formed from pre-existent chaos, the *khora* (as in Plato's mythic cosmology, *Timaeus*). While the theological doctrine of creation marks a significant break from ancient Greek cosmology, more recently some have argued for a congruence between creation *ex nihilo* and contemporary Big Bang theories and the notion that the universe had a temporal beginning in the form of a singularity.[1]

Does Big Bang cosmology confirm the doctrine of creation *ex nihilo* and the teaching that 'in the beginning, God created the heavens and the earth'? Numerous cosmologists seem to interpret Big Bang cosmology in a way which precludes the notion of creation and a creator. For example, some account for the Big Bang in terms of a fluctuation in a primal vacuum known as 'quantum tunnelling' from nothing, from which the universe expanded according to what is known as inflation theory. 'Nothing' is defined by the cosmologist Alexander Vilenkin as a state with no classical space-time in which the basic categories of physics – space, time, energy, entropy and so on – seem to lose their meaning. This utterly uncaused emergence of the universe from nothing apparently accounts for the universe's existence without reference to anything beyond the universe itself.[2] The universe is simply a brute fact.

[1] See, for example, Paul Copan and William Lane Craig, *Creation out of Nothing: A Biblical, Philosophical and Scientific Exploration* (Grand Rapids, MI: Baker Academic, 2004), pp. 17–19 and passim.

[2] See Alexander Vilenkin, 'Creation of Universes from Nothing', *Physics Letters* 117B (1982), pp. 25–28, cited in Mark William Worthing, *God, Creation and Contemporary Physics* (Minneapolis, MN: Fortress Press, 1996), pp. 98–100. See also Vilenkin, 'Boundary Conditions in Quantum Cosmology', *Physical Review* D 33:12 (1986), pp. 3,560–3,569; Vilenkin, 'Birth of Inflationary

An alternative to the inflationary theory of cosmic origins is offered by Stephen Hawking who, in *A Brief History of Time*, sets forth the case for a universe understood as finite and yet without beginning or end, rather like the surface of a sphere. Hawking famously states: 'So long as the universe had a beginning, we could suppose it had a creator. But if the universe is really completely self-contained, having no boundary or edge, it would have neither beginning nor end: it would simply be. What place, then, for a creator?'[3]

Whether one accepts the Big Bang understood as a temporal boundary to the universe, as in the inflationary theory, or the Hawking model of a beginningless universe which is nevertheless finite, neither approximates to the doctrine of creation *ex nihilo*.[4] Natural science cannot truly think the *nihil*. Scientific cosmology still operates with the Aristotelian notion that *ex nihilo, nihil fit*. The vacuum of modern particle physics which fluctuates to bring the universe to existence through so-called quantum tunnelling is not 'nothing', for this 'nothing' is apparently subject to fluctuation. As Thomas Hobbes famously maintained against Robert Boyle and the vacuum in Boyle's air-pump, even a vacuum is not 'nothing': it still maintains a material and political significance.[5] Even attempts by mathematical physicists to identify 'nothing' with the empty mathematical set fail because, as William Carroll points out, 'the empty mathematical set . . . is subject to the principles of logic and to the laws of quantum cosmology and, as such, cannot be identified with absolute nothing'.[6] Joseph Yciski puts it succinctly thus: 'The alleged nothing [discussed in contemporary cosmology by Hawking and others] turns out to be a complex reality of ordering principles without which there would be no uniformity in nature and no scientific study of natural phenomena would be possible.'[7] Contemporary cosmological speculation seems magically to reify the *nihil*.

Universes', *Physical Review* D 27:12 (1983), pp. 2,848–2,855; Alan Guth, *The Inflationary Universe: The Quest for a New Theory of Cosmic Origins* (Reading, MA: Perseus Books, 1997); and C. J. Isham, 'Creation of the Universe as a Quantum Process' in Robert John Russell, William R. Stoeger and George V. Coyne (eds.), *Physics, Philosophy and Theology: A Common Quest for Understanding* (Vatican Observatory Publications, 2005), pp. 375–408.

3 Stephen Hawking, *A Brief History of Time* (London: Bantam Press, 1988), pp. 140–141.

4 Big Bang theory and quantum cosmology do not conflict with creation *ex nihilo*. They provide a complementary, not alternative understanding of the origin of the universe, and of reality in general. See W. Stoeger's chapter in this volume for a defence of this claim from a scientific perspective.

5 See Stephen Shapin and Simon Schaffer, *Leviathan and the Air-pump: Hobbes, Boyle and the Experimental Life* (Princeton University Press, 1989).

6 William Carroll, 'Thomas Aquinas and Big Bang Cosmology', at www2.nd.edu/Departments//Maritain/ti/carroll.htm#N_12_.

7 Joseph Yciski, 'Metaphysics and Epistemology in Stephen Hawking's Theory of the Creation of the Universe', *Zygon* 31:2 (1996), p. 272, cited in Carroll, 'Thomas Aquinas and Big Bang Cosmology'.

Whereas those who first formulated the doctrine of creation *ex nihilo* had to attend to the ancient Greek understanding of a universe that has no temporal beginning, so we must likewise attend to the tendency to reify the *nihil* and the consequent difficulty of speaking of God's act of creation from nothing. How are we to express the utterly unique instance of the divine creative act, and so distinguish God's act of creation from any natural process or human contrivance, so maintaining the radical nature of the doctrine of creation shared by the ancient Abrahamic faiths?

In order to articulate the radical nature of *ex nihilo* and avoid any tendency towards understanding creation as in any way univocal with natural processes or human contrivances, I would like to consider the doctrine of creation *ex nihilo* with reference primarily to the doctrine of God. I will begin in the thirteenth century with Thomas Aquinas and the way in which he distinguishes between God's act of creation from nothing and the subsequent nature of the universe, namely through the category of motion. Creation is not, strictly speaking, a motion, whereas nature is understood by Aquinas in Aristotelian fashion as a principle of motion and rest.

I will offer a brief examination of Aquinas' understanding of motion, creative emanation and God's relation to a cosmos saturated with motion. This will present us with a question. If we are to claim that a study of nature involves, in the end, a study of motion, and creation *ex nihilo* does not fall into this category of motion (that is, it is not a natural process), are we establishing a division between the natural sciences on the one hand, and theology on the other? Is theology defined as that discourse about the motionless, divine origin of the universe, whereas the natural sciences are concerned only with motion, that is, natural processes which are, of necessity, absent from the divine?

I will attempt a tentative answer to that question by describing the way in which, for Aquinas, motion is analogically related to the eternal dynamism of the Trinity. I will describe Aquinas' understanding of creation as a 'motion' of emanation from God before considering emanation within created beings and its relation to the eternal emanation of the persons of the Trinity. We will see that, in the dynamism of the Holy Spirit proceeding from the Father and Son, we find the principle of natural motion. Motion, then, is not the wedge between creation and creator, but the means of creation's participation in the divine.

Having considered motion in relation to the divine processions, creation and emanation, I will turn to address the development of ideas latent in Aquinas' view by Hans Urs von Balthasar, referring particularly to

Trinitarian theology, the ontology of love and the structure of motion. I will suggest that Balthasar's emphasis on difference within the Trinity as the structure of love implies that motion, which, in its Platonic, Aristotelian and Thomist guise, requires difference, is also structured as a kind of kenotic self-donation.

In concluding this chapter, and in order to draw attention to the crucial place of the Trinity in thinking about the true nature of creation *ex nihilo*, I will examine the thought of Isaac Newton, the principle theorist of motion in early modern science, to suggest why his voluntarist, Arian and Unitarian theology prevented him from truly articulating the radical edge of the traditional Christian doctrine of creation. We will see that Newton's doctrine of God and understanding of motion paves the way for the separation of faith and reason, and therefore the separation of theological cosmology from the speculations of the natural sciences.

AQUINAS: CREATION AND EMANATION

Aquinas is frequently reluctant to describe God's act of creation as any kind of 'motion'. Why? To answer this question, we need to understand how Aquinas understands motion, which for us post-Newtonians seems to be a simple category belonging to physics with little, if anything, to do with theology or metaphysics.

Aquinas gleans much of his understanding from Aristotle. For Aristotle and his successors, motion – *kinesis* – is a mysterious and broad category which encompasses not only local motion of bodies through space, but also the changes of, for example, growing, learning or thinking. These different varieties of motion are analyzed by means of the categories which are fundamental to Aristotle's metaphysics, most particularly potency and act. At a general level, motion is passage from potency to act, and therefore the means of the actualization, or perfection, of creatures. A student, for example, is potentially knowledgeable concerning the history of France, and, by the motion of learning, becomes actually knowledgeable concerning the history of France. Aristotle identifies motion as 'the actualization of what potentially is, *qua* potentiality'.[8]

As far as Aristotle is concerned, every motion must be caused by something which is, in some sense, in act with regard to the motion concerned. For example, for something to move from cold to hot, it must be moved by

[8] Aristotle, *Physics* III.1.201a. On this definition of motion, see L. A. Kosman, 'Aristotle's Definition of Motion', *Phronesis* 14 (1969), pp. 40–62.

something which is actually hot. In other words, there is always something that is moved, and – in the end – there is always a mover. This is also why Aristotle maintains his motor-causality principle which is so central to later medieval natural philosophy: '*omne quod movetur ab alio movetur*' (whatever is moved is moved by another). Any motion can always be analyzed into the mover and that which is moved. So motion is always relational for Aristotle.[9]

Given an Aristotelian definition of motion which has at its heart the passage from potency to act and the postulation of a subject which preceded the motion, it is not surprising that Aquinas frequently avoids describing God's act of creation *ex nihilo* as any kind of 'motion'. However, on other occasions, Aquinas stretches his use of the term *motus* in such a way that it can be employed at least metaphorically, but without error, of the divine creative act and even of God's immanent and perfectly subsistent intellective life.[10] How can this be so? It is necessary to begin with an examination of the character of emanation, for – as many commentators neglect to mention – Aquinas refers to creation as 'the emanation of things from the first principle'.[11]

It is important to recall at this stage that emanation is a term with a very complex history. It is deployed in numerous ways in ancient pagan and Christian thought, particularly within the Neoplatonic tradition. What Aquinas means by this term is certainly not what Peter Lombard still maintained a century earlier, namely that created natures emerge from God in a hierarchy in such a way that creatures are created by those immediately above them in that hierarchy. Neither does emanation refer to a necessary emergence of creation from the Godhead. Emanation, for Aquinas, concerns self-expression. It refers to the active self-expression of a nature in relation to others in the production of another self. In the *Summa contra Gentiles* he begins by noting that 'one finds a diverse manner of emanation in things, and, the higher a nature is, the more intimate to the nature is that which flows from it'.[12] What does this mean? Take a fire, for

9 For a more detailed discussion of motion and the interpretation of the principle '*omne quod movetur ab alio movetur*', see Simon Oliver, *Philosophy, God and Motion* (London: Routledge, 2005), especially Chapters 2 and 4; and James Weisheipl, *Nature and Motion in the Middle Ages*, ed. W. E. Carroll (Washington, DC: The Catholic University Press of America, 1985).

10 For example, see Aquinas, *Summa contra Gentiles* (hereafter, *SCG*), I.13.10. See also *Summa Theologiae* (hereafter, *ST*), Ia.19.1, ad. 3 on the entirely subsistent movement of the divine will.

11 Aquinas, *ST* Ia.45: *De modo emanationis rerum a primo principio*. For a discussion of divine emanation and motion in relation to Aquinas' understanding of the perfections of being, life and knowing, see R. A. te Velde, *Participation and Substantiality in Thomas Aquinas* (Leiden: Brill, 1995), pp. 272–279.

12 *SCG* IV.11.1.

example. A fire necessarily emanates a likeness of itself and so moves another object from cold to hot. This emanation terminates outside the mover, in the heating of another object.

For Aquinas, however, the highest form of emanation is not that which terminates externally from the being concerned (for example, an inanimate object locally moving another object) but that which has an internal termination, for this implies an increasing degree of self-subsistence. We find a clear instance of emanation and return in the human intellect, for the intellect is capable of self-knowledge and understanding. Thus a human being is able to produce a communication of its nature, an emanation of another self, in such a way that *self*-reflection is possible. When we reflect on or think about ourselves, it is as if a version of ourselves emanates from our intellect in such a way that we can, as it were, 'look' at ourselves. Yet the human intellect is imperfect because it must take its first knowledge – even of itself – from without, namely through sense perception, before returning from the external object to arrive at knowledge of itself by its relation to the external object in question.[13] I know myself not through myself, but in my relation to external objects. I know myself, for example, as sat behind this desk.

Perfect emanation is found in God whose intellect and act of understanding, unlike those of angels, are identical with his being. Therefore, God's being, intellect and understanding are one.[14] For the divine to know himself and express himself through that knowledge is the divine essence, the very divine life itself. Aquinas goes on to maintain that God's self-knowledge, although perfect, unitary and eternal, still maintains distinction. This distinction consists in the God who expresses his self-knowledge in himself and the God who is expressed or conceived, namely the Son who is the expression of the self-knowledge of the Father. The former is a perfect emanation of the latter in such a way that the being of both is identical and this emanation remains entirely immanent.[15]

As well as God's knowledge of himself through himself, Aquinas elsewhere outlines the sense in which ideas subsist in the divine mind and are therefore known by him.[16] He claims that these ideas are forms of things existing apart from things, and that the form of a thing can either be the exemplar or pattern of the thing whose form it is said to be, or it can be the means of knowing the thing whose form it is by its residing in the knower. In both these aspects, ideas subsist in the mind of God. Yet, as

[13] *SCG* II.60. [14] *SCG* I.45.
[15] On the difference between divine and human self-understanding, see *SCG* IV.II.II. [16] *ST* Ia.15.1.

regards the latter, it can be seen that it is by God's interior self-knowledge, namely the emanation of the Son from the Father, that he knows other things by their proper ideas subsisting in him. In a sense, therefore, all things are known primarily and per se as they exist most perfectly in God's knowledge, and as they are therefore known in God's self-knowledge, in God's interior emanation.

Aquinas also describes the place of the Spirit within the divine emanations and creative act.[17] He seeks to make clear what we must understand of the Spirit with regard to God's immanent life and act of creation. Initially, Aquinas examines intellectual natures in general and states that there must be a will alongside intellect because such a nature must *desire* to know.[18] Crucially, intellects are not merely passive recipients of 'information'; all knowledge is at once *willed* or *desired* knowledge. Just as any natural thing has an inclination to its own proper operations, for 'it tends to what is fitting [*convenientia*] for itself', so too an intellectual nature has an inclination, which we call will, towards its own proper operation in knowledge.[19] Aquinas claims that, of all the acts which belong to the will, love (*amor*) is found to be a principle and common root. He describes this in terms of the 'affinity and correspondence' (*affinitatem et convenientiam*) between the principle of inclination in natural things and that to which they are moved. Thus, for example, if I am standing before a beautiful painting in one of Rome's magnificent churches, a 'species' or 'likeness' of the painting comes to reside in my mind. Meanwhile, the painting comes to reside in my will because there is a certain 'proportion and suitability' – a *convenientia* – between myself and the painting. My love of, or desire for, the painting draws me to knowledge of the painting. The *convenientia* between my intellect and will on the one hand, and the painting on the other, becomes the principle behind my intellectual nature's self-motion towards knowledge of the object, that motive attraction being a form of love.

However, in contrast to intellectual beings such as angels or humans, God is at one with his intellectual nature and, likewise, his will. The first and most appropriate object of the operation of the divine will – the object of God's desire – is the divine goodness, and so God, because God loves himself and is beloved and lover, must be in his will as the beloved is in the lover.[20] The beloved is in the will of the lover by means of a 'proportion and suitability' between the two. God has a most perfect proportion and suitability with himself because he is simple. Therefore, God is in his will with perfect simplicity. In addition, any act of will is, as Aquinas remarks, an

[17] *SCG* IV.15ff. [18] *SCG* IV.19.1ff. [19] *SCG* IV.19.2. [20] *SCG* IV.19.7.

act of love, but the act of the will is the divine being. So 'the being of God in his will by way of love is not an accidental one – as it is in us – but is essential being', hence the scriptural teaching that 'God is love.'[21]

Coupled with what has been said of God's self-knowledge in the emanation of the Son, we now have a twofold picture of the divine life. On the one hand, God loves himself because, as we have seen, the 'proportionate and appropriate' end of God's operative will is himself and his own goodness. Yet this would not be loved if it were not known, and God knows himself through conceiving of himself in the eternal emanation of the Word. Yet it is not quite adequate to say that it is God's knowledge which is beloved, for God's knowledge is his essence. Therefore, coupled with the emanation of the Word must be a love whereby the lover dwells in the beloved, both in God's knowing and in that which is known. The love by which God is in the divine will as a lover in the beloved 'proceeds both from the Word of God and the God whose Word he is'.[22] It is the Holy Spirit. It is as if the Father is the lover and the Son the beloved, but immediately and in eternity this is returned so the Son is the lover and the Father the beloved. This introduces a kind of circular dynamism to the inner divine life which Aquinas refers to as a kind of intellectual 'motion'.[23]

With regard to God's self-knowledge and self-love in the persons of the Trinity, we now have a flickering sense of how the universe can be said to have the divine nature as its cause. Aquinas states that 'effects pre-exist in a cause according to its mode of being. Since, then, God's being is his actual understanding, creatures pre-exist there as held in his mind.'[24] Thus he states, 'God's knowledge stands to all created things as the artist's to his products.'[25] However, in addition to the knowledge of things, Aquinas also notes that an act of will is necessary in the act of creating: creation *ex nihilo* is not a necessary emanation. God is so inclined because his own subsistent goodness wills that other things be in such a way that 'by his will he produces things in being' and his self-love thereby becomes the cause of the creation of things.[26] In a similar fashion Aquinas elsewhere states that 'It is . . . from the fact that the Holy Spirit proceeds by way of love – and love has a kind of driving and moving force – that the movement which is from God in things seems properly to be attributed to the Holy Spirit.'[27] It seems, therefore, that God's knowledge becomes the cause of creation and the ground of the continual subsistence of the cosmos, while the Holy Spirit, which proceeds from the Father and Son by way of love, is properly

[21] *Ibid.*; 1 John 4:16. [22] *SCG* IV.19.8. [23] *SCG* IV.19.12. [24] *ST* Ia.19.4, responsio.
[25] *ST* Ia.14.8, responsio. [26] *SCG* IV.19.12. [27] *SCG* IV.20.3.

described as the principle of the motion of nature.[28] This means that what moves all things to their characteristic operation is love, namely a desire for fulfilment in the beloved, a desire for fulfilment in God.

In what sense can this emanation and return to self in God be described as any kind of motion? In answer, Aquinas begins by stating that there are two kinds of action.[29] The first is that which passes to matter outside the agent concerned, for example locally moving another body or the heating of one body by another. The second is that which remains in the agent, for example understanding, sensing or willing. In the case of the first, the motion is completed not in the agent of the motion, but in another. In the second, the motion is the completion or perfection of the agent of the motion. However, this latter is not motion in the strict Aristotelian sense of the passage from contrary to contrary or the actualizing of the potential *qua* potential. In Aristotelian terms, it may be regarded as *energeia* (actuality), a kind of constant similar to seeing which is not temporally divisible into parts. It is an activity which, at every moment, is the same, not having an end outside itself.[30] Therefore, Aquinas concludes, this 'motion' is different from the strict Aristotelian definition of the *Physics*. However, he does seem willing to assimilate the Aristotelian view with the self-moving soul of Plato when he writes:

> Plato understood by motion any given operation, so that to understand and to judge are a kind of motion. Aristotle likewise touches upon this manner of speaking in the *De Anima*. Plato accordingly said that the first mover moves himself because he knows himself and wills or loves himself . . . There is no difference between reaching a first being that moves himself, as understood by Plato, and reaching a first being that is absolutely unmoved, as understood by Aristotle.[31]

Elsewhere, Aquinas explicitly states that life is especially manifested in motion, and specifically in self-motion and those things which put themselves into operation.[32] He states that, if love, drive and motion are particularly suited to the Holy Spirit, as Scripture suggests,[33] it is here that we find the dynamism of the Trinitarian life fully expressed and mediated.

In expounding Aquinas in this way I am not attempting to give an account of the causal mechanism of the universe's creation. Creation *ex nihilo* is not ordinary causality, so much as the intrinsic basis of all causality. Neither do I wish slavishly to follow modern science's tendency to privilege the temporal origin of the cosmos in giving an account of the universe's

[28] *SCG* IV.20.3. [29] *ST* Ia.18.3, ad. 1.

[30] On Aristotle's distinction between *energeia* and *kinesis*, see *Metaphysics* IX.6. [31] *SCG* I.13.10.

[32] *SCG* IV.20.6. [33] *Ibid.* Aquinas mentions John 6:64 and Ezekiel 37:5.

beginnings. Creation *ex nihilo* – the doctrine that creation, at *every* moment, is of nothing – as such privileges no *particular* temporal instant as revealing more acutely the nature of the cosmos as suspended over the *nihil*. Rather, my intention is to point to the way in which, for one of the most prominent theologians of the Christian tradition, effects analogically resemble their causes. Creation and motion are apparently opposed, for the former excludes the latter. Meanwhile, both are effects of something more real. They are reconciled and related, therefore, by their participation in the eternal and perfectly subsistent emanation of the divine persons. Yet, while Aquinas talks of emanation in creatures and God, he does so by analogy, always aware that, however great the similitude, the dissimilitude is always greater.

There is a sense, therefore, that if motion is the means of the perfection of creatures – their passage to actuality – then we might understand motion to be analogically related to the actuality of God's inner Trinitarian dynamic. I would now like to examine the way in which a more recent theologian, the Swiss Roman Catholic Hans Urs von Balthasar, develops this Thomist understanding of the doctrine of God and cosmic motion with particular reference to an understanding of both creation and motion as *relational*. More particularly, Balthasar moves beyond Aquinas in describing both motion and creation as related by analogy to the eternal kenosis within the Trinitarian Godhead.

BALTHASAR: DIFFERENCE AND THE DYNAMISM OF TRINITARIAN LOVE

The life of God, for Balthasar, is characterized by self-donation in the form of kenosis.[34] The revelation of this self-giving is recorded in the hymn to Christ's self-emptying in the incarnation in Philippians 2. Within the economy of salvation, this kenosis reaches its greatest intensity on Holy Saturday when God, in sovereign freedom, endures the dereliction of godlessness. Yet it is crucial for Balthasar that this kenotic moment is not an arbitrary act of God, as if the divine had suddenly become subject to godlessness in order to be fully himself (as in the thought of Jürgen Moltmann). Rather, it is suffering and dereliction which are made subject to God, and the godlessness of Holy Saturday is always the

[34] Hans Urs von Balthasar, *Theo-Drama: Theological Dramatic Theory*, trans. G. Harrison, vol. IV (San Francisco: Ignatius Press, 1994), pp. 325ff.

economic outworking of God's immanent and eternal kenosis.[35] It is at this moment in the economy of salvation that it is revealed that even that which is *not* God is brought to be subject *to* God. Moreover, as Graham Ward observes, this kenosis is not christomonistic, an act confined to Christ's incarnation and crucifixion. Rather, divine kenosis, as Trinitarian and eternal, is the possibility of God's self-giving within the economy of salvation.[36] As Aquinas refers to the eternal emanation of the Son from the Father, so for Balthasar the Father pours out his life without remainder in the Son's eternal begetting. The Son's response is kenotic *eucharistia*, thus constituting a 'eucharistic movement back and forth from the Father'.[37] Importantly, the self-donation of the Father is also the self-reception of the Son, thus constituting the relational nature of the eternal divine gift: self-donation and self-reception are one. This love cannot be contained within an enclosed dyad, but opens in eternity in the procession of the Spirit who maintains the infinite difference between Father and Son. This infinite *diastasis* is revealed in the Son's cry of dereliction on the cross and the silence of Holy Saturday.[38] Within that hiatus is contained not only sin, but the whole of creation, for the 'otherness' of creation – the ontological difference – is itself the *imago* of the infinite difference which is being itself, namely the difference of the divine persons. Balthasar writes:

If, within God's identity, there is an Other, who at the same time is the image of the Father and thus the archetype of all that can be created; if, within this identity, there is a Spirit, who is the free, superabundant love of the 'One' and of the 'Other', then both the otherness of creation, which is modelled on the archetypal otherness

[35] Balthasar, *The Glory of the Lord: A Theological Aesthetics*, trans. E. Leiva-Kerikakis, vol. I (San Francisco: Ignatius Press, 1982), p. 461: 'God's incomprehensibility is now no longer a mere deficiency in knowledge, but the positive manner in which God has loved us so much that he surrendered his only Son for us, the fact that the God of plenitude has poured himself out, not only into creation, but emptied himself into the modalities of an existence determined by sin, corrupted by death and alienated from God.' Crucially, in maintaining that Christ's kenosis on the cross is the economic outworking of God's eternal kenosis, Balthasar is *not* suggesting that there is an eternal suffering in God. Rather, within a sinful world, the cross is the way in which eternal love manifests itself. It is the way in which the eternal love of God, which has always flowed to creation, is maintained in its self-giving in the face of sin. I am grateful to D. C. Schindler for highlighting this point to me.

[36] See G. Ward, 'Kenosis: Death, Discourse and Resurrection' in L. Gardner, D. Moss, B. Quash and G. Ward (eds.), *Balthasar at the End of Modernity* (Edinburgh: T&T Clark, 1999), pp. 15–68, at pp. 44–45.

[37] Balthasar, *Theo-Drama: Theological Dramatic Theory*, trans. G. Harrison, vol. II (San Francisco: Ignatius Press, 1990), p. 268.

[38] See Balthasar, *Mysterium Paschale: The Mystery of Easter*, trans. A. Nichols (Edinburgh: T&T Clark, 1990).

within God, and its sheer existence, which it owes to the intradivine liberality, are brought into a positive relationship to God.[39]

In fact, for Balthasar, it is only the difference inherent within being itself which makes creaturely difference intelligible – especially the difference within all creatures, that between essence and existence.[40]

The Trinitarian difference within the Godhead and the difference of essence and existence in creation indicate, for Balthasar, 'both a *similitudo* (insofar as the multiplicity of creatures is one in *esse*) and a *maior dissimilitudo*, insofar as nondivine being necessarily cleaves in two and stands over against the divine identity in the form of non-identity'.[41] This is to say that the diversity within creation is not to be interpreted as a fall, but is rather a participation in the Trinitarian difference of the Godhead.[42] Yet, because of the ontological difference in which the essence of non-subsistent creatures is not one with their existence, the resemblance or *similitudo* is, as Aquinas would say, one of creatures to God, and not of God to creatures.[43] Likewise, Balthasar refuses to mitigate the ontological difference.

So what, for Balthasar, is the nature of the *analogia entis* through which creation is formed as an *imago* of the eternal Godhead? For Balthasar, this must be kenosis which is itself the form of love. As Ward notes, the view that love is kenotic has strong precedent in the early Church: love is self-abandonment and gift, whereas sin is the attempt at self-possession as a rejection of self-donation.[44] Kenotic love is a self-donation, not a 'giving-up'. This economy of love involves reception and therefore the relationality and difference of the giver and the recipient.[45] In a move seemingly beyond Aquinas, and with an eye on the dangers of subordinationism, it is kenotic love which is elevated to the heart of Balthasar's theology:

But if we reflect once more on the process of the intradivine processions, two approaches are barred to us: the idea of a Father who generates the Son in order to come to know himself as God and the idea of a Father who, because he has already

[39] Balthasar, *Theo-Logic: Theological Logic Theory*, trans. A. Walker, vol. II (San Francisco: Ignatius Press, 2004), pp. 180–181. See also Balthasar, *Theo-Drama*, vol. IV, p. 323.

[40] Balthasar, *Theo-Logic*, vol. II, p. 182. This is not to suggest in any way that 'difference' is a straightforward concept. It is beyond the immediate purview of this chapter to enter into a detailed discussion. For such an assessment of the difficulty of 'thinking difference', see R. Williams, 'Afterword: Making Difference' in L. Gardner, D. Moss, B. Quash and G. Ward (eds.), *Balthasar at the End of Modernity* (Edinburgh: T&T Clark, 1999), pp. 173–179.

[41] Balthasar, *Theo-Logic*, vol. II, p. 183. [42] *Ibid.*, pp. 184–185. [43] See, for example, *ST* Ia.4.3.

[44] Ward, 'Kenosis', p. 46.

[45] For an exacting theological analysis of the theology of gift, including a critique of Derrida's notion of the 'one-way' gift, see John Milbank, *Being Reconciled: Ontology and Pardon* (London: Routledge, 2003).

known himself perfectly, generates the Son. The first position would be Hegelianism, the second, thought through consistently, would be Arianism. For this reason, the immemorial priority of the self-surrender or self-expropriation thanks to which the Father *is* Father cannot be ascribed to knowledge but only to groundless love, which proves the identity of love as the 'transcendental par excellence'.[46]

As the 'transcendental par excellence', it is love alone which is credible as our means of understanding God's revelation of himself and creation's analogical relation to its divine source. Creation bears the marks of its origin: the love of God which is kenotic in nature. So created entities are understood to participate in the eternal kenosis of the persons of the Trinity by continually giving themselves to be seen, known, understood and delighted in. As Rowan Williams points out, reality is therefore kenotic and ek-static for Balthasar, for all things continually move out of themselves in self-donation.[47]

How might kenotic love at the heart of divine being, and its concomitant image in creation, illuminate the nature of cosmic motion? To answer this question, it is necessary to refer to the specifics of the Aristotelian–Thomist understanding of motion. It must be remembered that motion prior to the advent of modern natural philosophy is a broad category referring not only to the locomotion of bodies in space, but also to the motions of quality and quantity: learning, growing and maturing in character, for example, are varieties of motion. Central to Aristotle's and Aquinas' concept of motion is difference, which is also integral to Balthasar's understanding of love. For Aquinas, following both Plato and Aristotle, motion is always relational: there is a mover and that which is moved. Motion takes place between contraries (for example, black and white, ignorance and knowledge) and is passage from potency to act. It is a necessary condition for motion that there be something in act and something in potency with regard to the motion in hand.

Crucially, therefore, motion requires the difference of mover and moved, and the difference of potency and act. There is also a sense in which motion might also be described as ecstatic and even kenotic. I have already alluded to the distinction made by Aristotle between *energeia* (actuality) and *kinesis* (motion). The being of something in motion is always constituted by its relation to a mover as it passes 'beyond itself' from potency to act. At every

[46] Balthasar, *Theo-Logic*, vol. II, p. 177.

[47] See R. Williams, 'Balthasar and the Trinity' in E. Oakes and D. Moss (eds.), *The Cambridge Companion to Hans Urs von Balthasar* (Cambridge University Press, 2004), pp. 37–50, at p. 41.

moment of the motion, that which is in motion is exceeding itself as it receives a new form and progresses towards actuality. Therefore, Aristotle characterizes motion as an *ecstasis* in which a being may receive a new form which is bestowed by its mover. Because nature is identified more particularly with form rather than matter, motion for Aristotle and Aquinas is a genuine transformation whereby something may receive a new form. By contrast, the being of what is fully actual is self-contained and, unlike that which is in motion, it is at every moment self-identical. However, this is not to say that an energic being is self-enclosed. Quite the contrary is the case, for such actualized beings are the most potent and ready movers of those in potentiality.

In what sense might motion be kenotic in character? In any motion, the mover 'donates' the form it already possesses and pours this into that which it moves. For example, in the case of the motion of learning, the teacher donates knowledge or the means of thought in such a way that the student, who is moved to knowledge, receives a genuinely new form. It is not the case that the teacher 'gives up' knowledge in order to bring a student from potency to act; rather, this motion is brought about through self-donation. That which is moved receives and seeks a new actuality through desire. It is therefore not the case that creation is simply a series of ultimately passive objects which are moved or manipulated in mechanical fashion by a divine subject. Rather, creation participates in being moved by God, for in its cosmic motion creation exhibits the desire for its natural end in the divine. Where humanity fails of its own power to participate in its motion by God, the divine provides the gift of grace whereby humanity may once again seek motion to the beatific vision.[48]

Motion, therefore, requires difference and is ecstatic and kenotic in character. Motion is the temporal image of the differentiated, ecstatic and kenotic self-donation and self-reception which characterizes the Trinitarian divine life. Cosmic motion is the 'watermark' of creation's divine origin, representing a *similitudo* – which is yet a *maior dissimilitudo* – of the cosmos to the divine life. This 'watermark' is the kenotic self-donation of love which moves the sun and other stars.

Moving to the last brief section of this chapter, I would now like to contrast this understanding of cosmic origins and motion with the theology and cosmology of the greatest theorist of motion in early modern science, Isaac Newton. Following theologians including Michael Buckley, I see here

[48] On motion and grace, see Simon Oliver, 'The Sweet Delight of Virtue and Grace in Aquinas's Ethics', *International Journal of Systematic Theology* 7:1 (2005), pp. 52–71.

the beginnings of the separation of cosmology from issues in theology and metaphysics, and the sundering of faith and reason.[49]

NEWTON ON GOD AND MOTION

It is now commonly known that Isaac Newton, whose great work, the *Principia Mathematica*, was published in 1687, wrote far more theology than he did science. Because he denied the divinity of Christ and the doctrine of the Trinity – thus putting at grave risk his position at Trinity College, Cambridge – Newton, however, did not publish his theological manuscripts.[50]

Newton expounded his Arian views of Christ at least fifteen years prior to the publication of the *Principia*. There are two principal reasons why Newton held such an Arian view of God. The first relates to studies in biblical interpretation and religious history which he initially undertook in earnest between the late 1660s and the mid-1680s, and to which he was to return in the early part of the eighteenth century. Through his studies, Newton became convinced that the earliest Christian Church held an authentic and uncorrupted non-Trinitarian faith which understood Christ as an exalted and yet created mediator between God and the universe.

The second reason for Newton's Arianism, and one which was at the same time a consequence of this Christology, is more explicit and, although this view was undoubtedly formulated much earlier, it appears in the General Scholium of the second and third editions of the *Principia*. This was the belief in the utter supremacy, power and freedom of the will of the Lord God of Dominion.[51] It was a supremely free and sovereign will which, for Newton, was the supreme attribute of God. Because this will was supremely free, this entailed its inscrutability and arbitrary character. It was because of God's omnipotent wilful dominion alone that he was worthy of worship. This voluntarism featured a dualistic distinction between God's *potentia ordinata* and *potentia absoluta*. It was by the former that God ordained and preserved the regular workings of the laws of nature. However, in the latter was enshrined the absolute power of God's will to

49 See M. Buckley, *At the Origins of Modern Atheism* (Yale University Press, 1987).

50 At the time of writing, Newton's manuscripts are being made available on the Internet by a project substantially sponsored by the Arts and Humanities Research Council and the Royal Society, at www.newtonproject.sussex.ac.uk.

51 See Isaac Newton, *The Principia: Mathematical Principles of Natural Philosophy*, trans. I. B. Cohen and A. Whitman (Berkeley: University of California Press, 1999), pp. 939–944.

suspend or change these laws at any moment. This was a kind of arbitrary 'addition' to God's *potentia ordinata*.

Newton's voluntarist Lord God of Dominion as described above was utterly remote and transcendent. This concept of the divine fitted neatly with Newton's physics in which the universe was seen to be filled with discrete objects whose particular motion required no reference to a relation with any other being. Interaction between discrete objects constituted change brought about by conflictual forces. Remember that, according to Newton's first law of motion, a body will continue in its state of motion or rest until it is subject to another force. Motion is a state, and any body will naturally resist a change in that state. What Newton is primarily concerned with is not motion per se, but forces which change a state of motion. Through the natural resistance to change possessed by bodies, the universe exhibited some degree of stability and changelessness, this being a reflection of the divine nature itself. However, this left a theological gap for Newton which was somewhat unpalatable: how was he to describe a mode of divine action within such a world so as not to make God incidental to cosmology?

Newton gave two apparently different answers to this question. The first, in typical Arian fashion, saw the divine as utterly remote and acting through Christ as an intermediary. God and Christ were not one in substance, but one in unity of will and dominion. Newton states that, on this view, Christ is understood as the 'viceroy' of God, putting into action the dictates of the divine will. The second means of divine action, however, is direct within absolute space. J. E. McGuire has argued that this latter form of divine action shows that Newton's Arianism was limited in its effect upon his cosmology.[52] However, I will suggest that the latter notion of divine action is also the result of Newton's Arianism and that this conception of God reinforces his understanding of motion.

Absolute space is the context and basis for motion in Newton's universe. He outlined his notion of space in *De Gravitatione et Aequipondio Fluidorum*, a treatise which was to form the basis of many arguments in the first edition of the *Principia*.[53] Newton explains that space is neither substance nor accident, but rather 'an eminent effect of God, or a disposition of all being'.[54] Space is ultimately characterized as extension. We are

[52] See J. E. McGuire, 'The Fate of the Date: The Theology of Newton's *Principia* Revisited' in M. J. Osler (ed.), *Rethinking the Scientific Revolution* (Cambridge University Press, 2000), pp. 271–295.

[53] This text is available in A. R. Hall and M. B. Hall (eds.), *Unpublished Scientific Papers of Isaac Newton: A Selection from the Portsmouth Collection in the University Library, Cambridge* (Cambridge University Press, 1962), pp. 89–156.

[54] *Ibid.*, p. 132.

able to abstract 'the dispositions and properties of a body so that there remains only the uniform and unlimited stretching out of space in length, breadth and depth'.[55] Space is also 'eternal in duration and immutable in nature, and this because it is the emanent effect of an eternal and immutable being'.[56] In a fashion which appears to consider space as 'begotten' of God, Newton explains that, 'If ever space had not existed, God at that time would have been nowhere; and hence either he created space later (in which he was not himself), or else, which is less repugnant to reason, he created his own ubiquity.'[57]

Thus it can be seen that, in the absence of a fully divine Christ, absolute space becomes the basis of creation, forming the 'disposition of being *qua* being', for such space is eternal in duration and immutable in nature, and this because it is the emanent effect of an eternal and immutable being. While space is not literally God's sensory medium, it is difficult to avoid the conclusion that Newton has described a spatial and three-dimensional Godhead. Indeed, Newton's absolute space – eternally of God, as it were – takes on the characteristics of an orthodox second person of the Trinity. Whereas, for Aquinas, God creates and sustains the world through the Son's emanation from the Father, so for Newton, God creates the world in a co-eternal and uncreated absolute space through the exercise of his will.

It seems, therefore, that absolute space coupled with the action of the divine will is the ontological precondition of all being. It is by means of co-eternal and infinite space that God is able to operate and instantiate a material cosmos. Whereas, for Aquinas (and those in the broad Thomist tradition such as Balthasar), the motion of a body is itself a participation and effect of the knowledge of the body's form in the perfect 'motionless motion' of God, namely in the emanation of the Son from the Father, for Newton, creation occurs through the inscrutable and arbitrary 'motions' of the divine will. This is expressed in a recent article by J. E. McGuire in which he states that, for Newton, 'God does not recreate similar conditions in successive regions of space; he maintains the same formal reality in different parts of space through a succession of times. In this way the continuity of motion is the real effect of God's motion.'[58]

Yet what divine motions can these be within Newton's Arian voluntarism? They can only be the motions of an arbitrary and inscrutable divine will. Whereas, for Aquinas, the 'motionless motion' of the divine emanation was able to provide the ontological basis and goal of all motion, for Newton, who has already discounted the possibility of relationality within the

[55] *Ibid.*, p. 133. [56] *Ibid.*, p. 136. [57] *Ibid.*, p. 137. [58] McGuire, 'The Fate of the Date', p. 282.

Godhead, motion can only be the effect of the imposition of divine volition. The lack of Trinitarian relationality in Newton's conception of God means that the universe cannot be thought of as a hierarchy and system of related motions which are images of the divine life, but rather as the action of one being, God, within absolute space to instantiate a material body, whereupon the created being retains a primitive state of motion which is discrete and self-explanatory.

CONCLUSION

Where does this leave us? There is a question which pervades the traditional reflection on creation which is pertinent: could a single, monadic, non-relational divinity of Newtonian variety 'create'? Some, including recently Tom Weinandy in the spirit of Balthasar, argue no.[59] Weinandy states that:

> If God were a solitary monad existing in complete self-isolation, the 'thought' of creating something other than himself could never arise. It would be ontologically impossible for the thought of 'another' to arise, for there would be no ontological ground upon which this thought of 'another' could arise. Being the sole being that existed, it would be impossible for a single-person God to conceive of anything other than himself.[60]

This is why one might suppose that a monadic personal God must create of necessity in order to be personal, for being personal necessitates relationality. Alternatively, a monadic God, in order to conceive of something other than himself, must create not *ex nihilo*, but out of a non-temporally bounded, always existent 'other' in the form of a pre-existent material nature akin to Aristotle's eternal cosmos or Plato's *khora*. It would then be God's relation to this eternal Aristotelian cosmos which was the basis of God's creating of an other.

Because Newton proposes just such a deity – a God devoid of relationality and characterized by freedom understood in terms of an arbitrary, all-powerful and inscrutable will – he cannot properly think creation *ex nihilo*. Rather, creation emerges within a co-eternal absolute space which then forms the basis of God's relation to his creation, an absolute space which, bizarrely, takes on the characteristics of an orthodox Christ. Moreover, there can be no reason intrinsic to God himself concerning *why* he would create. This is beyond intelligibility and reason, for the divine will, in being sovereign and free, is not bounded by 'reasons' for creating. The

[59] See Balthasar, *Theo-Logic*, vol. II, p. 181.

[60] Thomas Weinandy, *Does God Suffer?* (University of Notre Dame Press, 2000), pp. 139–140, note 75.

consequence of the combination of Newton's theology and natural philosophy is a sense that creation – as a theological doctrine – stands outside the realm of reason, whereas the natural processes under examination in the *Principia* are merely the instantiation of an inscrutable divine will and the subject of a wholly autonomous natural philosophy. Moreover, with the central characteristic of nature – motion – understood non-relationally and through the category of force, there seems no basis of relating such motion to the life of God, as there had been in Aquinas where motion is understood as an analogue of the supreme relationality of the Trinity. It therefore comes as no surprise that early modern science divested itself so easily of metaphysical and theological concerns.

Properly to think creation *ex nihilo*, one requires a doctrine of God which is sufficiently rich, such that God himself is the full and wholly adequate reason not only for the universe's temporal beginning (if, indeed, we can properly conceive of such a thing), but also for God's continual sustaining of creation over the *nihil*. This, I would suggest, following Aquinas and Balthasar, is found only in a fully Trinitarian doctrine. The relation of God to the kenotic act of creation is analogically related to God's kenotic self-relation in the emanation of the persons of the Trinity. This much is proposed by, among others, Barth, Pannenberg and Torrance. Going just a little further, what I have also suggested is that the dynamic eternal emanations within the Godhead are also related by analogy to cosmic motion – the means of creaturely perfection – where motion is understood as fundamentally relational and the key characteristic of the cosmos. We might even suggest that God continually 'moves' creation from nothingness to being. Because such a doctrine of God is sufficiently rich that we need not postulate anything other than God to account for creation, this can be the only way of truly thinking creation which is of nothing, thereby maintaining the distinctiveness of theological cosmology and avoiding the reification of the *nihil*. As I have argued in more detail elsewhere, this also allows us to understand the subject matter of physics – motion – as included and taken up within the subject matter of theology by virtue of motion's analogical relation to the doctrine of God.[61] Meanwhile, we would do well to remember that, for theologians such as Aquinas and Balthasar, the doctrine of creation *ex nihilo* is first a doctrine of God and only then a cosmology.

[61] See Oliver, *Philosophy, God and Motion*, esp. Chapter 6.

CHAPTER 10

The Big Bang, quantum cosmology and creatio ex nihilo

William R. Stoeger, S. J.

INTRODUCTION

There is compelling evidence that our universe emerged from an extremely hot, dense primordial state about 14 billion years ago – the *Planck era*, which is often considered the direct result of the *Big Bang*. From that fiery epoch it has gradually expanded and cooled. And as it has cooled it has become more and more lumpy, and more and more complex. As ever lower temperatures were reached, simpler more basic entities and systems combined and formed an ever more complex and diverse array of evolving systems – particularly in cooler, more protected, more chemically rich environments.

But what is the Big Bang? Strictly speaking, it is the past limit of the hotter, denser phases we encounter as we go back farther into the history of the universe. Not only is it observationally inaccessible, but it also lies outside the reliability of the classical (non-quantum) cosmological models we depend upon. What will quantum cosmology be able to tell us about it? By considering the recent educated scientific speculation on what may have led to the Big Bang and the Planck era, we shall find that quantum cosmology – and the physics upon which it relies – promises to reveal a great deal, but cannot provide an alternative to the traditional philosophical notion of creation, *creatio ex nihilo*, in accounting for the universe's ultimate origin. Any understanding it might provide, no matter how physically fundamental, will require a deeper explanation or basis for its existence, order and properties. In other words, it will not be self-subsistent or self-explanatory. But at the same time, quantum cosmology indirectly poses these ultimate questions, which it cannot answer, and in so doing points towards – and is consonant with – *creatio ex nihilo*.

In what follows we shall briefly describe the basic ideas and findings about our universe that physicists and astronomers – especially observational and theoretical cosmologists – have uncovered. Some of these are very well substantiated scientifically, and others – particularly those concerning the Planck era and what led to it – are the fruit of educated intuition, speculation and continuing exploration. Though these latter do not yet constitute reliable theories, they have already contributed important and compelling insights into the character of physical reality before space, time and matter as we know them emerged from the Planck era. From there we shall go on to reflect upon these findings and models from a philosophical point of view, particularly with regard to their explanatory depth. To what extent do any of them constitute or provide an entrée to ultimate explanations of existence or order? As we just mentioned, we shall find that they do not. In fact, we shall argue that physics and cosmology as we know and practice them are in principle incapable of providing such explanations.

Finally we shall briefly present the basic components of *creatio ex nihilo* and show that it does not – and cannot – conflict with authentic and observationally supported scientific findings and conclusions. Instead it is deeply consonant and complementary with what the natural sciences discover – and is indirectly suggested and supported by the character of natural process, which manifests dynamical integrity and autonomy but requires ultimate ontological and nomic grounding. Thus, the Big Bang, quantum cosmological models of the primordial processes generating it, biological evolution, and the emergence of intelligence and consciousness are not alternatives to divine creation, but rather complementary accounts, filling in the concrete details left open by that fundamental but very unadorned and semi-apophatic insight.

THE UNIVERSE AND ITS EVOLUTION

If we probe the history of the solar system, of our galaxy the Milky Way, of the universe itself, what do we find? Astronomy, geology, physics, chemistry enable us to do this – both because of the information about past epochs which is hidden in the make-up of the planets, meteorites, stars, galaxies (we are immersed in relics of the distant past) and because the farther out we observe in doing astronomy, the farther back in time we are looking. For instance there are some quasars which are of the order of 10 billion light years away – the signals we are now receiving from them began their journey towards us 10 billion years ago. Thus, we can in principle obtain direct information about the way the universe was at all epochs of the distant past. Astronomy and observational cosmology (the astronomy and physics of the universe as a single object of study) provide us with a core sample of the universe, reaching from the present back to within 100,000 years of the Planck era itself.

And so, what do we find?[1] We have discovered that our observable universe is immense, consisting of the order of at least 100 billion galaxies, each with billions, or in many cases hundreds of billions, of stars, and spread out over tens of billions of light years. Furthermore, it is becoming clear that it is almost certainly only a small part of a much larger "universe as a whole." On microscopic levels, the matter it contains is made up of 92 natural elements – from hydrogen, through helium, carbon, oxygen, iron, etc. to uranium. There is compelling evidence that most of the matter, however, is not made up of these elements but is constituted by non-baryonic (not composed of protons and neutrons) dark matter, which rarely interacts with itself or with anything else except through gravity. This dark matter is clustered near and around galaxies and clusters of galaxies in massive haloes, which extend to larger distances than the visible part of the galaxies themselves. Finally, there is fairly solid evidence that this baryonic and non-baryonic matter is complemented by smoothly distributed dark energy – possibly vacuum energy – which has negative pressure and is thus inducing the expansion of the universe to accelerate.

It is notable that on both macroscopic and microscopic levels, the cosmos is intricately clustered. There are moons orbiting planets; planets, comets, asteroids orbiting stars; stars orbiting one another (binary systems); dozens, hundreds, thousands and even hundreds of thousands of stars either densely or loosely clustered; these clusters marshalled into spiral, elliptical and irregular galaxies; the galaxies often collected into clusters of galaxies; and these clusters linked together in superclusters. On the microscopic, or chemical, level the 92 natural elements are often found combined into small, or in some environments very large, molecules. And the molecules are frequently organized into systems of tremendous intricacy and variety – some very simple and some extremely complex, such as those composed of cells, like the plants and animals on earth.

[1] There is a vast professional and popular scientific literature summarizing the cosmological discoveries of the last hundred years. Some of the introductory professional references would be: Edward W. Kolb and Michael S. Turner, *The Early Universe* (Redwood City, CA: Addison-Wesley, 1990); Andrew R. Liddle and David H. Lyth, *Cosmological Inflation and Large-Scale Structure* (Cambridge University Press, 2000); M. P. Hobson, G. Efstathiou and A. N. Lasenby, *General Relativity: An Introduction for Physicists* (Cambridge University Press, 2006), pp. 355–466. Among the recent popular accounts are: George F. R. Ellis, *Before the Beginning: Cosmology Explained* (London: Boyars/Bowerdean, 1993), and Martin J. Rees, *Just Six Numbers: The Deep Forces that Shape the Universe* (New York: Basic Books, 2001).

By measuring the redshifts of distant galaxies, we have come to realize that our universe is expanding – that the galaxies farther away from us are receding much faster than those which are closer. They are not moving away within a static absolute spatial framework. Rather there is strong evidence that space itself is expanding and carrying the galaxies along with it. And as we have just briefly mentioned, we have strong evidence that the expansion is now accelerating, instead of decelerating, as many guessed fifteen or twenty years ago.

We also have discovered and confirmed that, as the universe has been expanding, it has also been cooling – that as we go back into the past, the universe was not only much denser, but also much hotter. The presence of the cosmic microwave background radiation (CMWBR) – which is radiation that originates from the almost perfectly smoothly distributed hot ionized gas from a time before there were stars and galaxies (about 13.7 billion years ago) – assures us of this. At that time, when the primordial radiation in the universe on average last scattered from matter, the universe was about 4,000 K. There was a time long before that, between one and three minutes after the Big Bang – when the universe began expanding and cooling – during which the temperature of the universe was much hotter, more that a billion degrees Kelvin. We know this because of the large amount of helium we have detected throughout the cosmos – about 24 percent by weight of all the baryonic matter in the universe is helium – and a trace amount of deuterium. That amount of helium, and the little bit of deuterium, could not have been produced by stars. But in that brief window a couple minutes after exiting the Planck era, the temperature and density would have been just right to produce lots of helium, and some deuterium.

Our ever more precise measurements of the CMWBR on various angular scales assure us of another amazing fact. As I have already indicated, for at least the first several hundred thousand years after the Big Bang – or perhaps the first couple of million years of the universe's 13.7-billion-year history – there were no galaxies or stars. The universe at that time was simply a large ball of hot, expanding, gradually cooling gas with no discernible lumps in it. There were very slight lumps – density fluctuations – however, which would eventually stop expanding and collapse under the force of gravity to become galaxies and clusters of galaxies. But at that early time these fluctuations were very weak, with a density of only about 1 part in 100,000 different from the background density of the universe.

This means that at that early time there were no elements heavier than helium, and perhaps a little bit of lithium. Chemistry had very little to work with! All the elements heavier than helium and lithium were produced later, either in the cores of stars or in supernova explosions which terminate the life of large stars. Such explosions also serve to scatter those heavier elements throughout the universe, enriching the gas out of which succeeding generations of stars and planets form.

In physics we study the various forces which enable matter to interact, combine and undergo transformations. We find that there are only four basic interactions – gravity, electromagnetism, the weak nuclear interaction and the strong nuclear interaction, which binds protons and neutrons together into the nuclei of atoms. These form the necessary basis for all the other interactions in more complex systems, whether they be chemical or biological. Interestingly enough, these four basic interactions apparently were not always distinguishable. In the very, very early universe – in the Planck era, when the cosmic temperature was above 10^{32} K – it is likely that they were identical, that is *unified*. There was probably only one "superforce" – and furthermore everything was quantized, including time and space. As yet we have no adequate theory reliably describing this early extreme epoch. However, there is a great deal of work being done to fill this important gap, using a number of different approaches. Superstrings, loop quantum gravity, twistors, non-commutative geometry are the names of some of the leading programs aimed at constructing an adequate description of the Planck era. Chaotic inflation, eternal inflation, the original Hartle–Hawking "no-boundary" proposal, and suggestions connected with these are limited semi-classical approaches attempting to arrive at conclusions about the Planck era – or about how our universe began to expand and cool immediately after emerging from it – based on what we understand about gravitation, space-time and quantum theory from the reliable but limited theories we already have. More about these later!

Once the temperature fell below 10^{32} K (in four space-time dimensions, if there are more than three spatial dimensions effective at very high temperatures, then the Planck epoch would be reached at a much lower temperature), according to the standard picture, gravity would separate off from the grand unified force (GUT, Grand Unified Theory), and space and time as we know them would emerge. A little later, as the temperature slides below 10^{26} K, the strong nuclear force becomes distinct, separating from the unified electro-weak force. At a much lower temperature, around 10^{15} K, the electro-weak interaction splits into the weak nuclear force and electro-magnetism. In the standard model, all this diversification of physical interactions occurs well within the first second after the universe begins to expand out of the Planck era. It is important to point out that we already do have a reliable theory of electro-weak unification, the Weinberg–Salam model, which has been confirmed experimentally. A great deal of work is being done on constructing and testing an adequate GUT, as well as on the full unification of GUT with gravity. As yet, although there has been significant progress, we are far from full and reliable unified theories of these kinds.

Right as the expanding universe emerged from the Planck era, or shortly thereafter – certainly before the GUT transition at 10^{26} K – the universe probably underwent a very brief but significant *inflationary phase*, during which it expanded extremely rapidly for a very short time – by a factor of the order of 10^{30}. This period of inflation would have been driven by a high vacuum-energy (or by some other form of dark-energy) density, which possesses a comparably high *negative* pressure, thus sourcing a repulsive gravitational force. Though there is not yet adequate confirmation that inflation occurred, there are many indications that the detailed characteristics of our universe are consistent with it. Furthermore, there are no compelling alternative explanations for several puzzling features of our universe. Among the most prominent of these are the fact that the CMWBR is almost the same temperature in every direction, and the presence of the tiny temperature fluctuations in it, which code for small density fluctuations in the ionized gas at that time, roughly 300,000 years after the Big Bang. These are the seeds from which galaxies and clusters of galaxies developed later on. Inflation ended and the universe reheated (the extremely rapid expansion during inflation would have understandably been accompanied by supercooling) quite quickly, restoring the temperature to a level above 10^{26} K, followed by *gradual* expansion and cooling from that point down to the present time. Formation of the galaxies and stars, delayed because of the strong coupling between the free electrons and radiation while the gas of the universe was ionized, slowly commenced once most the gas became neutral, below about 4,000 K, right around the time the CMWBR last scattered from the cosmic plasma. As soon as that transition occurred, the slight density enhancements began to grow (relative to the expanding background) under the attractive influence of gravity, eventually collapsing to form galaxies and clusters of galaxies.

THE PLANCK ERA AND "THE BEGINNING" OF THE UNIVERSE

But what about the Planck era and the Big Bang? What generated this extreme primordial state? Was this the very beginning of the universe?

The standard models of the universe, which are called the Friedmann–Lemaître–Robertson–Walker (FLRW) models, have worked very, very well in describing its large-scale structure and its history back to a time when the universe was enormously hot, greater than 10^{26} K. Such models are smooth (homogeneous – the density of matter at any given time within large volumes is constant) and isotropic (they look the same to any observer in all directions) on the largest scales. Of course, our universe is presently very lumpy – there are galaxies, clusters of galaxies, and stars and clusters of stars within the galaxies. However, on the largest scales, the FLRW model still works better than any other. And it can be easily modified on such scales to include this lumpiness as little fluctuations, or perturbations, which become galaxies and clusters of galaxies at later times. Locally, on small scales, such lumps strongly disrupt the smoothness, but averaged over very large scales, they still constitute very small fluctuations and thus do not markedly change the behavior or characteristics of the universe as a whole. This is even more obvious at very early times, when the universe was less than a few million years old. Then there were only small fluctuations on all scales – even the smallest. These only stopped expanding and collapsed into galaxies later, but probably before the universe was a few hundred million years old.

If we use this standard FLRW model to go all the way back in time as far as we can go, we find that at a certain point it describes the universe as having infinite temperature and infinite density. In the version which best fits what our universe is like, this point, which is often referred to as "the initial singularity" or "the Big Bang," would have occurred, about 13.7 billion years ago – but only the tiniest fraction of a second before the universe was at the temperature of the Planck era, 10^{32} K.

There is a problem, however, in taking this "initial singularity" or "Big Bang" point seriously. The fact that it involves infinite temperature and infinite density serves as a warning that this did not actually happen. It is simply a "prediction" of the model which does not represent what really occurred. In fact, there are very strong indications, as I mentioned at the outset, that the key assumptions upon which the FLRW model is based – those of Einstein's theory of gravitation, general relativity – break down when the universe is at or above the Planck-era temperature. The model is very reliable below that temperature, but severely fails in describing its physical state and behavior during the Planck era itself, or during any era preceding it.

Thus, we have firmly established evidence and a reliable description of the hotter denser cosmic phases we encounter as we go back farther and farther into the past. In fact, we can define the Big Bang as the past limit of these hotter denser phases – a limit, however, that is outside the acceptable range of the FLRW model. For the Planck era (at 10^{32} K) and anything earlier, it is completely inadequate. As yet we have no reliable way of complementing the model at these extreme energies. Quantum cosmologists, as we have already seen, have been working for decades to provide one.

From this discussion we can clearly see, then, that the Big Bang, or even the Planck era, is *not* "the very beginning" of the universe. It certainly *is* "the beginning" according to FLRW models of our universe. But those models are completely inadequate precisely in the region of the Big Bang! Thus, on the basis of what we know so far we can say very little about the Big Bang and Planck era, or about what generated them. As we shall see, however, research in quantum cosmology – though not yet yielding complete and reliable results – has begun to shed some significant light upon some possibilities and some of the characteristics of that primordial cosmic state.

Eventually, from a philosophical point of view, we shall want to determine whether or not an adequate theory of the conditions in the Planck era, and a reliable account of what led up to it, will ever be able to model an "absolute beginning" of the universe. Or, more fundamentally, are physics and cosmology capable of providing an ultimate explanation for the universe and its principal features? If so, then they would be viable alternatives to the philosophical *creatio ex nihilo* idea of creation, which constitutes the basis for the theological doctrine of creation in Judaism, Christianity and Islam. If not, then they would be complementary, and not on a level equivalent to that of philosophical or theological explanation. Before we delve more deeply into that issue, we look briefly at what quantum cosmology is suggesting. First, however, we comment on the use of models in the sciences.

We have already referred often to the FLRW standard models of our observable universe, and frequently used the word "model" in other contexts throughout our discussions. We shall continue to do so! Why is that? We rarely, if ever, in our quest for knowledge and understanding deal with reality as it is in itself – certainly not in the natural sciences. We observe and measure certain features and phenomena it manifests – from particular perspectives, looking for certain indicators and using certain instruments, which have certain capabilities and limitations. From what we learn, and using our informed imaginations, we construct certain models of the universe, or of other systems, and its evolution.

We then test those models with further observations and measurements, gradually refining them, so that they reliably and accurately represent the reality we encounter and measure. But these models are never perfect, nor definitive. We shall find that they always suffer from important limitations. Thus, we must clearly recognize that, though models represent reality with *some* reliability – they have been constructed that way – they are *not* the reality they represent. In talking about the universe as we are doing, it is tempting to identify – or confuse – the model with the reality. Even though the model reveals something about the universe, it also possesses features and deficiencies which fall short of, or misrepresent, the reality itself. Models are, instead, tools we use and modify to probe and gradually come to understand that reality. There is really no other way we have discovered to arrive at a detailed testable understanding of the world around us.

INSIGHTS FROM QUANTUM COSMOLOGY

Why does the basic physics underlying the FLRW standard cosmological models, and their modifications (e.g., additions of an inflationary epoch), break down at the very high temperatures, or energies, which characterize the Planck era? One simple answer is to say that the universe is too hot for space and time (or more correctly space-time) to exist as smooth continua. The fluctuations in geometry are so large that the concept of space-time as we usually model it – as a smooth, connected manifold – is no longer valid. Instead we have to find an adequate way of representing this highly energetic state with a discrete, broken-up, foam-like structure, which becomes space-time when the temperature falls below 10^{32} K, and the universe emerges from the Planck epoch. In other words, we need a quantum description of space-time and therefore of gravity. This is because the basic physics of space and time is intimately linked with the gravitational field, which in turn is determined by the mass-energy distribution throughout the universe. (Remember mass and energy are equivalent – $E = mc^2$!) Mass-energy generates gravity and therefore space-time, but space-time and gravity in turn tell mass-energy how to move. We thus need to somehow marry Einstein's gravitational theory, which wonderfully and accurately describes this fundamental link, with quantum theory, which deals with the particle-and-wave-like character of reality at submicroscopic levels. So far this challenge has proved extremely difficult, and has not been met.

Towards the beginning of our discussion, we saw that there are good reasons for supposing that at very high energies, or temperatures, the four fundamental physical interactions (gravity, electromagnetism, and the strong and weak nuclear interactions) gradually become unified – that is, identical. As we go backward in time towards higher and higher temperatures, first electromagnetism and the weak interaction become the electroweak force. At an even higher temperature, we suspect the electro-weak interaction unites with the strong nuclear force, yielding the unified GUT interaction. Finally, it seems that at roughly 10^{32} K, as we have already discussed, gravity unifies – becomes indistinguishable from – the GUT interaction. It is as this point that we need a quantum theory of gravity to describe what became space-time at lower temperatures.

In order to begin to understand what a unified quantum theory of gravity, and therefore what quantum cosmology, involves, it is helpful to discuss briefly some of the key characteristics it will have. Since it will be a quantum theory, a probability description of phenomena will be essential. It will not describe or predict unique outcomes, but rather the probability of a range of allowed outcomes in each case. This probability aspect is incorporated in the theory by what is often referred to as a *wavefunction*, whose square is just the probability of a given physical state, or outcome, being realized. And so in quantum cosmology there will be a *wavefunction of the universe*, which describes the probability of different universes "being observed" or, better, emerging from the quantum state described by that given cosmic wavefunction. The theory determines the character of that wavefunction and how it evolves – that is, how the probabilities it describes evolve or develop.

But how are specific classical outcomes to be understood and explained? In standard quantum mechanics, this is an unsolved problem – often referred to as "the measurement problem." When the wavefunction is detected or measured by interacting with a detector, or with something in its environment, it "collapses" and yields one of the allowed states with the probability given by the theory (repeating a given measurement over and over again under identical conditions, or recording the diffraction pattern of a stream of electrons passing through a slit and impacting a screen, has confirmed this). However, there is, as yet, no completely satisfactory or well-substantiated account of how this collapse is effected, except that it is somehow triggered in the wavefunction's interaction with the detector or the surrounding physical context. There is now some agreement that the elimination (decoherence) of the non-zero interference cross-terms among the allowed states (those entangled states are also allowed by quantum theory) is due to the rapid interactions with the environment, but there is no real progress in explaining how just one of the allowed states emerges from the collapsed wavefunction. This measurement problem is even more severe in quantum cosmology, for a variety of reasons – most obviously because it is very unclear with what detector or environment the cosmic wavefunction would interact in order to trigger collapse. There is nothing except the cosmic wavefunction!

Second, another quantum-based characteristic of these theories is that key properties of reality take discrete – not continuous – values. We are familiar with this in standard quantum physics, with the wave-particle character of the constituents of matter and its interactive forces. They are made up of *quanta*, bundles of mass or energy. We have electrons, protons, photons, etc. In quantum gravity there will be, besides, an irreducible minimum length, and perhaps a minimum interval of time – often referred to as the *Planck length* and the *Planck time*, respectively – smaller than which distance and time are undefined or unrealized. There is also a particle which communicates gravity, and is associated with a gravitational wave – the graviton. Thus, gravity, space and time at such submicroscopic scales are *foamlike*, discontinuous and quantized. The breakdown of our smooth model of space-time is a direct consequence of this. Another is that the initial singularity – the point in the past where the volume of the universe goes to zero, and its density and temperature become infinite – predicted by FLRW models cannot be considered real.

Third, since we are dealing with relativistic gravity, there is no absolute time – nor absolute space. In fact, space-time, as we have already emphasized, is determined by and evolves with mass-energy. Time, therefore, is a parameter *internal* to the system, not external or detached from it. It is instead to be identified with intrinsic properties of the system – such as volume or temperature. Thus, there is no unique choice for what we choose as time, or how we parameterize it – in fact, there are an infinite number of ways in which we can slice a general space-time into constant-time, purely spatial leaves, each leaf representing a definite value of the time we choose. Furthermore, well-tested theory demands that it be treated very much like any other dimension, intimately associated with the other spatial dimensions. Classically, in Einstein's gravitational theory, general relativity, and in special relativity, it is distinguished from the spatial dimensions in the metric tensor by designating it with a sign opposite to the one we use for the spatial dimensions, since classically it *does* have some unique characteristics (e.g., unique directionality).

However, it turns out that, when we go to quantum theory, we often need to include in our considerations the wavefunctions when time is imaginary – that is, when time is exactly like another spatial dimension, with the same sign. This is true in quantum field theory, even apart from quantum gravity and quantum cosmology. When applied to the universe, this strongly indicates – though still in a preliminary way – that, in the Planck era, time may have been very much like space and that it only became what we identify as time once the universe cooled enough for space-time to enter the non-quantum, or smooth classical, regime. If this is correct, it means that there was a beginning of time as we know it, separate from the beginning of the universe, if indeed the universe even had an ultimate temporal beginning. That is, there may very well have been a very early stage of our universe in which there was no time, except as another space-like dimension. Only later did it "flip over" to become classical time.

Over the past forty years or so there have been a number of different approaches which have been taken towards developing a fully reliable theory of quantum gravity which could be used by quantum cosmology to describe the very early universe, and therefore the Planck era and what may have preceded it. At present the most highly developed and promising of these are superstrings, loop quantum gravity and non-commutative geometry. I shall not spend time here describing these fascinating and tantalizing ideas in any detail.[2] There is just not space here for that. All of these incorporate, in one way or another, the three basic insights we just discussed, which seem to be essential to any description of reality at these extremely high energies and temperatures. Here I shall just mention some of the other consequences, or preliminary conclusions, such theories suggest for quantum cosmology.

But first we must realize there have been a number of significant contributions to quantum cosmology apart from those directly connected with developing a full and adequate theory of quantum gravity, or a fully unified theory of all four fundamental interactions. These have been what might be called semi-classical quantum cosmology treatments. These incorporate some of the basic insights from standard quantum theory and from Einstein's general relativity we summarized just above, and may indicate some of the key features which characterize the Planck era and

[2] For a readable introduction to these ideas in this context, see Lee Smolin, *Three Roads to Quantum Gravity* (New York: Basic Books, 2001).

what led to it.[3] These approaches are enabled by the requirement that any quantum cosmology or quantum theory of gravity must, as the temperature or energy decreases, yield the reliable classical, or non-quantum, models we already have – like the FLRW models. Working the other way, we can construct the semi-classical quantum versions of these classical models and see what sort of quantum corrections are expected to occur as we go to slightly higher temperatures which trigger the transitions to the quantum-cosmological regime.

Among some of the key people who contributed to such approaches are John Archibald Wheeler, Bryce DeWitt, Stephen Hawking and James Hartle, and Alex Vilenkin. Wheeler and DeWitt formulated the very elegant and suggestive Wheeler–DeWitt equation which describes in simple terms the behavior of the quantum-mechanical "wave-function of the universe."[4] This cosmic wavefunction would under certain conditions have a definite probability of issuing in our classical universe, which would then expand and cool, as general relativity and the FLRW models prescribe. It is important to realize that the Wheeler–DeWitt equation does not contain time as such, as we have already implied. In the purely quantum regime the wavefunction of the universe in some sense "just is." However, there is a sense in which time can emerge from the Wheeler–DeWitt equation as the transition between the wavefunction of the universe and the classical universe itself occurs. Hartle and Hawking[5] later extended this work, and showed, by using the concept of imaginary time we have already explained – by which one treats time exactly like a spatial dimension – and by conceiving that there was no initial three-dimensional spatial boundary to the universe, that we can in a consistent way obtain from the cosmic wavefunction a universe like the one we inhabit. They also obtain a very early inflationary phase for this universe, which seems to be required. This is called "the Hartle–Hawking

[3] As Chris Isham has emphasized, "certain general properties" – like those we have mentioned – "are expected to hold in any quantum gravity theory." See C. J. Isham, "Quantum Theories of the Creation of the Universe" in Robert John Russell, Nancey Murphy and C. J. Isham (eds.), *Quantum Cosmology and the Laws of Nature: Scientific Perspectives on Divine Action* (Vatican City State: Vatican Observatory Publications and Center for Theology and the Natural Sciences, 1993), pp. 49–89, at p. 65.

[4] See B. S. DeWitt, "Quantum Theory of Gravity I: The Canonical Theory," *Physical Review* 160 (1967), pp. 1,113–1,148; Carlo Rovelli, *Quantum Gravity* (Cambridge University Press, 2004).

[5] J. B. Hartle and S. W. Hawking, "Wave Function of the Universe," *Physical Review* D28 (1983), pp. 2,960–2,975; see also C. J. Isham, "Creation of the Universe as a Quantum Process" in Robert John Russell, William R. Stoeger, S. J., and George V. Coyne, S. J. (eds.), *Physics, Philosophy and Theology: A Common Quest for Understanding* (Vatican Observatory Publications, 1988), pp. 375–408, for a non-technical description.

no-boundary proposal" for the origin of the universe, an amazing idea and result, but one which depends on a number of assumptions which are not easy to justify. The Vilenkin scenario[6] is similar in some respects. It specifies a certain type of boundary condition on the space of all three-dimensional spaces (superspace) such that a given universe, which traces a path through superspace as it evolves, cannot begin at a singularity. However, it can originate in a region of superspace, where time is imaginary, and where the cosmic wavefunction is therefore oscillating.[7] As the universe leaves this region, when it gets large enough, it transitions to a classical universe with time as we know it emerging, and begins to expand and cool as ours has done.

Some of the underlying geometry and physics in these ideas are very reminiscent of black-hole physics, to which these physicists also contributed in important ways. In particular, as a particle falls into a black hole – as it passes through the event horizon, which defines its "surface" – there is a sense in which the time dimension, as seen from outside the black hole, becomes spatial. Furthermore, the event horizon itself, from the semi-classical quantum point of view, is the site for quantum evaporation events, through which a bath of particles is emitted from the black hole. In other words, the black-hole event horizon has a temperature which enables it to emit radiation and particles. This behavior has been reproduced by more complete – but still inadequate – theories of quantum gravity, such as loop quantum gravity.[8] These connections have served to encourage quantum cosmologists and others to take the Wheeler–DeWitt and Hartle–Hawking approaches with provisional seriousness – as well as the closely related educated guesses about what happens in the very early universe.

It is notable that the Hartle–Hawking proposal has been touted by some as indicating that physics and cosmology now *can* provide a universe emerging from "nothing." Because there is no boundary, nor any classical time, that can be defined, there is a sense in which the physics seems to indicate that it "just appears from nothing." However, this is an illusion, at least from a philosophical point of view. At the very least one needs the existence of the wavefunction of the universe and the ordered behavior described by the Wheeler–DeWitt equation itself. Where did these come from, or why are they as they are, rather than something else?

[6] A. Vilenkin, "Quantum Cosmology and the Initial State of the Universe," *Physical Review* D37 (1988), p. 888; see Isham, "Quantum Theories" for a non-technical account.

[7] See Isham, "Quantum Theories," pp. 71–74.

[8] See Rovelli, *Quantum Gravity*, pp. 308–311.

Furthermore, as two well-known workers in the field point out, this proposal really does not eliminate the singularity, which they accept as "a point of creation."[9] This is clear because the wavefunction does not vanish at the singularity. The Wheeler–DeWitt equation, and proposals for solving it, like those of Hartle and Hawking, and Vilenkin, present simplified models, or descriptions, of some features we might expect from the quantization of the gravitational field, and of the early universe. But they are by no means adequate. They should approximate what happens far from the singularity,[10] but they certainly are incapable of describing what happens near it. Much less do they describe "the process" by which the creation of the universe took place, understood in the radical philosophical sense.[11]

String theory has recently generated two other popular but still inadequate scenarios for triggering the Big Bang and providing a possible way of understanding the emergence of the universe from the Planck era.[12] One is "the pre–Big Bang scenario" and the other is "the ekpyrotic scenario." Because of symmetries in string theory, including time-reversal and what is called "T-duality," two completely different phases of the universe are allowed – a pre–Big Bang phase,[13] in which the universe collapses from an almost empty state an infinite time ago, to become very dense and very hot leading to the Planck era. However, like many other quantum gravity theories, string theory does not allow a singularity – the volume has a minimum, and the density, temperature and curvature have maxima. When these are reached, the universe bounces and enters the post–Big Bang phase. Thus, according to this suggestion, it is very clear that the Planck era and the Big Bang are not the beginning of the universe, nor even of time. One of the principal difficulties with this suggestion is that there is not yet a satisfactory account of how to effect the transition (the bounce!) from one phase to the other. In the ekpyrotic scenario,[14] our universe is simply one of many large membranes

[9] M. Bojowald and H. A. Morales-Técotl, "Cosmological Applications of Loop Quantum Gravity" in N. Bretón, J. L. Cervantes-Cota and M. Salgado (eds.), *The Early Universe and Observational Cosmology* (Berlin: Springer, 2004), pp. 421–462, at p. 431.

[10] Bojowald and Morales-Técotl, "Cosmological Applications," p. 445; Isham, "Quantum Theories," p. 72.

[11] Isham, "Creation of the Universe."

[12] Gabriele Veneziano, "The Myth of the Beginning of Time," *Scientific American* 290:5 (May 2004), pp. 54–65.

[13] Veneziano, "The Myth of the Beginning of Time"; Maurizio Gasperini and Gabriele Veneziano, "The Pre-Big-Bang Scenario in String Cosmology," *Physics Reports* 373:1–2 (2003), pp. 1–212.

[14] Veneziano, "The Myth of the Beginning of Time," pp. 64–65; Justin Khoury, Burt A. Ovrut, Nathan Seiberg, Paul J. Steinhardt and Neil Turok, "From Big Crunch to Big Bang," *Physical Review* D65 (2002), 086007, pp. 1–8.

(D-branes) floating in a higher dimension space. These "branes" are a natural consequence of string theory. Periodically, because of the gravitational attraction between them, these branes collide with one another triggering a Big Bang-like event. However, not any pair of colliding branes will yield the Big Bang and the universe we have. For two branes to do that would require that the branes themselves and the collision between them be "finely tuned" or carefully orchestrated. For instance, the branes involved should be almost exactly parallel.[15]

This brief overview of quantum cosmology reveals a number of important things about our understanding of the very early universe. First of all, we see that we cannot take the Planck era, or the initial singular point of the standard FLRW model we sometimes call the Big Bang, as the beginning of the universe. In fact, we cannot even consider it to be realized in reality – it represents a limit which falls outside the physical reliability of the model. Second, at some stage before the universe began to expand and cool, it was in a state where the smooth and continuous character of space, time, matter and energy no longer holds – where everything is discrete, quantized and wildly fluctuating. Furthermore, the transition from this state to the classical cosmic state of smooth space-time was governed by inherently probabilistic laws of physics. Considering whatever wavefunction which described that primordial quantum state, there was a certain probability that it would lead to our universe, and certain complementary probabilities that it would lead to other types of universes. Third, though something that would develop into time existed, it is likely that it was not like classical time, but probably more like another spatial dimension. However, because space and time were not smooth, but more foamlike and disconnected, it is probably misleading to even refer to primordial time being a "space-like dimension" in the sense we might imagine it geometrically. The main point here is that time as we know it may very well have begun only in the transition from the Planck era, as gravity separated from the other three unified interactions. Fourth, this reminds us that, in the Planck era, all four fundamental physical forces were probably unified in a single "superforce."

There is a fifth consequence that we should also point out. It is that many of these scenarios strongly imply that our observable universe is not the only one. In fact, they seem to indicate that there may be

[15] I am indebted to George Ellis, a well-known cosmologist from the University of Cape Town, for this qualification via a private communication.

trillions, if not more, other universes or universe domains. Almost any scenario which we invoke for the origin of our universe domain seems to automatically produce many others.[16] It is likely that, if such is the case, these universes would be very different from one another in terms of their coupling constants, geometry and other characteristics. These many other universes have been frequently invoked as a scientific explanation for the apparent fine-tuning of our own universe for complexity and the emergence of life ("the anthropic principle"). Of course, such a multiverse cannot be an ultimate explanation, since, as is already clear, its existence and character will require a more fundamental physical explanation – some generating process, which in turn will require a physical underpinning.

This leads us to a more general and fundamental conclusion we can draw from quantum cosmology. Any more reliable scenario for the origin of the Planck era, and the triggering of the expansion and cooling of the universe from that state, requires other detailed physics describing some physical structure or states which in some sense underlie or explain the Planck era itself. Any such account will always demand some further explanation or physical foundation – and ultimately an adequate metaphysical foundation or ground. As George Ellis has remarked, quantum cosmology assumes that all the structures of quantum field theory, superstrings or other organizing structures, pre-exist the universe itself, since they determine its emergence. So where does all of this structure reside? And how does it trigger the coming into being of the whole physical universe? We might also ask, with Ellis, where these structures reside after the universe has emerged. These questions push us beyond where the natural sciences, or perhaps any human inquiry, are able to take us.

Physics as such can specify in great qualitative and quantitative detail how we get from one physical state to another, or what the underlying constituents or factors of a given state are. It can do this if it has adequately modelled the regularities and relationships involved. However, it cannot in principle account ultimately for their existence or for the particular form those structures, regularities and relationships take. To put this in temporal terms, which are not essential to the issue,

[16] We cannot go into this here, but see G. F. R. Ellis, U. Kirchner and W. R. Stoeger, "Multiverses and Physical Cosmology," *Monthly Notices of the Royal Astronomical Society* 347 (2004), pp. 921–936, at p. 921, and W. R. Stoeger, G. F. R. Ellis and U. Kirchner, "Multiverses and Cosmology: Philosophical Issues," at http://arxiv.org/abs/astro-ph/0407329, and references therein.

physics can never tell us how we get from absolutely nothing – nothing like space or time, matter or energy, wavefunction or field, nothing physical at all – to something that has a particular order.

There is no physics of "absolutely nothing." Thus, though physics can shed a great deal of light on many other questions having to do with the universe, it evidently cannot help us in illuminating the ultimate ground of order or of being. This is precisely why physics in general, and quantum cosmology in particular, do not provide an alternative account of the creation of the universe, philosophically or theologically speaking.

And so now we turn to discuss the philosophical concept of "creation from nothing" – *creatio ex nihilo* – as a complementary, *not* an alternative, understanding of the origin of the universe, and of reality in general.

THE BASIC INSIGHT OF *CREATIO EX NIHILO*

The basic reason why *creatio ex nihilo* is complementary to any scientific explanation, including whatever quantum cosmology theoretically and observationally reveals about the "earliest" stages of our universe – or multiverse – and not an alternative, is that it does not and cannot substitute for whatever the sciences discover about origins. It simply provides an explanation or ground for the existence and basic order of whatever the sciences reveal. The Creator empowers or enables the physical processes – including whatever primordial originating processes and entities, whatever they are – to be what they are. The Creator does not and cannot replace them. Nor, as we have just seen above, can what quantum cosmology discovers and models ever substitute for what *creatio ex nihilo* accomplishes – that is providing an ultimate ground of existence and order. In our discussion at the end of the previous section we found rather strong indications that any physical process or dynamical structure that would account for, or generate, the extreme conditions marking the Planck era, or triggering "the Big Bang," requires a more fundamental physical explanation or grounding. Nothing we are familiar with in the physical or biological worlds – or in reality generally – stands on its own without requiring some cause and context. Nothing we can investigate scientifically completely explains its own existence and characteristics. Thus, whatever we find in quantum cosmology will always raise further questions for understanding, and an infinite regress of questions of physical origin is inevitable. And no member of this chain of origins, nor the entire chain itself – even if its infinity were realized – would provide an ultimate grounding for existence and order.

George Ellis[17] has raised a connected issue that may require *creatio ex nihilo*, or something like it (see our discussion of *creatio continua* below). It involves the issue of reductionism. Can appeal to fundamental particles and forces really adequately account for the emergence of complexity, life, consciousness, human values and meanings? Or are these in some sense "created out of nothing"? Instead, do they shadow what already exists in some other realm of reality? Or, finally, are they in some sense implicit in the nature of existence of material reality even at its most basic level?[18] Non-physical realities exist and come into being. They then require some explanation or grounding. Is their existence an aspect of *creatio ex nihilo*? From our elaboration of this idea below, I think we can say it is, though not unmediated.

What *creatio ex nihilo* provides, then, is an ultimate ground of existence and order for the universe – and for reality as a whole. It does this by proposing a self-subsisting, self-explanatory "cause" – the Creator – which is the fundamental source of being and order, and in which all existing things participate. As such, this ultimate ground of being and order is not another entity or process in the universe, which can be discerned or isolated from other physical causal factors and entities. It is not scientifically accessible! And yet it is causally distinct from them, because, without it, nothing would exist. And yet it does not substitute for created causes – it endows them with existence and efficacy. One way of putting it is that this Creator, however we attempt to describe it, is the necessary condition for everything, and the sufficient condition for nothing. Events and changes occur, and entities and systems emerge and subside into their components, only through the created, or "secondary causes" which the Creating Primary Cause sustains. In fact, the rich philosophical tradition shared by Judaism, Christianity and Islam uses the complementary categories *primary cause* and *secondary cause* in just this way.[19]

Let us explore this somewhat rarefied philosophical realm a bit more deeply. First, many people object to asking questions for the ultimate ground of being and order, maintaining that an answer is not scientifically accessible or even possible. We have just emphasized, indeed, that

17 Private communication.

18 These are substantially Ellis' questions. I am grateful to him for reading the manuscript, and suggesting that I include his perspective on these issues.

19 For example, recall Aquinas' distinction between primary and secondary causality in *Summa contra Gentiles* III, cc. 66–70, esp. c. 69; *Summa Theologiae* I.45.5 and 8; I.47.2bis; I.105.5; and *De Potentia* III.7. See also James Pambrun's and Thomas Tracy's chapters in this volume.

it is not. However, in order for this objection to be valid, we have to show that science provides the only way of knowing or understanding – that there are no other ways of knowing. But it seems clear that there are – including areas like commonsense knowledge from experience, intuitive knowledge, philosophical knowledge and perhaps even theological knowledge. Strictly speaking, *creatio ex nihilo* falls within philosophical knowledge, which is then employed by theology to try to understand in a very limited way who the God who reveals God's self to us is.

Second, others may object that such questions for an ultimate ground of being and order are simply meaningless. But for what reason are they meaningless? Is a self-subsisting reality a meaningless concept? Is the concept of an ultimate explanation for being and order inherently meaningless? Is something meaningless simply because we cannot find it in definitive form within our experience? It seems very hard to justify a positive answer to these questions. Furthermore, it very much seems that our quest for understanding continues beyond what is given – or can be given – by the sciences. If nothing we can potentially describe or model scientifically promises to yield the ultimate ground to existence and order, is it illegitimate to search for such understanding elsewhere – even if it means pointing towards some transcendent reality which we cannot adequately describe, but which seems to "fit the bill"? To terminate our quest when faced with this ultimate issue seems very arbitrary and unsupported.[20] Do we simply abandon the principle of sufficient reason at this point? If so, on what grounds?

Presuming for the moment that there are no serious reasons for dismissing the basic concept of *creatio ex nihilo*, how can we understand it better?[21]

[20] For detailed arguments along this line, see W. Norris Clarke, S. J., "Is a Natural Theology Still Possible Today?" in Robert John Russell, William R. Stoeger, S. J., and George V. Coyne, S. J. (eds.), *Physics, Philosophy and Theology: A Common Quest for Understanding* (Vatican Observatory Publications, 1988), pp. 103–123.

[21] For brief summary treatments of *creatio ex nihilo*, see: Catherine Mowry LaCugna, *God for Us: The Trinity and Christian Life* (Harper-SanFrancisco, 1993), pp. 158–167; Langdon Gilkey, "Creation, Being, and Nonbeing" in David B. Burrell and Bernard McGinn (eds.), *God and Creation: An Ecumenical Symposium* (University of Notre Dame Press, 1990), pp. 226–241; William R. Stoeger, "The Origin of the Universe in Science and Religion" in Henry Margenau and Roy A. Varghese (eds.), *Cosmos, Bios, Theos: Scientists Reflect on Science, God, and the Origins of the Universe, Life and Homo Sapiens* (La Salle, IL: Open Court, 1992), pp. 154–259; William R. Stoeger, S. J., "Conceiving Divine Action in a Dynamic Universe" in Robert John Russell, Nancey Murphy and William R. Stoeger, S. J. (eds.), *Scientific Perspectives on Divine Action: Problems and Progress* (Vatican City State: Vatican Observatory Publications and Center for Theology and the Natural Sciences, 2008), pp. 225–247.

First, it is crucial to realize that when we talk about God, or "the Creator," we will never be able to have an adequate concept of that. It will always be beyond us – radically transcendent. But at the same time, we can point to the mystery of existence and order at the depths of reality and of our experience, and say something very tentative about creation and what it requires. There will be some ways of speaking about God and God's creative action which are less inadequate than others! In the same vein, we have to acknowledge that, when we talk about God "causing" or "acting" when God creates, we are speaking metaphorically or analogically. God acts or causes in a very different way from the way in which anything in our experience acts or causes. And yet there is some legitimate content to those assertions, in the sense that God somehow endows things with existence and with their specific being in the ultimate sense, but also through the action of other created causes, which God also holds in existence. Without God, they would not exist! Thus, God as primary cause is a cause unlike any other cause – unlike the created, or secondary, causes which God sustains and enables. God is their necessary condition.

Second, *creatio ex nihilo* is not primarily an answer to the question of temporal origin. It is an open philosophical question whether or not there was something like a temporal beginning to creation – a first moment, as it were. Certainly, as we have already seen, quantum cosmology points to the separation of the first moment of time as we know it from the origin of the universe itself, if there was one. *Creatio ex nihilo* is, instead, about the ultimate ontological origin of reality – most fundamentally it describes in a very bald and unadorned way the *ultimate dependence* of everything on the Creator. It is not about a creation event, but about a *relationship* which everything that exists has with the Creator.[22] So *creatio ex nihilo* is also *creatio continua*, continuing creation. The relationship between the Creator and created continues as long as something exists. The Creator sustains or conserves reality – and the universe – in existence. Without God, it would not exist. It has been helpful to conceive the relationship of creation as a *participation* in the being of the Creator.[23] In this regard, it also seems clear that it is better to conceive of the Creator more like a verb than like an entity. In some ways, the Creator is pure, self-subsisting being, activity or creativity, in which all things participate. Traditionally, some philosophers and theologians have referred to God as "Pure Act."

[22] See LaCugna, *God for Us*, p. 160. [23] See, for instance, David Burrell's chapter in this volume.

Third, it is also critical, as we have already implied, to avoid conceiving of the Creator as *controlling* creation, or as *intervening* in its dynamisms. God, instead, enables and empowers creation to be what it is – and both ultimately endows and supports all the processes, regularities and processes of nature with their autonomous properties and capacities for activity. Thus, God as Creator does not substitute for, interfere with, countermand or micro-manage the laws of nature. They possess their own integrity and adequacy, which God establishes and respects.[24] We might say, but again metaphorically, that God is working in and through the laws of nature – including the probabilistic and statistical laws of quantum mechanics and of random mutations in genomes – by empowering them and giving them freedom to operate.

Fourth, it is often claimed that God as Creator, though transcendent, is immanent in creation and in its activity. Though God as Creator does not function within nature or history as another created (secondary) cause, God is present and active in and through the whole network of processes and relationships, precisely because God is sustaining them and enabling them. We can better understand this by pointing out that transcendence is not about being above and beyond creation as detached from it, but rather being free from any barriers, limitations or obstructions. Thus, there is no barrier to the ground of being and order being immanent – deeply present and active, but present and active as Creator, not as another created cause – within all aspects of creation. Transcendence does not impede or contradict immanence – it enables it!

Fifth, the relationship of ultimate dependence and creative immanence is not uniform, but instead is highly differentiated – that is, it is different with respect to each entity, organism, system, person and process. God sustains them all in being, but God is sustaining different things in being, with different properties, capacities and individualities – and through different constitutive relationships with the world around them. And each responds to its environment and to the situation within which it finds itself – and therefore to God – in different ways.

There is much more that could be discussed about *creatio ex nihilo* and how it is to be coherently understood. But what I have presented here captures the essence of the approach in a way which helps us appreciate the fundamental question it attempts to answer, and why, if properly understood, it cannot be in competition with cosmology or the other

[24] Stoeger, "Conceiving Divine Action."

natural sciences in explaining the origins of the universe, or of anything emerging within it.

Of course, like anything, *creatio ex nihilo* has been strongly criticized on several fronts.[25] I shall briefly reflect on just one of them – the one most relevant for our purposes – in order to shed further light on how *creatio ex nihilo* should be understood, and not understood. The objection I shall explore is that *creatio ex nihilo* is "metaphysically incoherent." The charge is often based on the presumed contradiction between the Creator's transcendent character and what *creatio ex nihilo* asserts regarding God's immanence and knowledge, especially if creation is also relatively autonomous and free to be itself.[26] Langdon Gilkey perceptively reveals the root of the problem.[27] He emphasizes, as many philosophers and theologians before him have done, that God simply cannot be described, conceptualized or objectified as other beings can be. When we refer to God or God's action we can do so only "symbolically" or "analogically." God is intrinsic mystery, inexhaustible richness, whose depths can never be completely plumbed and which is continually being revealed in nature and in history. In order to conceive God as Creator we are tempted simply to extrapolate naively from the sort of being we know and experience to an infinite degree. This is a mistake. We end up defining God by God's "unconditional and absolute character rather than by God's mystery, and the dialectical nature of the relation of that mystery to the being of God is lost – as the continual relatedness of God to finite being is also sacrificed."[28] Thus, we delude ourselves into thinking we have adequately described God but, in so doing, we have "overaffirmed" the being of God in terms of finite being.[29] This analysis helps us radicalize the distinction we must preserve between God as primary cause and the secondary causes we experience directly – a distinction we have insisted upon, but which it is easy to gloss over.

CONCLUSION

Now that we have looked carefully at the way physics, cosmology and quantum cosmology probe the origins of the universe and the objects

[25] See John J. O'Donnell, S. J., *Trinity and Temporality: The Christian Doctrine of God in Light of Process Theology and the Theology of Hope* (Oxford University Press, 1983), pp. 17–21, for a brief summary of these critiques.

[26] Stoeger, "Conceiving Divine Action."

[27] Gilkey, "Creation, Being, and Nonbeing," pp. 231–236; see also, Stoeger, "Conceiving Divine Action."

[28] Gilkey, "Creation, Being, and Nonbeing," p. 232.

[29] Gilkey, "Creation, Being, and Nonbeing," pp. 234, 236; Stoeger, "Conceiving Divine Action."

and systems that emerge within it, and explored the essential contents and limitations of *creatio ex nihilo*, we can see more clearly how different they are from one another. In particular, we begin to appreciate the detailed scenarios which quantum cosmology constructs and must eventually test, as well as the need to find a physical explanation for any stage of cosmic development, no matter how primordial. By their very nature, physics and cosmology, as do the other sciences, will always focus on how we get to a particular outcome from another physical configuration by some transition, process or change. Thus, they attempt to describe in qualitative and quantitative detail the first configuration and the physics that enables the transition to the outcome in question. This has proved extremely powerful. However, it has the limitation that it can never deal with the essential ground of being and order, upon which all else rests. *Creatio ex nihilo* as a philosophical – not a scientific – approach attempts to do that. Properly applied it is not about changes, processes or transitions – it does not, and cannot, substitute for anything that the sciences legitimately accomplish and validate. It merely – but powerfully – complements our quest for understanding and explanation of origins by supplying a "bare-bones" but compelling resolution to the basic issue of the ultimate ground of existence and order.

Thus, quantum cosmological scenarios or theories – which describe the Planck era, and the Big Bang, or which describe the primordial regularities, processes and transitions connected with these extreme very early stages of the universe – are in principle incapable of being alternatives to divine creation conceived as *creatio ex nihilo*. They simply do not account for what *creatio ex nihilo* provides – the ultimate ground of existence and order. Reciprocally, *creatio ex nihilo* is not an alternative to the processes and transitions quantum cosmology proposes and provides – these are models of the physical processes which generated our universe and everything emerging from it. *Creatio ex nihilo* by itself cannot, and was never intended to, usurp the role these, and the laws of nature upon which they depend, play in the universe. Instead they are precisely the expressions and channels of its continuing operation. Thus, quantum cosmology and *creatio ex nihilo* contribute deeply complementary and consonant levels of understanding of the reality in which we are immersed. Exactly the same point can be applied to divine creation and biological evolution – they are not exclusive alternatives, but rather complementary accounts, linking the ultimate ground of being and order with their elaboration in concrete structures, dynamisms, processes and transitions.

CHAPTER 11

What is written into creation?

Simon Conway Morris

INTRODUCTION

It is difficult to see what science can usefully say about *creatio ex nihilo*. Even to describe it as an 'event' begs the question of prior nothing as against historical something. The latter is patently open to scientific investigation, but the former and any conceivable connecting factor are matters (so to speak) for metaphysical discussion. Even the fashionable suppositions of a universe emerging via the agency (again so to speak) of a quantum perturbation would seem to fall into the category of metaphysics, given that any proposed 'mechanism' apparently possesses no prior explanation, and would not be open to any sort of experimental verification. Those subscribing to naturalistic, if not materialist, world-pictures seem seldom to perceive a problem; broadly they regard the material universe as a brute fact. *Creatio ex nihilo* might be an embarrassment, but it is only a potential stumbling-block; as already noted, given it is beyond scientific discourse, the scientists have nothing to contribute.

Even so, no scientist can avoid being embedded in a metaphysical framework (even if it is ostensibly nihilistic or solipsistic), and it is not surprising that the apparent peculiarities of our universe (famously in terms of the apparent 'fine-tuning' of the physical constants) sharpen the desire to find an 'escape clause' from the ominous sense of a world designed for our habitation and understanding. It is hardly surprising, therefore, if many scientists believe the best course of action is to appeal to multiverses, endlessly generated, with no ultimate beginning and without a conceivable end. Yet should this latter view be true, in itself this need not speak against God's action. It may indeed be consistent with plenitude, not least if there

I am most grateful to Janet Soskice for the invitation to attend the conference in Castel Gandolfo, and also warmly thank George Coyne and his fellow Jesuits in the Vatican Observatory for their hospitality. I thank Vivien Brown for expeditious typing of numerous versions of this manuscript. My work is supported by the John Templeton Foundation and St John's College, Cambridge.

are innumerably different universes that are all 'inhabited' by creatures (in the strict sense of the word) that can worship God. Even if one allows oneself just one universe, the theological consequences may be more inescapable than is sometimes imagined. It is certainly no coincidence that the enthusiasm for steady-state universes, as most famously set forth by the astronomer Fred Hoyle, is also strongly linked to theologies, notably Hinduism, that are attuned to eternities and as often as not a cyclic return to catastrophe and destruction. Nor incidentally is such a prior commitment by any means unusual. A number of distinguished scientists (and philosophers) are famous for their insistence that their method cannot allow divine causation: it is simply inadmissible. But even this may be premature. To return to the conceit of a single universe, as it happens ours, it is far from clear that, if God chose to instantiate the universe by what we perceive as a quantum perturbation (and here we might find an echo of how the incarnation was similarly instantiated; see below), this must automatically rule out his agency, any more than multiverses rule out his creative fecundity.

Nevertheless, present scientific evidence strongly points to our universe having (from our temporal perspective) a defined beginning and, because it was not thereafter invariant, also a history. All we see around us is thus a product of the Big Bang. Rightly we are warned against the risk of conflating the evidence for the Big Bang, not least the extraordinary implications of the cosmic microwave background data, with *creatio ex nihilo*. The former may be a consequence of the latter, but no scientist needs to be reminded that all hypotheses are provisional, and even supposedly watertight data may be interpreted in radically new ways. Such caution is more than justified when we remember that cosmologists are still searching for most of the universe, in the form of dark energy and dark matter.

CAN SCIENCE MEET THEOLOGY?

Yet, despite these introductory and cautionary statements, I will suggest that the concept of *creatio ex nihilo* remains of central importance to all our discussions. First, it allows us to think in terms of an intervention (again speaking temporally) preceded by a decision (so far as it is humanly possible to speak in such terms), and by implication a plan (to reduce the glory of the universe to a bureaucratic memo). This obviously has a congruence with the Big Bang and the ensuing history of the universe (notwithstanding the cautionary remarks made above). It is, however, clearly discrepant with the existing orthodoxy that also readily accepts the Big Bang but also posits (from its perspective reasonably enough) an expansion of the universe that will continue for ever. As we shall see, this assumption may be premature.

The second strand of enquiry is more immediate, if not down-to-earth, and this is to explore whether in terms of its *creatio ex nihilo* there are at least consistencies, if not consequences, for the world about us. After all, we live in a real universe that in its various ways is highly ordered. How has this come about? More significantly, at least from our perspective, we have life. Some is evidently sentient, and at least one species (or at least some of its representatives) believe *creatio ex nihilo* is a valid concept for discussion. Given who we otherwise are – deracinated apes – perhaps this is rather surprising. Paradoxically, the reason this need not be an occasion for surprise is that this sentient species is scientific, i.e., it employs a technique that has an uncanny knack of revealing the unexpected. We wish to know why the world is as it is, and science is remarkably successful in revealing its intricacies. *Creatio ex nihilo* may be a metaphysical statement, but it makes it inevitable that we consider, if only to dismiss, God's action in the world. If the world is our arena of investigation, then we are entitled to continue to search for this activity (albeit reminding ourselves that for all we know it is either hidden or simply opaque to our minds), so at least we can claim to find (or not find) consistencies and congruencies. Here too a theological dimension may be closer than sometimes realized. If the argument that science could only emerge in a monotheistic, if not Christian, context is accepted, then we can also remind ourselves why this might have been so. In approaching the question of *creatio ex nihilo*, it is surely relevant that science itself could not possibly operate unless the universe is underpinned by rationality. How it would otherwise be possible for an ostensibly meaningless universe to be open to reliable investigation, when we have no grounds for thinking that anything we know is true, is equally central to this presupposition.[1]

Creatio ex nihilo obviously produces something but, if it remains as a fog of quarks (or whatever the primary particles are deemed to be), this is arguably of little interest. What matters (literally) is the emergence of complex and organized forms, and ones that may show a pronounced tendency to increase the levels of complexity and organization. From our privileged perspective such emergences look to be inevitable, but is this based on familiarity as against any deep understanding? Consider the iconic case, at least for biologists, of DNA. Its emergent properties as a

[1] V. Reppert, *C. S. Lewis's Dangerous Idea: A Philosophical Defense of Lewis's Argument from Reason* (Downers Grove: Intervarsity Press, 2003).

conformable double helix with appropriately weak hydrogen bonds are far beyond what any well-informed organic chemist might predict.[2] And given that the acid test for science is successful prediction, then we immediately perceive that, by lacking a general theory of emergence, creation is deeper than we may imagine; ultimately, if paradoxically, I suggest that we will only understand its operation if creation is not eternal but originated out of nothing. In other words an eternal creation, although theologically apparently acceptable, may simply not give us the same sort of universe as the one we inhabit.

ARTIFICIAL SYSTEMS

This failure to grasp emergence seems to manifest in other ways, notably in artificial systems. Here I will pass by that graveyard of ambition, the search for artificial intelligence, as this ostensibly has some bearing on the emergence of consciousness, a topic to which I will return towards the end of this chapter. But consider the programme devoted to artificial life, particularly so-called *in silico* evolution. Paradoxically the results are strangely lifeless. To be sure these simulations do some quite interesting things, but they never seem to 'take off'. Now this seems quite strange, for two reasons. First, there is a general insistence that the world around us is governed by simple algorithms. To be sure there is a counterpart of chaotic behaviour whereby the initial conditions are very sensitive but, despite this, systems typically do not remain chaotic but rapidly stabilize. The proverbial butterfly's wing may generate hurricanes on the opposite side of the planet, but hurricanes themselves are well-defined, and within certain parameters predictable, heat engines. Second, returning to artificial life, if evolution is a self-governing process that is ostensibly autocatalytic then, in principle, we should see a runaway process of diversification. We do not. One can always argue, of course, that the real world is much larger and more variable than the contents of any test tube, virtual or otherwise. Yet science as a whole is quite familiar with finding the particular and extrapolating to the universal. To date, artificial life seems to lack this characteristic; it simply does not reflect reality.

It may be, therefore, as already hinted, that *creatio ex nihilo* involves not only the instantiation of a material world but one that is necessarily underpinned by eternal principles (scientists vaguely intuit this when they waffle

[2] C. Y. Switzer, S. E. Moroney and S. A. Benner, 'Enzymatic Recognition of the Base Pair between Isocytidine and Isoguanosine', *Biochemistry* 32 (1993), pp. 10,489–10,496. See also S. Conway Morris, *Life's Solution: Inevitable Humans in a Lonely Universe* (Cambridge University Press, 2003), pp. 27–28.

on about 'the mind of God'). It might still be argued that science aims to identify just such principles, but this claim needs to be met with scepticism, for at least three reasons. The first would argue that this is equivalent to the oxymoronic Theory of Everything, an enterprise that is greeted with general scepticism. Nothing indicates that the world is so reducible: the collapse of black holes *and* the origin of species? Second, and addressing a topic that was touched on earlier, there is the perennial fascination with the physical constants that govern the world, some of which are so finely adjusted that a small deviation would lead to an uninhabitable universe. The identification of this 'fine-tuning' has unsurprisingly generated both anthropic enthusiasm and a grim reassertion that the world is no other than it can be if we are to be here as observers. Less regarded is Neil Manson's insistence that we have no idea why the physical values we observe are what they are, nor why they vary in ways that seem to be unrelated.[3] Quite possibly there are other combinations, in our eyes equally arbitrary, that are just as sustainable when it comes to functioning universes. Or maybe not, but even if we are the trillion-trillionth of all possible physical combinations that just happens to work, we are still none the wiser as to how these particular combinations come about *creatio ex nihilo*. Finally, our endeavour to understand the universe may need to seek what we perceive as intangible 'things both visible and invisible'. Oddly, perhaps, science accepts the mysteries of gravitational attraction and quantum entanglement, but is reluctant to address the concerns of philosophers, be it the platonic archetypes or the harmony of the spheres. Yet these are arguably as much part of the universe as the supposedly familiar. Recall how G. K. Chesterton insists that, behind the everyday, lie the impenetrable mysteries of being.

UNDERPINNING OF LIFE

There may, therefore, be a little more to creation, and its emergence *ex nihilo*, than is at first expected. Nevertheless, before departing to the higher levels of speculation, i.e., how matter becomes conscious, I would like to examine briefly what we think of as the material world. This is simply because it provides the underpinning of what we regard as being sentient. Life itself depends critically on only a small number of the elements within the periodic table. Life thus is carbon based, and a well-known extension of the anthropic principle is its surprisingly abundant production in stellar nuclear synthesis. The 'surprise' lies in the fact that the general principles of

[3] N. Manson, 'There Is No Adequate Definition of "Fine-tuned" for Life', *Inquiry* 43 (2000), pp. 341–352.

nucleosynthesis suggest that only small quantities of carbon would be expected to form inside stars. The so-called triple-alpha process whereby three helium-4 nuclei combine to form an atom of carbon-12 is only possible by the curious coincidence that the resonance energies of helium-4, carbon-12 and the intermediate beryllium-8 are 'fortuitously' similar. This is crucial because beryllium-8 is very unstable, but the resonance ensures enough survives to allow the crucial step to carbon-12 to occur. Without that coincidental resonance the likelihood of carbon-based life forms is extremely low: we would not be here.

There are, however, other aspects of the periodic table that bear inspection. Consider just two elements, both 'minor' but essential to life. 'Why Nature Chose Phosphates' is Westheimer's[4] succinct summary of why phosphorus (as phosphate esters and anhydrides) is a universal in biology, be it DNA (and RNA), ATP (adenosine triphosphate), many co-enzymes, as well as innumerable compounds that serve in different metabolic pathways. Their versatility is a reflection of their ability to ionize molecular compounds (thereby enabling them to interact) and allow, as the circumstances demand, widely variable rates of hydrolysis. As Westheimer writes, 'No other residue [that is potentially available] appears to fulfil the multiple order of phosphate in biochemistry.'[5]

The other element is apparently far more idiosyncratic. Zinc is biologically widely distributed, occurring among other places in the jaws of worms.[6] But in at least one context, although it appears to be apparently incidental, it is actually essential. The importance of carbon has already been addressed, and we can be sure that on any planet the principal 'currency' will be carbon dioxide. An important biological stage is the hydration of carbon dioxide, and life's solution is to employ a natural catalyst, an enzyme known as carbonic anhydrase. Unsurprisingly this enzyme is ubiquitous, and plays obvious roles in such areas of physiology as respiration and photosynthesis, as well as such processes as biomineralization. While catalysts by definition accelerate chemical reactions, even among enzymes carbonic anhydrase is remarkably efficient, acting with astonishing speed and efficiency. The action of carbonic anhydrase depends crucially on the employment of a zinc atom. In passing, we might also note that this enzyme has evolved not once, a rather reasonable assumption given

4 F. H. Westheimer, 'Why Nature Chose Phosphates', *Science* 235 (1987), pp. 1,173–1,178.

5 *Ibid.*, p. 1,173.

6 G. W. Bryan and P. E. Gibbs, 'Zinc – a Major Inorganic Component of Nereid Polychaete Jaws', *Journal of the Marine Biological Association, UK* 59 (1979), pp. 969–972.

that carbon-based life would have been faced with this challenge from the first metaphorical day, but at least four (and possibly six) times.[7] The similarity is to do with not the overall molecular structure of the enzyme, but the details of the active site that involves an atom of zinc and three amino-acid residues, usually histidine. Clearly one of life's more successful solutions. The association between zinc and histidine also points to a more widespread convergence in as much as metal and amino acid show a characteristic association in numerous other molecular systems, including the byssal threads of the mussel.[8] The principal point is that these two key elements of phosphorus and zinc (and indeed one could have extended this list to include at least copper, iron, molybdenum and selenium) could not possibly exist without the supporting 'scaffold' of the periodic table. Elements such as argon or scandium may be technically, if not technologically, 'useless', but the entire biological world would be inoperative unless these key elements could be embedded in the chemistry of the universe.

Given biological systems are strongly hierarchical it is unsurprising to learn that the apparently complex systems are underpinned by relatively simple building blocks. In the context of this discussion it is necessary to stress that typically at the time of their appearance these building blocks had some different function from ones that have subsequently been adopted. In other words, although evolution represents a triumph of novelty, its underpinnings are remarkably conservative, so that evolution is just as much about co-option as it is about innovation. A classic example concerns the crystallins.[9] As their name suggests, these are proteins that confer transparency and so are central for the operation of the eye. Not only that: although we think of an eye allowing light to pour into the head, recall that the so-called reverse eye has also evolved. This is where a luminescent organ needs to pour light in the opposite direction, into the outside world, as a display or warning. Once again, crystallins are employed to confer the transparency.[10] The point to stress here, however, is that these proteins

[7] A. Liljas and M. Laurberg, 'A Wheel Invented Three Times: The Molecular Structure of Three Carbonic Anhydrases', *EMBO Report* 1 (2000), pp. 16–17. See also B. C. Tripp, K. Smith and J. C. Ferry, 'Carbonic Anhydrase: New Insights for an Ancient Enzyme', *Journal of Biological Chemistry* 276 (2001), pp. 48,615–48,618; and A. K.-C. So and G. S. Espie, 'Cyanobacterial Carbonic Anhydrase', *Canadian Journal of Botany* 83 (2005), pp. 721–734.

[8] K. J. Coyne, X.-X. Qin and J. K. Waite, 'Extensible Collagen in Mussel Byssus: A Natural Block Copolymer', *Science* 277 (1997), pp. 1,830–1,832.

[9] J. Piatigorsky, 'Gene Sharing, Lens Crystallins and Speculations on an Eye/Ear Evolutionary Relationship', *Integrative and Comparative Biology* 43 (2004), pp. 492–499.

[10] M. K. Montgomery and M. J. McFall-Ngai, 'The Muscle-derived Lens of a Squid Bioluminescent Organ is Biochemically Convergent with the Ocular Lens', *Journal of Biological Chemistry* 267 (1992), pp. 20,999–21,003.

evolved long before the first eye, or indeed the first animal, in organisms where typically they provided protection from physiological stress, such as heat shock. They were pre-adapted for a completely different function, in the lens, because these proteins combined the invaluable properties of long-term stability with a relatively small size and solubility in water. This allows them to be orientated so effectively that the tissue not only is rendered transparent but also can remain in this condition for years, even decades. One might, however, further expect that all eyes would be drawn to a particular crystallin. In fact, we find the exact opposite: a considerable variety of crystallins have been recruited from completely different sources. So far as can be told, one is as pretty good as another, so the universal property of tissue transparency does not reside in any historical determination.

I would suggest that this example of the crystallins may point to a much more interesting principle, and this particular versatility of function is actually the tip of a largely unregarded molecular iceberg. There is now growing evidence that there are many more instances where effectively the same molecular toolkit can be employed for markedly different purposes. It is as if a metaphorical spanner was used to not only undo bolts, but also tighten screws, open bottles, serve as a straw, mend carpets, clean stains and provide a source of light. This is not to say that in principle one bio-molecule could actually do everything, but it is to stress that the versatility of bio-molecules is under-appreciated.

This malleability of bio-molecules is, of course, one of the distinctions between life and any machine analogy. But I suspect that, although it will seem to have echoes of vitalism, it does hint at a neglected aspect of creation, not only in terms of life's fecundity, but also in terms of a 'language' of molecules whereby the same 'word' in a new context can mean something markedly different. In this sense, although the reductionist approach necessarily identifies *the* function, as investigations proceed, so more and more functions are identified using, if not the identical molecular substrate, one that is little different. Interestingly, a somewhat similar conclusion is emerging from genes. Long regarded as 'particles of destiny', matters are now turning out to be rather different. Here too the same gene may do different things at different times, or different sections of the same gene may be employed for different purposes. Not only this, but the entire molecular system is embedded in a 'nano-factory' of quite extraordinary complexity where innumerable chemical reactions are conducted not only cheek by molecular jowl, but without interference. In this way we see the emergence of an exceedingly complex system, one part of which must underpin sentience and consciousness, topics to which I return below. As importantly, the theme of co-option and versatility in both genes and bio-molecules suggests that in a certain way these structures possess abstract properties that may conceivably reflect a much deeper structure to our universe.

THE ENDURING MYSTERY OF CONSCIOUSNESS

Nowhere is this deep structure more obvious, nor more problematic, than the utterly familiar but equally mysterious quality of consciousness. There has, of course, been no shortage of 'explanations' that as often as not strike the disinterested observer as 'explaining away'. But disinterested observers oxymoronically cannot exist, and it is self-evident that the stubborn core of our consciousness, embodied so to speak in the refractory question of the haecceity of qualia, simply eludes any satisfactory physical explanation. What we know, let alone intuit, simply evades any reductionist framework.

Yet metaphysicians should beware. After all, a large part of the rout of theology has ostensibly been placed at the door of ever-widening rationalist explanations. Seemingly intractable mysteries vanish as easily as the early morning mist, even if the revealed landscape seems oddly one-dimensional: a sickly sun that casts no shadows and provides no warmth. No matter! Liquefying blood of saints, miraculous cures, flying monks, bi-locationism, not to mention the Turin shroud, let alone the Oviedo sudarium; all belong to the mindset of credulous peasants, crafty priests and the gullibly ill-educated. Sensible people, epitomized by the Bloomsbury circle and their liberal–agnostic descendants, know so much better. And happily they know so much better, not least if they are biologists. Here recent work would seem to throw the most material light on that difficulty of difficulties, the explanation of consciousness. I am thinking here, of course, of the results from brain imaging, such as MRI or PET scans. Fascinating as these results are, they surely tell us nothing about the realities of consciousness. Again the question slips through our metaphorical fingers. Moreover, and as I will discuss below, there are other brain states that seem to be very difficult to reconcile with the glib materialist accounts of what consciousness is meant to represent.

SENSORY EVOLUTION AND CONVERGENCE

So given the haecceity of consciousness, is there actually anything worth discussing? The initial approach I wish to consider is considerably more prosaic, and indeed at first sight does not seem to have a major bearing on the problem. Yet, as I will further argue, its very success in drawing together what appear to be disparate strands of enquiry paradoxically reinforces the fundamental problem of what it is to be conscious. The focus of attention now moves, therefore, to the evolution and function of sensory systems, simply because, although the roots of sentience must lie even deeper – we know, for example, of single-celled organisms that already employ molecules such as acetylcholine[11] that are key components in the operation of the nervous system of animals – the *sine qua non* of the consciousness must be predicated on the basis of some sort of sensory perception. In passing I should note that, while this is apparently correct, we may be radically underestimating the spheres of sensory perception. This is because evidence is now emerging that those stupid vegetables, i.e., plants, may be far more 'sensitive' to their surrounding environment than was once thought.[12] This is not to equate animal sentience with any other sort of sensory perception, but only to remind ourselves that our obsession with activity, neural circuits, synapses and electrical activity may only be an obvious (and necessarily familiar) manifestation of a more widespread phenomenon.

Yet even restricting the discussion to animals means that only the briefest of outlines is possible, if not desirable. But the evidence for features in common is intriguing. To begin with, we have striking evidence for the evolutionary convergence of sensory systems.[13] By this I mean that effectively unrelated animals have arrived at very familiar functional solutions. The classic case is the camera-eye of the vertebrates, of which of course the humans are one representative, as compared with that of the squid and octopus (a group referred to as the cephalopods). The evolutionary history of both groups is sufficiently well known as to put it beyond all reasonable doubt that the common ancestor could not possibly have possessed a camera-eye, and at most was equipped with simple eye-spots. In point of fact, the camera-eye has evolved independently about seven times, perhaps most remarkably in a jellyfish.

An interesting corollary of this concerns not only the employment of crystallins, which as noted above have been recruited numerous times independently of each other, but in the present context even more importantly that of colour vision. Once again, for the great majority of readers, this

[11] I. Wessler, C. J. Kirkpatrick and K. Racke, 'The Cholinergic "Pitfall": Acetylcholine, a Universal Cell Molecule in Biological Systems, including Humans', *Clinical and Experimental Pharmacology and Physiology* 26 (1999), pp. 198–205.

[12] F. Baluška, S. Mancuso and D. Volkmann (eds.), *Communication in Plants: Neuronal Aspects of Plant Life* (Berlin: Springer, 2006).

[13] Conway Morris, *Life's Solution.*

attribute is so familiar that we lose sight of its sheer peculiarity. Given the prevalence of convergence, it is perhaps less surprising that colour vision has evolved independently a number of times. In at least the case of the vertebrates this type of perception is based, at least in a proximal sense, on only a handful of changes at about five key sites in the 'vision molecule', that is the protein rhodopsin. This so-called 'five-site rule' is convergent across the vertebrates. Interestingly, fully fledged trichromatic vision is indeed rare, but once again is convergent. Most strikingly it has emerged independently in ourselves, some New World monkeys (where in some species there is a further subtext of dichromatic males and trichromatic females) and certain marsupials. In any event, these analyses suggest that different animals presumably see the same colour, say red, and so in principle experience the same qualia. What is even more interesting is that the ability to detect different frequencies of light is phylogenetically very ancient. Even in bacteria the equivalent light-sensitive protein (bacteriorhodopsin, which is probably convergent on our opsin) allows a spectral shift from a blue to an orange colour.[14] It is not my intention to suggest that bacteria 'experience' such qualia, but to indicate that the inherency of this property lies close to the roots of all life.

Such convergences in sensory systems are by no means confined to eyes, illustrative though they are. Even when the organs of perception, such as those involved with hearing, olfaction or taste (not to mention 'alien' perceptions such as echolocation or electro-reception), are strikingly different, the underlying mechanisms of audition, smell or gustation turn out to be remarkably similar. Not only that, but it appears that, while the mechanisms, especially at the molecular and neural level, are often very similar, the underlying genetic architecture is quite different.

It may, or may not, be reassuring to learn that a fly hears, sees and tastes in very much the same way as we do. Yet even more intriguingly there is also evidence for even deeper similarities between apparently quite disparate modes of perception. It is perhaps somewhat less surprising then to learn that these disparate modes can then be integrated to form a single 'image'. Possibly the best-known example of the former instance, that is of fundamental similarity, is the neurological convergence between the highly tactile nasal tentacles of the star-nosed mole and the eye. As Ken Catania has stressed, this is a mole that uses its nose as an eye.[15] And why not? After all,

[14] L. Vogeley, O. A. Sineshchekov, V. D. Trivedi, J. Sasaki, J. L. Spudich and H. Luecke, '*Anabaena* Sensory Rhodopsin: A Photochromic Color Sensor at 2.0 Å', *Science* 306 (2004), pp. 1,390–1,393.

[15] K. C. Catania, 'A Nose that Looks like a Hand and Acts as an Eye: The Unusual Mechanosensory System of the Star-nosed Mole', *Journal of Comparative Physiology A* 185 (1999), pp. 367–372. See also Conway Morris, *Life's Solution*.

any sensory system depends on transduction of external stimuli, say photons or touch, into electrical signals that are processed to inform the animal about the outside world – what we choose to call reality. Accordingly, when we learn (to give just one instance) that in the dolphin the sensory inputs, derived from the familiar vision and decidedly unfamiliar echolocation, are integrated to form what we can only assume is a single 'image',[16] so we intuit that however we make sense of the outside world the same mental substrate must emerge.

These deep and pervasive similarities suggest that the mental states accessed (the reason why I use this word will become apparent) by nervous tissues that are dedicated to different sensory inputs are most likely universal. Nor is it particularly obvious why this should not be the case. This conclusion also finds a parallel in the perception of numbers whereby the property of numerosity (a sensory process of 'how many?') and the distinction of numbers of different things (a cognitive judgement: 'two gin and tonics' as against 'two books') both follow the same psycho-physical laws (and are determined by analysis of factors known as numerical distance and numerical magnitude, as enshrined in Fechner's Law), again suggesting that sensory perception and cognition (aka understanding) are, somehow, fundamentally equivalent.[17] It would appear, therefore, that Thomas Nagel's celebrated uncertainty that we could ever know the mind of the bat is premature. Nervous systems (and quite possibly non-nervous analogues such as we see in hunting ciliates)[18] on this planet point to deep-seated commonalities that hint at how mental processes, and by further implication mind, must be universal. We should not necessarily assume, however, that this conclusion represents a closure. This is because Nagel's other point in his celebrated essay has received less attention, but may be more fundamental. This is to the effect that the neural substrate, even if it is as I argue a universal, may in itself impose absolute restrictions on cognizance, so that some things will forever remain beyond our comprehension.

[16] H. E. Harley, H. L. Roitblat and P. E. Nachtigall, 'Object Representation in the Bottlenose Dolphin (*Tursiops truncatus*): Integration of Visual and Echoic Information', *Journal of Experimental Psychology: Animal Behavior Processes* 22 (1996), pp. 164–174.

[17] A. Nieder and E. K. Miller, 'Coding of Cognitive Magnitude: Compressed Scaling of Numerical Information in the Primate Prefrontal Cortex', *Neuron* 37 (2003), pp. 149–152.

[18] For single-celled organisms, see I. Walker, *The Evolution of Biological Organization as a Function of Information* (Manaus: INPA, 2005). For communicating plants see Baluška, Mancuso and Volkmann, *Communication in Plants*.

UNIVERSAL MENTALITIES?

The suggestion of a potential for universal mentalities is still in its infancy, although the identification of what appear to be very similar cognitive landscapes in birds (notably crows and parrots) and great apes (and also dolphins) is consistent with this conclusion. But is any of this really relevant to how we determine consciousness, how we know qualia are real? The observed commonalities may reassure us that qualia are not simply freaks of human consciousness; even if a universal mental landscape is identified, however, this seems only to exacerbate the problem of how out of matter emerges mentality.

And indeed, put that way, the only realistic programme would appear to be panpsychism. Largely ignored in post-Cartesian discourses, the new evolutionary framework would seem to be not only consistent with it but in tune with the mantra of emergence. Yet it is far from clear that, despite Skrbina's[19] excellent overview, panpsychism can ever be taken seriously again. We now know beyond all reasonable doubt that crows, for example, are conscious and probably have the same 'theory of mind' as we do. If so, it is hardly surprising to find our closer relatives also stepping into the same cognitive world. Elephants' ability for self-recognition, what appears to be an awareness of death, as well as such tricks as plugging the bells they wear with mud to prevent them from alerting the farmer of an ongoing raid on his crops, all point to advanced cognitive abilities. Dogs? Well, at least conscious, and certainly with emotions. Lizards? Some evidence. Fish, again yes, but sea anemones, or amoeba, or bacteria? Stones, atoms, quarks? If we were vitalists, then panpsychism would have its attractions, but to imagine a conscious emerging from ultimately an atom (or quark) effectively provides no explanation at all.

THE BRAIN AS AN 'ANTENNA'

One might also note that a panpsychic agenda could have gnostic undertones. And here I would suggest that all attempts to understand consciousness will fail until we not only abandon a naturalistic framework, but also re-frame our question in the context of a much wider (and stranger) universe that is not only thoroughly supernatural, consisting of worlds both visible and (to us) invisible, but also only explicable by the agency of *creatio ex nihilo*. Suppose we were to think of the brain, which is by implication

[19] D. Skrbina, *Panpsychism in the West* (Boston: MIT Press, 2005).

ultimately 'only' a chemical 'machine', as an 'antenna' that has evolved (convergently!) for life to 'discover' the mental world and thereby become conscious by default. From a naturalist perspective this would be described politely as 'intriguing', but in private as 'bizarre'. Quite so, and at first sight with good reason. Properties such as memory and sleep clearly have some physical basis. Neither, however, readily explains such matters as the construction of a 'memory palace' (as by Matteo Ricci), unprompted recall (as in Coleridge's[20] famous instance of a servant girl spouting Latin, Greek and Hebrew, that upon investigation was 'learned' when employed by a savant, but only emerged much later when she was in the grips of fever), or, in the case of sleep, its pre-cognitive dreams. So too imaging studies of the brain may indeed localize some activities; other activities, however, are far more diffuse, and in no case does the region of neural activity reveal anything of the qualia, be it the chess piece or the antiphonal singing. Not only that: even when we feel we are the most intensely conscious, almost the entire brain remains a 'black box', silent and ostensibly entirely unengaged. And this latter paradox is perhaps less surprising with the discovery that in vegetative states, where by definition there is no brain activity, the patients still appear to be conscious.[21] That too makes it more believable that in well-documented 'out-of-body' experiences, where the individual may be technically 'dead', conscious experience clearly continues for the simple reason that it is subsequently reported.

All this seems inexplicable from a panpsychic, let alone naturalist, perspective. If, however, there is a mental world and the brain is the 'antenna' that makes first contact with it, then not only do we have access to new realities, which the intuition of qualia has long indicated, but we find a world where theological discourse is not divorced, but integral. It is true that, even if this idea wins further acceptance, it could in principle be applied to any world-picture that accepts the supernatural. On the other hand, there are rival explanations for our perception of such worlds. These are notoriously not easy to reconcile with each other, apart from via some syncreistic mishmash, of which the present day supplies some splendid examples. Christianity, of course, makes some highly specific claims that are built on both Judaic experience and wisdom, but argue uniquely for particular interactions between the divine and the mundane. These

[20] S. T. Coleridge, *Biographia Literaria, or Biographical Sketches of My Literary Life and Opinions* (London: Everyman's Library, 1965).

[21] A. M. Owen, M. R. Coleman, M. Boly, M. H. Davis, S. Laureys and P. Pickard, 'Detecting Awareness in the Vegetative State', *Science* 313 (2006), p. 1,402.

certainly find echoes, resonances and rumours in other traditions, but none approaches (even remotely) the concrete specifications of the Christian claim for the incarnation and the resurrection. Indeed, so far as they are even entertained, they are rejected as a monstrous scandal, if not an insult. In addition, but I believe consistently with these tenets, Christianity embraces the concept of *creatio ex nihilo*. This too is in conflict with Aristotelian philosophy (which still is the main underpinning of science), as well as many eastern religions.

As already noted, *creatio ex nihilo* is simply not open to scientific investigation. Yet, as also noted, we are entitled to look for consistencies, such as the Big Bang and anthropic principles of fine-tuning. Even if they are revised and ultimately overthrown we are also entitled to predict that their successors will be yet more consistent with the underlying precept of *creatio ex nihilo*, albeit in ways that at present are simply past our imagination. So too our very ability to understand the universe as rational creatures persuades me that there is an underlying rationality, an argument famously put forward by C. S. Lewis and subsequently refined in his debate with Anscombe and further commentators.[22] I believe my suggestions with respect to the roots of consciousness, emerging as they do from my interest in the evolutionary convergence of sensory systems and cognitive landscapes, point in the same direction. All this also points to a universe entirely dependent on God, and from our perspective a product of *creatio ex nihilo*. Yet just as many are deeply offended by the Christian scandal of particularity (although I suspect the scandal tells one more of a given perspective on the world), so scientists are justly suspicious of singularities. Does this not apply to *creatio ex nihilo*? At first sight it does, but the Christian narrative seems to point to instances where, from our stance, *creatio ex nihilo* has recurred. I would hesitate to even begin to explore this area, not only because of my manifest lack of expertise, but simply because to talk of *creatio ex nihilo* 'happening' forces the discussion to a mundane level. Yet I believe the discussion is important both because of the present science and religion debates, but more importantly because of Aquinas' insistence on universal truths that ultimately cannot make sense outside the parameters of Christianity.

Thus, standing (as I hope I do) within the walls of Christian orthodoxy, I would suggest the most compelling examples of *creatio ex nihilo* are the incarnation via Mary and the resurrection. In one strange way, their 'familiarity' offers a slight straw to grasp as we attempt to understand how

[22] Reppert, *C. S. Lewis's Dangerous Idea*.

something comes out of nothing, albeit intruding into existing creation. It remains manifestly the case that beyond the metaphorical walls we are met (then, as now) with sheer disbelief (in its own way understandable) that cannot, or will not, accept the internal consistency of the evidence. This perceived impossibility, and the recurrent slide from scepticism to disbelief, serve to derail any thoroughgoing supernaturalism that insists that God's intervention is utterly other. But I would speculate that the Transfiguration and Ascension may also help to define *creatio ex nihilo*, i.e., as the time-line that not only serves to link the incarnation and resurrection, but also points to its culmination. Our perception of these events is begged in the very term 'time-line', but when we approach the eternal and ineffable our language predictably fails. A metaphor of a 'time-line' for *creatio ex nihilo* does have a further advantage, however, in not only reconciling our imagination to the ostensibly impossible, but also reminding us that Christian orthodoxy claims to identify a narrative – one set in a historical context in which the story developed, culminated and apparently ended. So too the 'time-line' of *creatio ex nihilo* argues that since its original definition in Roman Judaea it has remained temporarily accessible to all via the Eucharist but must also terminate in the Eschaton. At that point, when time ends, we will fully understand *creatio ex nihilo*.

CHAPTER 12

Creatio ex nihilo *and dual causality*

James R. Pambrun

INTRODUCTION

The notion of causality plays no small role in conversations between scientists and theologians. For scientists, the notion of causality reflects, at least implicitly, an anticipation of a sense of order in the universe and how such an order lends itself to scientific investigation. Accompanying such an anticipation is an assumption about the intrinsic integrity to this order, namely, that whatever can be known about such order falls within the horizon of scientific learning. With respect to the natural order of the world, scientific knowledge enjoys a high degree of autonomy. For theologians, the notion of causality has been drawn upon in order to refer to God's universal and efficient cause. The notion of *creatio ex nihilo* elaborates the meaning of this by affirming the primacy of divine agency. On one level, this implies that there is no other reason for, no other cause involved in, the creation of the universe other than God's own desire that this universe be; that it exists. At a further level, it affirms that this world as created persists in its act of existence by virtue of God's abiding and intimate relation with this world. We have, then, two distinct disciplines which appropriate, at least at first sight, the same notion, causality, in order to affirm two interpretations about the order of the cosmic universe.

In this light, William Stoeger has identified one of the immediate questions that the encounter between these two disciplines poses regarding causality: "It is essentially this: How can we have two adequate agents causing the same effect – God as primary cause and the secondary causes through which God is working? How can we speak of divine causality within the world as we know it, without compromising scientific and philosophical principles – without using an interventionist model, for instance?"[1]

[1] William R. Stoeger, "Describing God's Action in the World in Light of Scientific Knowledge of Reality" in Robert John Russell, Nancey Murphy and Arthur R. Peacocke (eds.), *Chaos and*

The aim of this chapter is to develop a way of approaching this question that allows for a conversation, an encounter to take place between theology and science. If such an encounter is possible, it assumes that each discipline has something to offer on behalf of a fuller understanding of the world in which we dwell. But how can such a conversation be pursued, and on the basis of what kind of approach? An initial clue, in my judgment, is also provided by Stoeger, namely "through the common ground of understanding and language."[2] Why such an approach? In the first place, such an approach recognizes that a conversation will not take place purely on the basis of relating the findings of modern science to the confessional beliefs of a faith tradition. There is no direct or immediate route between science and theology. The reason is that each discipline constitutes distinct forms of questions with respect to distinct kinds of data. Both, I would maintain, do refer to the same world. However, the kinds of sources, data, models of investigation each appropriates to fulfill its requirements of being a scientific discipline are quite different. In this respect, each reflects the work of a distinct strategy of meaning given the nature and configurations of the questions appropriate to each discipline. This is the first point, namely, the recognition of the difference, perhaps even the discontinuity, between both disciplines. This said, Stoeger's approach also implies a point of continuity. Such a continuity resides in the empirical fact that both disciplines appropriate acts of understanding and acquire their status as a discipline by adhering to the criteria of acts of understanding.

For this reason, while I argued that no immediate relation can be established between the findings of science and the confessional beliefs of a faith community such as that of *creatio ex nihilo*, there remains nonetheless the philosophical moment evident in each discipline whereby both reflect an act of meaning at work. Given this approach, the question then arises about how to effect a conversation which attempts to relate a scientific account of order and the affirmation of God as universal and efficient cause. From the side of the work of the theologian, this calls for two distinct operations. The first involves an attempt to understand what modern science understands when, through its own disciplines, it appeals to and draws upon a notion of causality. The second calls for theology to refine its own understanding of how *creatio ex nihilo*

Complexity: Scientific Perspectives on Divine Action (Vatican City State: Center for Theology and the Natural Sciences, 1995), pp. 239–261, at p. 254. See also T. Tracy's chapter in the present volume on this very issue with focus on human freedom.

[2] Stoeger, "Describing God's Action," p. 242.

qualifies divine agency. These two considerations frame the steps to be taken in this chapter.

In the first part I shall draw upon the work of the philosopher and historian of science, Ernan McMullin. One of the main virtues of McMullin's work is the attention he has given to the forms of inference that have defined the history of science and the nature of the epistemological developments within modern science. McMullin has identified three main stages in the development of scientific inference: deductive, inductive and, following Charles Peirce, retroductive inference. A consideration of these forms of inference will provide more critical precision to the meaning of the notion of causality.

The second part of the chapter will consist of an elaboration of the import of retroductive inference for clarifying the manner in which modern science develops causality in the form of "verified intelligibilities." In this part of my argument, I shall turn to reflections of the chemist Frank Budenholzer. The critical issue at this point will be the very meaning of the notion of the world and reality to which scientists advert when they are engaged in scientific inquiry and understanding. The merit of Budenholzer's contribution will be the way in which he emphasizes what is actually known. The world as known by science is not an object out there to be broken down into smaller and smaller parts. Rather, it consists of the world, an understanding of which is mediated by verified intelligible relations. The world is what is affirmed in light of the fulfilling conditions to be met given the form of intelligible relations configured by a scientific discipline. The very notion of causality, as we shall see, is co-extensive with an understanding of such structured patterns of relations, their intelligibility and their verification in concrete instances.

These two sets of reflections will constitute the first task of the theologian, namely to attempt to understand what is going forward in the act of scientific understanding, especially as this understanding refers to a notion of causality. The second task of the theologian brings us to the third part of this chapter and asks how such a reflection on the form and praxis of scientific inquiry opens a door to an encounter with the meaning of *creatio ex nihilo* and dual causality. *Creatio ex nihilo*, too, is a notion which reflects meaning at work. As such, it too is the work of intelligible meaning with respect to the interpretation of our cosmic world. The specificity of this notion, however, is the manner in which it brings into play not only a theological notion of causality, God as universal and efficient cause, but also how this notion of causality has a bearing on the meaning of existence of the world as such. Here emerges the notion of dual causality. For, given a respect for the explanatory findings of modern science, how is it possible to refer to God's agency with the understanding that such an agency is not that of an initial first moment of the universe, rather is an abiding relation that sustains the structured patterns of relations known by modern science? The challenge is not simply to find a way of affirming both. The challenge goes deeper. If creation refers to this same world, is it possible to integrate within an understanding of creation a further intelligibility that allows for the integrity of modern science's own notion of causality? For this to be possible, a double openness is called for – one on the side of science, the other on the side of theology.

The argument of this third part will consist of the way in which theology works with philosophy in order to identify and bring to the surface a presupposition accompanying scientific investigation in all its acts. What is this? It is the presence to scientific inquiry of the abiding awareness that *some thing exists* which, as such, becomes the subject of scientific inquiry. However far back scientific investigation goes, however radical it becomes, it always takes for granted that it investigates some phenomenon of reality. Modern science cannot outrun this fact of life. Is existence not what is implicitly affirmed whenever scientific investigation reaches, in Frank Budenholzer's terms, a judgment of "verified intelligibility"? My hypothesis is that it is possible that the theologian meet the scientist precisely at that moment when the very foundation, the very intelligibility of reality, always there prior to our questioning, becomes a topic for consideration in its own right. The notion of *creatio ex nihilo* speaks to the inherent intelligibility of existence as a property of every phenomenon that is investigated or is to be investigated by modern science. This chapter wishes to take up the lines of such an investigation.

PART I: CAUSALITY AND MODES OF INFERENCE IN THE HISTORY OF SCIENCE

The meaning of theoretical terms and their relations is normally a function of the kind of explanation sought in scholarly investigation. For this reason, my aim in this first part is to identify a systematic framework within which I shall invite us to explore the notion of causality itself. The systematic framework will focus on the act of understanding, in particular, how the history of science has been shaped and defined by a commitment to acts of understanding. In order to provide some measure to this framework, I shall refer to Ernan McMullin's own "systematic" account of this history which he has adopted and in turn somewhat refined from his reading of Charles Sanders Peirce.[3] McMullin refers to three distinct forms of inference that have defined the history of scientific investigation: deductive (Aristotelian), inductive (from the fourteenth to the seventeenth century) and retroductive (abductive), which identifies the form of inference that defines contemporary science. I shall develop my remarks by first saying a word about retroductive inference as a basis for contrasting it with deductive and inductive inference. I shall then return to retroductive inference and highlight a number of features relevant for an initial definition of causality.

(a) Retroductive inference

One of the critical characteristics of retroductive inference[4] is the way it integrates a complex process of inquiry, a process that incorporates "a whole series of discrete and well-defined operations."[5]

> The principal way in which natural science enlarges our world is ... through retroductive inference to structures, processes and entities postulated to be causally responsible for the regularities established by the experimental scientist or for the individual "traces" with which historical sciences like geology and evolutionary biology are concerned.[6]

In this way, retroduction is a *method* of inquiry which incorporates distinct processes and operations (observation, theory, affirmation). It is a refined way of asking questions, identifying theories and validating these theories. Consequently, it also incorporates a reflexive approach, for it also asks about the very criteria engaged in the process of validating theories.[7]

[3] Ernan McMullin, "Conceptions of Science in the Scientific Revolution" in David C. and Robert S. Westman Lindbert (eds.), *Reappraisals of the Scientific Revolution* (Cambridge University Press, 1990), pp. 27–92; Ernan McMullin, "The Impact of Newton's *Principia* on the Philosophy of Science," *Philosophy of Science* 58 (2001), pp. 279–310, at p. 284. With respect to McMullin's account of the different forms of inference, see in particular Ernan McMullin, *The Inference that Makes Science*, The Aquinas Lecture (Milwaukee: Marquette University Press, 1992); Ernan McMullin, "Structural Explanation," *American Philosophical Quarterly* 15:2 (1978), pp. 139–147; and Ernan McMullin, "Models of Scientific Inference," *CTNS Bulletin* 8:2 (1988), pp. 1–14.

[4] For a good analysis of McMullin's use of retroduction and its role in his thought, see Paul L. Allen, *Ernan McMullin and Critical Realism in the Science–Theology Dialogue*, Ashgate New Critical Thinking in Religion, Theology and Biblical Studies (Aldershot: Ashgate, 2006), pp. 67–94.

[5] McMullin, *The Inference that Makes Science*, p. 97.

[6] Ernan McMullin, "Enlarging the Known World" in J. Hilgevoord (ed.), *Physics and Our View of the World* (Cambridge University Press, 1994), pp. 79–113, at p. 101.

[7] McMullin, "Enlarging the Known World," pp. 102–106; McMullin, *The Inference that Makes Science*, pp. 91–92.

One of the more significant features of retroductive inference is its use of hypotheses where hypotheses refer to theories which are integrated patterns of asking questions. On the basis of such questions, retroduction works from effects to causes by way of postulating and hypothesizing about the explanatory causal structures underlying these effects. In addition, the hypotheses and postulates configured by theoretical entities – let us call these intelligibilities – have taken us well beyond the world of observable entities.[8] Indeed, this theoretical dimension, while appearing more abstract and more and more remote from the immediate or what can be sensed, has, in fact, led to an enrichment and enlargement of our comprehension of the world as real.

These developments have educated our more spontaneous notions of cause and effect. Since retroduction employs a complex process for disclosing underlying explanatory structures, it has challenged notions of causality that would otherwise invite us to look for immediate links between effect and cause or immediate and contiguous relations among visible bodies or an identifiable influx of relations whereby one body impacts another and thereby produces an effect. In order to invite us to focus more precisely on what that notion of causality is with which we actually work, I would like to contrast very briefly retroductive inference with deductive and inductive.

(b) Deductive and inductive inferences

Associated with Aristotle, deductive inference represented a rather tightly conceived relationship between cause and effect. It was governed by the rules of logic that allow one to move from premises to conclusions. Premises are self-evident propositions. The process hits upon an insight which stops a movement of regressive steps in the syllogism. No further appeal to ongoing steps in reasoning back to further explanations is needed. The insight is a grasp of the idea of the universal in light of which the particular conceptual moments and linguistic definitions are comprehended.[9] Now, if the premises are necessary, then the conclusions,

8 "Another function of structural explanation ... allows us to enlarge our world in an effective way ... It proposes to explain by introducing entities that are not observed and may, indeed, be unobservable," Ernan McMullin, "Materialist categories," *Science & Education* 8 (1999), pp. 37–44, at p. 39.

9 McMullin refers to the moment of *epagōgē*. It consists of a grasp of the universal in the particular. McMullin, *The Inference that Makes Science*, p. 5. It also consists of a recognition of that moment of insight by virtue of which an insight calls for no further demonstration. But what kind of proposition meets such a requirement? McMullin identifies the role of a "convertible" premise, that is, one of the conditions is "reciprocally predicable" (McMullin, *The Inference that Makes Science*, p. 18). On the role

governed by the logical rule-governed link between premise and conclusion, are themselves necessary. Causes – what Aristotle referred to as material, formal, efficient and final – are insights, seized upon by the mind (*nous*), into the relationship between the kinds of premises and their relation to universals. "They [the premises] must specify in a unique way the cause of the effect or property of which scientific knowledge is desired."[10] Deductive inference was an achievement. It held a strong appeal in our quest for causal explanation. However, its rather tight link between cause and effect enjoyed more success when studying large-scale cosmic movements than it did in the study of living forms. In these latter cases, it tended to fall short of explanatory success.[11]

Inductive inference progressively took shape from the fourteenth to the seventeenth century. McMullin identifies the key figures in this narrative: the nominalist thinker, D'Autrecourt, as well as Bacon, Hume and Mill.[12] Inductive inference reached prominent practical expression in the work of Newton (*Principia*) and his mechanistic view of nature. Rather than seeking self-evident principles, this form begins with an attention to concrete observables. It consists of selecting and classifying a set of observations and then identifying that set of relationships which explains why these observations happen to co-occur. The main operation of this form of inference is one of generalization. On the basis of observed particulars and a classification of similar types of observed realities, one identifies the relationships or correlations that hold among these

of first principles, see Patrick H. Byrne, "Hunting for First Principles" in *Analysis and Science in Aristotle* (Albany, NY: State University of New York Press, 1997), pp. 123–163. Also Frederick E. Crowe, "Universal Norms and the Concrete *Operabile* in St. Thomas Aquinas" in Michael Vertin (ed.), *Three Thomist Studies*, supplementary issue of *Lonergan Workshop*, vol. XVI, ed. Fred Lawrence (Boston: Lonergan Workshop, 2000), pp. 1–69, at pp. 15–17.

10 "From his general theory of nature he concluded that there were just four broad types of explanation; they coincided (he claimed) with the ways people actually *do* answer the question 'why?' . . . What counted as explanatory was thus determined by the choice of ontology as well as by a reference to customary practice. Explanation for Aristotle is thus causal *by definition*, since each mode of explanation is linked with a characteristic sort of 'cause' . . . It must be remembered, of course, that the terms 'cause' and 'causal' are much broader here than they would be in modern usage," Ernan McMullin, "The Explanation of Distant Action: Historical Notes" in James T. Cushing and Ernan McMullin (eds.), *Philosophical Consequences of Quantum Theory: Reflections on Bell's Theorem, Studies in Science and the Humanities From the Reilly Center for Science, Technology, and Values*, vol. II (University of Notre Dame Press, 1989), pp. 272–302, at pp. 274–275. McMullin, *The Inference that Makes Science*, p. 5.

11 As McMullin has argued, developments in scientific inference will occur as a result of developing insights into the rules of logic but even more fundamentally as a result of ongoing questions and developments in the history of science. Certain premises represented oversights with respect to the full set of logical possibilities. To reach a self-evident premise prescinded at times from other possible ways of interpreting a phenomenon.

12 McMullin, *The Inference that Makes Science*, pp. 66–80.

observations. Thus, from the particular cases, one progressively expands or generalizes to an entire set or class of observables for which particular relationships hold.[13] Based on these generalizations of co-occurrence, correlations or law-like patterns are postulated which "explain" why the observed regularities co-occur, behave or are ordered the way they are.

Since the process begins with an attention to particulars and moves to generalization, the notion of cause that is implicated is different from that notion of cause intended by deductive inference. There remains a search for explanation. However, inductive inference does not look to universal and necessary self-evident premises. It attempts to account for, based on the operation of generalization from a set of particular observables, the law-like character that holds among the relationships. Increasingly, the appeal of inductive inference to the role of hypothesis began to postulate unobservable entities, smaller and smaller bodies, that played a role in the observed effects and so, it itself, became the occasion for introducing an increasing host of questions and problems which sought some resolution.[14]

McMullin shows how thinkers such as Kepler and Boyle increasingly began to refer to hypothetical entities and unobserved and "hypothetical causal reasoning."[15] In particular, McMullin has examined the question of action at a distance and the way in which questions about matter were transposed in order to take into consideration such emerging categories as mass, force, attraction, gravity.[16] An inherent tension continued to strain the resources of inductive reasoning. The reason why a development in inference occurred was that the existing forms of inference could not themselves respond to the questions arising within the fields of scientific investigations. More was needed than the further generalization of the law-like character of the world. The kind of explanation required and its corresponding notion of cause would involve a leap in the order of understanding. In this respect, McMullin reminds us that inductive inference remained bound largely to a focus on "observed" entities. Inductive inference had to yield to the developments in the history of modern science.

(c) Back to retroduction

Developments since the nineteenth century have demonstrated that explanations call for a penetration into the order and structure of reality

[13] McMullin, "The Impact of Newton," p. 281.
[14] McMullin, "The Impact of Newton," p. 288.
[15] McMullin, "The Impact of Newton," p. 285.
[16] McMullin, "The Explanation of Distant Action."

which takes us well beyond what is observable or what can be conceived as smaller and smaller entities, albeit unobserved. Newton himself resisted the appeal to such theoretical hypotheses. But, as McMullin argues, the evidence on behalf of the leap into the more theoretical realm was already present in the *Principia* itself – perhaps not in what Newton was prepared to admit, but certainly in the very structure of the *Principia* itself as a form of inquiry. The book itself may well be regarded as an instance of such a hypothesis at work.[17] The history of science and the exigencies engaged by acts of understanding would undercut the mechanistic presuppositions which precluded Newton from radicalizing further his own presuppositions.[18]

The more recent combination of classical and statistical methods has enlarged the scope and power of theoretical postulates and has further refined our understanding of the causal explanatory underlying structures which account for how things come about. The reach of modern scientific hypotheses stretches toward theoretical entities.[19] At this junction, McMullin refers to the transpositions from a focus on logic or technique[20] to a method of inquiry capable of identifying structural explanations.[21] Moreover, the theoretical feature of structural explanation cannot be assessed in the same way that one affirms the validity of observed co-occurrences. Retroduction involves a theoretical *novelty*.[22] One of the virtues of retroduction as a mode of inquiry is its ability to clarify and integrate earlier scientific efforts and set the basis for further learning. Consequently, while retroduction has appeared in its fuller form only recently, it is not simply a process that follows chronologically upon deductive and inductive inferences. Even more significantly, it integrates these prior forms of inference as moments within its own act of reasoning.[23]

Accordingly, inductive inference has not been completely abandoned. It remains a first step integrated within retroductive inference. The kinds of classifications and the form of imaging which represents this operation

[17] McMullin, "The Impact of Newton," p. 307.

[18] In Newton's work, inductive inference itself would develop and undergo refinements. Among these is the role and scope of hypothesis. Newton "had already provided a conceptual structure whose further development would occupy the best mathematical minds for decades to come" (McMullin, "The Impact of Newton," p. 296, p. 297). See also McMullin, "The Explanation of Distant Action," p. 302.

[19] McMullin, "Structural Explanation," p. 143.

[20] McMullin, *The Inference that Makes Science*, p. 92.

[21] Worth re-emphasizing is McMullin's observation that induction privileges "observed" realities. *The Inference that Makes Science*, p. 90.

[22] McMullin, "Structural Explanation," p. 145.

[23] McMullin, *The Inference that Makes Science*, p. 20, p. 91.

of classification yield images for insight. But, as I shall discuss in the second part of this chapter, how retroduction incorporates a return to that moment of classification, which represented a form of ordering on the basis of empirically observed data, will be critical. For, if retroduction calls for a return to concrete, "observable" data as if we simply affirm what is already known by the first, inductive, descriptive account, nothing really new is added to our understanding. Retroduction enriches and enlarges our understanding of the world.

Furthermore, retroductive inference adds a realist character to investigation. By contrast, to identify in inductive inference why things co-occur is hardly an explanation of why these things co-occur. "Induction [writes McMullin] is only in a very weak sense explanatory."[24] Retroduction, on the other hand, seeks not simply to identify what relations account for co-occurrence – it also seeks to explain why these relations actually occur and how this leads us to affirm what exists. It is "because cause is . . . affirmed as real cause, that retroduction functions as a distinct form of inference."[25] How this occurs is a question which I shall turn to in the second part of this chapter. At this point, and given this systematic and historic overview, we may ask: What is a cause? Or: What is causality?

The meaning of the notion of cause, like science, is related to an interpretation of a history of scientific investigations. Our reading of the history of inference in scientific inquiry shows that our understanding of the nature of the relationship between cause and effect, as well as what we look for as explanatory, has changed. It has developed from self-evident premises to postulated theoretical entities or explanatory structures – law-like regularities, underlying reality.[26] Causal explanation became increasingly a function of a use of inference that has been transposed from logic to method of inquiry.[27] McMullin has identified in retroduction "the account of inference towards which all of this (history) has been

[24] McMullin, *The Inference that Makes Science*, p. 90.

[25] McMullin, *The Inference that Makes Science*, p. 94. Further, McMullin writes, there is "else little to distinguish induction and retroduction" (p. 95).

[26] McMullin remarks that "the quest for causal explanation in terms of underlying structures and processes has been an invariant in the natural sciences since the seventeenth century" (McMullin, "Enlarging the Known World," pp. 105–106). At the same time, McMullin has identified how the very notion of cause, due not least to philosophical presuppositions, was highly debated by such thinkers as Berkeley, Hume, Reid and Kant. On these debates, see McMullin, "The Impact of Newton," pp. 299–308.

[27] "Structural explanations . . . afford a causal understanding, since the underlying structure can be regarded as a cause of the regularity to be explained" (McMullin, "Materialist Categories," p. 38).

tending."[28] In light of this, I would suggest that causality is an intelligibility and that in a sense it is an explanatory finality.[29] That is, it stands for a form of explanation of the order of things, what brings things about, a counterpart to questions for understanding.

What is the significance of this overview for our question of *creatio ex nihilo* and dual causality? Just as there is a refinement in our understanding of causality, so too must there be a refinement in the way we ask our question about dual causality. In this regard, the historical developments of the forms of scientific inference as outlined by McMullin are noteworthy in at least two respects. First, an understanding of causality whose focus is explanatory structures has refined our comprehension of the integrity of the order of contingent existence. We are better able to account for not only why certain things exist as they do, but also how new patterns of life emerge. This has consequences for the theological form of the question. For, the more science refines its understandings of the natural order, the more theologians must identify with greater precision what exactly they are adverting to when they refer to God's own universal and efficient causality as it relates to this world. This is a question we shall have to take up in the third part of this chapter.

Second, the developments in the history of science provide us with data about the correlation between acts of understanding and the development in our comprehension and image of the world. In other words, acts of understanding have become a subject of reflection in their own right. By reflecting on the data of understanding *as it works*, we shall have an opportunity to reflect upon how different orders of intelligibility are possible. This will provide us with a way of thinking about dual causality in such a way as to follow McMullin's proposal that with increased understanding comes an enriched and enlarged understanding of our world. At this point, and in view of clarifying how the meaning of dual causality will relate to a form of intelligibility about our world, it is worth taking up this reference to intelligibility and exploring further its implications with respect to what we understand when we refer to our world as known. For this reason we turn in the next section to a reflection on the meaning of "verified intelligibility" and how such a reflection can further enrich the notion of causality as structural explanation of our world.

[28] McMullin, *The Inference that Makes Science*, p. 81.

[29] Bernard Lonergan, *Insight: A Study in Human Understanding* (New York: Longmans, 1958), p. 651.

PART II: "VERIFIED INTELLIGIBILITY" AND THE SIGNIFICANCE OF DISTINCT DISCIPLINES

A fascinating feature of modern science is the diversity and plurality of its own forms of inquiry. McMullin remarks that there is no such thing as science in general. Empirically, science consists of particular scientists engaged in particular scientific inquiries within specific scientific disciplines. In order to set the scene for exploring the intelligibility of a notion of dual causality, I wish to examine the significance of the diversity and autonomy of distinct sciences that make up modern science. In the long run, the question of dual causality will consist of whether there is a possibility of an encounter between two distinct "disciplines" – those disciplines that make up modern science and that of theology. I shall proceed in three steps. First, I shall refer to what is common among the scientific disciplines, namely, their search for "verified intelligibilities." Second, I shall explore how such intelligibilities involve an understanding not only of certain kinds of relationships but also of schemes of relationships. But no one science can account for the full set of concrete schemes and their properties. For this reason I shall turn, in the third step, to an examination of the role of the distinct sciences and the import of this diversity for our affirmations of this world and for our understanding of causality. In order to frame my remarks in this section, I shall draw upon recent publications of the chemist Frank Budenholzer who himself has drawn upon the work of Bernard Lonergan.[30]

(a) Verified intelligibilities

One of the main theses of Budenholzer's contribution is his emphasis on the meaning of "verified intelligibility."[31] Verified intelligibility directs our attention away from commonsense, descriptive knowledge of the object of investigation, to an explanatory knowledge. Retroduction, as we saw, invites us to shift from a knowledge whose focus was primarily on observables to one whose focus is on theoretical interpretation. This

[30] It is important to emphasize that Budenholzer's remarks draw significantly on the work of Bernard Lonergan. Frank Budenholzer, "Science and Religion: Seeking a Common Horizon," *Zygon* 19:3 (1984), pp. 351–368. The two principal texts to which I shall refer in what follows are: Frank Budenholzer, "Some Comments on the Problem of Reductionism in Contemporary Physical Science," *Zygon* 38:1 (2003), pp. 61–69; and Frank Budenholzer, "Emergence, Probability, and Reductionism," *Zygon* 39:2 (2004), pp. 339–356.

[31] Budenholzer, "Some Comments," p. 64, p. 65.

invites us to shift from an attention on how things appear to us to an attention on how things relate to one another. The use of the word "things" is deliberate. For the shift from observation to theory involves a corresponding shift from thinking about knowledge as something directed to what we see "out there" to some "thing" that possesses a certain intelligibility and integrity.[32] Budenholzer reminds us, though, that modern science holds these two references, the descriptive and the theoretical, together. Scientific inquiry begins by referring to something that can be described and classified, and remains a consistent reference throughout the entire process of inquiry. Moreover, theoretical knowledge is knowledge that develops some insight into a consistent pattern of data. At the same time, however, modern science moves toward explanatory intelligibility. Still, in this movement forward, a tension between the two distinct references is maintained, for it is important to be aware that one is moving between the two and knows when one is referring, on the one hand, to descriptive understanding, and when, on the other hand, one has moved into the world of theoretical understanding.[33] Given this complex process, a third moment occurs when the scientist affirms that the structural pattern of relationships identified by the theoretical model is present in the data as configured. That is, this pattern of structural relationships occurs in the thing, namely, in some unity, identity, whole. This is what Budenholzer refers to as "verified intelligibility." It will be precisely by moving from the descriptive to an imaginable pattern that the scientist will be able to begin to identify *at the scientific level* more explanatory patterns of relationships, models, which will in turn allow the scientist to affirm an explanatory intelligibility in this concrete reality. This is the basis of what McMullin identified as a moment of novelty which, by virtue of abstracting from the concrete, does not impoverish our interpretation of the world. Rather, it enlarges and enriches it. For this reason, once inquiry passes through the explanatory, theoretical

[32] "Things exist on various levels and are the unities that are explained – subatomic particles, atoms, molecules, cellular organisms, sensitive organisms, human persons that can transcend themselves in knowing and loving" (Budenholzer, "Emergence," p. 341). For what may be the origin of Lonergan's own use of the term, see William A. Mathews, *Lonergan's Quest: A Study of Desire in the Authoring of* Insight (University of Toronto Press, 2005), p. 347. On the notion of a thing, see also Joseph Flanagan, *Quest for Self-Knowledge* (University of Toronto Press, 1997), pp. 95–119. "Now the notion of a thing is grounded in an insight that grasps, not relations between data, but a unity, identity, whole in data ... [T]his unity is grasped ... by taking them in their concrete individuality and in the totality of their aspects" (Lonergan, *Insight*, p. 246).

[33] Joseph Flanagan, "Body to Thing" in Matthew L. Lamb (ed.), *Creativity and Method: Essays in Honor of Bernard Lonergan* (Milwaukee, WI: Marquette University Press, 1981), pp. 495–507.

moment, the scientist does not return to the object as if the scientist comes to know what was already "seen" or apprehended at a descriptive level. For that would simply undo, from the perspective of scientific understanding, the deeper and richer knowledge of the known world. What are the implications for our understanding of causality? In order to refine our understanding of causality, it is helpful to explore further what is implied in "verified intelligibility." Such an intelligibility directs our attention to the kinds of relations that constitute scientific knowing and to how these relations are known due to the work of distinct sciences.

(b) Verified intelligibility and relations

In seeking structural explanation, science reaches explanatory levels by identifying structured patterns of relationships. In so doing, each science names these relationships by developing theoretical terms specific to the scientific discipline concerned. Lonergan has suggested that each science develops these terms such that each "grasp[s] the higher and the more remote correlations."[34] Because relations are involved, Budenholzer, following Lonergan, refers to these scientific terms as explanatory conjugates, which refer to a set of terms or properties that specify a set of relations.[35] These conjugates "are the particular subject of the science at that level – physics, chemistry, biology, sensitive psychology, and so on."[36]

The development of explanatory conjugates represents in fact the novelty of insights which lead to the emergence of distinct scientific disciplines. Because there is a moment of genuine novelty involved, biology cannot be "explained" by simply expanding or generalizing laws in chemistry, nor can chemistry be "explained" by generalizing the laws or conjugates of physics. Much of Budenholzer's texts consists in helping us to remain at the level of explanatory intelligibility and to attend to the role of the diverse disciplines that make up modern science.[37] There is a further feature to this novelty. Explanatory conjugates name relations and their structural pattern. But, as we know, there is more to it than that. Our understanding of a thing involves more than its conjugates. A science identifies the properties or conjugates of a thing because a

34 Lonergan, *Insight*, p. 245.

35 "To describe the properties of things and events, Lonergan employs the technical term *conjugates*" (Budenholzer, "Some Comments," p. 65).

36 *Ibid.*, p 66.

37 In my judgment, much of McMullin's own effort to distinguish between inductive and retroductive inference is related to identifying this problem and to showing a way through it.

certain stability has emerged, such that we say something exists. Yet this stability itself further presupposes schemes insofar as any thing, as a unity, identity, whole, presupposes fulfilling conditions by virtue of which this thing emerged in the first place. For this reason, explanatory conjugates presuppose an entire scheme of relations, i.e., recurrent schemes.[38] This appeal to the fuller set of conditioned schemes enlarges our account of what is a cause.[39] When events themselves become ordered into a sequence of events or the possibility, over a sufficient expanse of space and time, that a sequence of events will occur, we refer to probabilities. A good, albeit simple, example comes from meteorology, whose elements are as follows:

> [There is a] circulation of water over the planet. The water rises out of the warm, tropical seas steaming upward, forming clouds that are carried on wind currents to the northern and southern hemispheres where the rains fall on the land, run down the mountains into rivers and lakes, flowing out to the ocean where the water circulates back to the tropical seas to repeat the scheme.[40]

A number of features are worth identifying here. First, the relations are not just a pattern or structure. They are also a pattern which exists in relation to a particular environment such that the pattern recurs as a systematic and regular scheme of operative relations. Second, it is worth distinguishing between classical and statistical patterns or laws. The former is more systematic and predictable: all things being considered, such relations are sustained. These are similar to Newton's classical laws and the development of theoretical correlations postulated by contemporary science. The latter refers to the event occurring and the probabilities according to which such and such an event can be anticipated to occur. This is statistical. This invites us to comprehend a thing not simply as a descriptive object but also as an event which occurs. For example, there is a probability of a certain amount of rain in a certain region at certain times of the year. So we anticipate that rain will fall with sufficient probability such that we say there is "a non-systematic deviation from an ideal norm."[41] Such patterns *normally* hold and recur. Third, and more importantly for our purposes, since these relations interact with or are bound by an environment, they

[38] Budenholzer, "Emergence," p. 341, p. 344. The term is borrowed from Lonergan. On Lonergan's own comments on schemes of recurrence, see *Insight*, pp. 118–121.

[39] See, for example, Flanagan, "Body to Thing," p. 498.

[40] The example comes from Flanagan, "Body to Thing," p. 497.

[41] "Statistical heuristic structure rests on an assumption of non-systematic relations and it aims at determining an ideal frequency from which actual frequencies may diverge but only non-systematically" (Lonergan, *Insight*, p. 110).

stand as practical solutions to the problem of living. In this context, Lonergan refers to the emergence of a species. A species represents the development of the flexibility and the habitual skills that allow some thing to live and act in an environment. It can impact the environment such that new sets of relations emerge along with their corresponding conjugates. But, just as there is a leap in the order of skills, complexification and adaptability in relation to changing and more demanding environments, so too is there the development of new disciplines which, by way of a new and distinct set of explanatory conjugates, can identify these skills and their properties.[42] We come to realize, in turn, that specific recurrent schemes themselves depend on a whole host of other schemes and their recurrence. Thus, we speak of a conditioned series or sets of sets of schemes. So what is the cause in each case – whether we refer to the emergence of a scheme, to its sustainability or to its role as a condition among a set of conditions sustaining other schemes?

It is important to recall Budenholzer's insistence that a thing does not consist of parts, smaller and smaller chunky little bits.[43] A thing is a unity, identity, whole, constituted by an entire complex of conditioned sets of recurrent schemes. "The basic understanding of cause is not that of particles in collision, whether molecules in a gas or the exchange of photons in quantum electrodynamics. Cause is simply an intelligible relationship of dependence."[44] Cause is an intelligibility, an explanatory structure, known by virtue of a *verified* intelligibility. This said, we begin to understand why we need so many distinct scientific disciplines, for our explanation of one "thing" can comprehend the properties identified by different conjugates. But such properties are never lumped together as belonging to one science. Rather, distinct sciences emerge with their own corresponding theoretical and skill set for identifying specific patterns of structural intelligibilities. These identify specific kinds of properties which surface with the emergence of more complexly organized life forms. At any point, we may be employing one particular science, but it is possible that that scientific understanding in its study of a particular thing would need to draw upon the properties identified by a range of sciences. Still, this does not imply that one science has denied the autonomy and assumed the responsibility of other sciences. To this final point, I now turn.

42 Mathews, *Lonergan's Quest*, pp. 357–360. 43 Budenholzer, "Emergence," p. 340, p. 350.

44 Budenholzer, "Emergence," p. 348. Or, in Flanagan's own words, "things exist only in and through their recurring schemes" ("Body to Thing," p. 500).

(c) The significance of distinct sciences in accounting for verified intelligibility

As I have indicated, a discipline is defined by the terms which name explanatory conjugates, the ordered set of relations. But those sets of terms, their relations and their derived relations are what a science is.[45] If a change occurs in naming the terms and their relations determined by the explanatory conjugates, a different science takes form. Nor does one move from one discipline to another by simply adding a new set of conjugate terms. For the definition of a discipline *is* the set of explanatory conjugates. So, again following Budenholzer, we have a set of explanatory conjugates which are associated with physics (atoms and subatomic levels of reality whose properties are "mass, energy, spin, color, charm"); we have a set associated with chemistry (molecules whose properties are "valence, reactivity, molecular symmetry"); we have a set associated with biology (cells: "gene expression, metabolic pathways, evolutionary niche").[46]

By and large, the knowledge of each of these disciplines is engaged in our knowledge of concrete things. To be sure, there are things for which our knowledge of physics is adequate. However, once we move up the scale of the complexification and the emergent genera of living things, we draw upon different and distinct disciplines. Thus, the knowledge of a cell integrates physical and chemical conjugates and the knowledge of animals as sentient beings integrates knowledge from among biology, chemistry and physics. The "higher" disciplines, in the act of inquiry, sublate the properties of the lower in their own study of a thing. This kind of understanding is quite different from attempting to break something down into smaller and smaller relationships. The distinct scientific disciplines did not emerge in response to questions about smaller and smaller parts that make up a body. Rather, they emerged as answers to questions in search of distinct patterns of intelligibility in our interpretation of a concrete thing. Intelligibility of the distinct disciplines is a matter of bringing greater systematic understanding to what is otherwise regarded at a lower systematic level as a coincidental manifold of disparate data or information. The movement from a coincidental manifold to a systematic intelligibility is the result of an insight reached by the scientist. Cells, for example, known by the biologist, are higher-level

[45] McMullin refers to Newton's work as a whole as a form of hypothesis. McMullin, "The Impact of Newton," p. 307.

[46] On these specifications, see Budenholzer, "Some Comments," p. 65.

integrations of what appears to be a coincidental manifold, say, of molecules. What appears coincidental for the chemist can become a systematic scheme for the biologist.[47] Because a higher-order science is a systematic organization of novel relations, it calls for a new set of terms or explanatory conjugates which in turn are a function of a new level of systematic understanding. We may ask once again: What is the cause of a thing affirmed by scientific understanding? What is affirmed is the concrete thing under all its aspects, that is, that which takes into consideration all the data and all the relevant schemes for affirming this thing. But what is that data? If we take the example of an animal: "An animal is a concrete unit whose basic conjugates are the subject of zoology."[48] "[A]n animal . . . is a unity in which each of the various levels of matter are integrated."[49] The various levels are represented by the knowledge of the distinct sciences. We can see in such an example how both the integrity of the concrete thing and the autonomy of distinct disciplines are respected.

Finally, in the light of these remarks, I think it important to say a final word about the sequence of intelligibilities as a sequence. The relationship among the disciplines and their intelligibilities opens up the possibility of referring to the notion of direction and examining its relevance for our notion of causality. To say that distinct sciences incorporate distinct conjugate forms and their verifiability in things should not lead us to overlook the intelligible relations among the disciplines themselves. Physics draws upon mathematics and geometry. Chemistry draws upon both mathematics and physics. Biology draws upon all three. These disciplines correspond to levels of reality and the affirmation of such levels. Now it is possible to identify conditioned sets of sets of schemes of recurrence whose intelligibilities identify conditions for the emergence of a higher set. But it is also possible to recognize that the properties of the higher intelligibilities are really operative as a form of direction in the lower levels and in turn act as operators which set the conditions for the emergence of further levels.[50]

The basis for affirming this is our experience of how a higher intelligibility emerges from what is apparently only a coincidental manifold at a lower level. A good example is the very history of retroductive inference I outlined in the first part of this chapter. In his account of the

[47] Budenholzer, "Emergence," p. 351. [48] *Ibid.*, p. 345. [49] *Ibid.*

[50] There is a limit by virtue of the potentialities of the lower levels. At the same time, these represent novel possibilities with respect to direction. *Ibid.*, pp. 350–351.

development of three distinct forms of inference in the history of science, McMullin identifies a plot line which demonstrates how retroduction is a response to the quest for explanatory understanding. McMullin maintains that this understanding reached by retroductive inference was operative as a search for causal explanation from the beginning. Indeed, this finality was present in data about how knowing occurs in deductive reasoning. Deductive reasoning held until someone recognized another set of regularities involved in the act of reasoning that could not be accounted for simply by the procedures of deductive reasoning. McMullin refers to a "Progressive elaboration of specific structures."[51] Retroduction identified not only the emergence of the complex process of method in modern science – it also identified an orientation in the acts of thinking and knowing present in the original data of seeking explanation. A normative power of intelligibility is evident in earlier understanding. In this respect, Stoeger writes, "If there were no end-directed, or end-seeking, behavior in physical reality, there would be no regularities, functions, or structures about which we could formulate laws of nature."[52]

My aim in this section was to bring into focus the relationship between our understanding of the cosmic world and the emergence and development of scientific disciplines. The power of modern science resides in its capacity to develop intelligible understanding and their verifications. While some would regard this as a form of abstraction, our aim was to underscore, in continuity with our opening reflections based on the work of Ernan McMullin, that such understanding both enriches and enlarges our comprehension of the concrete world. We now return to our question: How does this contribute to our understanding of *creatio ex nihilo* and dual causality? If what we have just outlined has some merit, a clue to the response is to return to *human understanding at work* and ask about the presence of disciplines which define yet expand the horizons developed by modern science. In short, does the world of verified intelligibilities identified and opened up by modern science lend itself to further

[51] McMullin, "Enlarging the Known World," p. 106.

[52] William R. Stoeger, "The Immanent Directionality of the Evolutionary Process, and Its Relationship to Teleology" in Robert John Russell, William R. Stoeger, and Francisco J. Ayala (eds.), *Evolutionary and Molecular Biology: Scientific Perspectives on Divine Action* (Vatican City State: Center for Theology and the Natural Sciences, 1998), pp. 163–190, at p. 187. At this juncture a series of questions that deal with emergence, supervenience, top–down causality, non-linear causality, analysis and synthesis, reductionism, etc. present themselves. However, these would be questions to pursue in another reflection.

horizons of meaning? Our reflections both on the structure of scientific inquiry and on the order and emergence of disciplines reflect, in my judgment, a further question regarding intelligibility. Modern science enlarges our understanding of the world. Still, such understanding can ask not only about the world as it manifests itself but also about the very fact of its existence, namely, that there is a world. Here the very notion of origin attested to by the notion of *creatio ex nihilo* comes into play. Given this affirmation and consistent with our reflections on the developments in the diversity of sciences themselves, it remains possible to inquire whether there exist explanatory conjugate terms which define a further discipline whose aim is to reflect on the intelligibility of such an originating relationship itself. With these considerations in mind, I turn to the third and final part of this chapter.

PART III: *CREATIO EX NIHILO* AND THE INTELLIGIBILITY OF DUAL CAUSALITY

The aim of this part is to bring the elaborations of the first two parts to bear on the subject of *creatio ex nihilo* and dual causality. The fundamental issue here is whether there is a further intelligibility to be discerned in the same concrete data, the same world, which is investigated by the natural sciences. To recall Stoeger's question, "How can we have two adequate agents causing the same effect?" The aim of the previous two parts was to identify the framework within which a response to this question is possible. In general, both consisted in inviting us to reconsider our presuppositions about the meaning of causality and, at the same time, to advert to the work of intelligibility that governs the patterns of inquiry adopted by modern science. In order to bring the resources of these investigations to bear on an answer to our question, I shall proceed in three steps. First, I shall identify in very brief terms our understanding of the implications of *creatio ex nihilo* as the backdrop to our question. In the second and third steps, I shall draw upon two directions of thought Stoeger has elaborated which arise from the notion of *creatio ex nihilo* and attempt to show how both relate to reflections on causality as they arose in the first two parts of this chapter. These directions consist of a reflection on contingency with respect to ultimate intelligibility or primary cause and a reflection on secondary causality with respect to God's sustained presence to creation as primary cause.

(a) *Creatio ex nihilo: a brief overview*

Historically speaking, the notion of *creatio ex nihilo* emerged as a response to the challenges presented by Gnostic speculations.[53] According to a seminal study by Gerhard May,[54] *creatio ex nihilo* aimed to affirm two fundamental tenets: that God was omnipotent; that matter was not evil. The first of these tenets denied that there exists in the act of creation any other power or any other material than God's own desire and God's effective Word that this universe be. God alone in God's omnipotence is the origin of creation. The second tenet affirms the integrity and goodness of this world as a world in its own autonomous relation with God. In his work entitled *The Gift of Being*, Zachary Hayes cites a passage from St. Augustine in which Augustine explains that the world was created *de nihilo*, that is, it was not created *from* the Trinity.[55] Were such the case, the world itself would be both eternal and divine. The phrase "from nothing" was also intended, then, to maintain that the world exists as world, distinct from God in its own integrity as world such that a real relation is possible between the world and God. The history of theological reflection has clearly borne out that neither of these tenets implied an attempt to explain the temporal beginnings of the universe. The refined form of questioning about time in Augustine's celebrated *Confessions* already understood that the world was not created *in time*. Time itself, for Augustine, is co-extensive with the act of creation, for there never was a time which existed prior to the creation of our universe. God neither creates nor acts in time. Some seven hundred years later, Aquinas further elaborated upon the notion of creation by claiming that creation was fundamentally an intelligibility about a relation established by God by virtue of which the universe is both called into existence in its own autonomy as world, and sustained by God's abiding fidelity to this relation.[56] At issue is the foundation and meaning of the very *existence* of the world. The world is pure generosity and gift! For the purpose of our own investigation in this chapter, the basic feature of our world that

[53] See other chapters in the present volume for a more detailed discussion of the origin of this doctrine in the three Abrahamic faiths.

[54] Gerhard May, *Creatio ex Nihilo: The Doctrine of "Creation out of nothing" in Early Christian Thought* (Edinburgh: T&T Clark, 1994).

[55] Zachary Hayes, *The Gift of Being: A Theology of Creation*, New Theology Studies 10 (Collegeville: Liturgical Press, 2001), p. 44.

[56] A.-D. Sertillanges, *L'Idée de Création et Ses Retentissements en Philosophie* (Paris: Montaigne, 1945).

arises from these theological affirmations is that this concrete universe of ours is a contingent one. What are the implications of this?

William Stoeger in his own reflections on *creatio ex nihilo* has, as a result of such qualifications, identified two basic directions coming out of *creatio ex nihilo*.[57] The first concerns the way in which *creatio ex nihilo* brings into play the question of ultimate cause; the second concerns the way in which it brings into play the relationship between ultimate cause and all contingent events. I shall take up each of these topics in turn.

(b) Creatio ex nihilo *and ultimate cause*

The question arises from our previous qualifications regarding temporal beginnings. Once we begin to understand that *creatio ex nihilo* is not focused on temporal beginnings, we also understand that we are engaged in questions about a different order of meaning. My presentation, in the first part of the chapter, on the history of inference was intended to bring to the fore how the very question of causality itself is co-extensive with the developments within the history of science. Given the historicity of reason, we deepen our appreciation of how human understanding itself is intrinsically contingent. As contingent it depends upon fulfilling conditions just as, in its own understanding of the universe, it recognizes the contingency of structured patterns of relationships that define any event.

But this experience both of the contingency of modern science and of the world only begs, as Stoeger argues, a further question. Is all understanding and reality merely contingent reality? A more radical question confronts us. While modern science identifies fulfilling conditions, is there a further intelligibility about the work of intelligibility? The same question concerns the nature of our world. McMullin has demonstrated that retroductive inference moves from data through theory to affirmation. Data as pure data is without intelligibility. Why? Because intelligibility and its affirmations are based not simply on data but on a complex pattern of operations that relate data to affirmation. To admit that something is purely data and leads to no further questions is to affirm that it is without potential meaning. Thus, we ask: What about our world, the world investigated by modern science? Is it just "there"? Is it assumed to

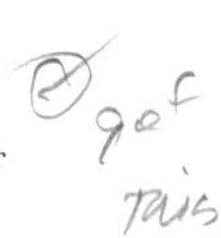

[57] William R. Stoeger, "The Origin of the Universe in Science and Religion" in Henry Margenau and Roy Abraham Varghese (eds.), *Cosmos, Bio, Theos: Scientists Reflect on Science, God, and the Origins of the Universe, Life, and Homo Sapiens* (La Salle, IL: Open Court, 1992) pp. 254–269, at pp. 257–261.

be simply another contingent piece of data? Or does it admit of intelligibility? The answer lies within the act of scientific inquiry. The whole work of modern science is grounded on the premise of intelligibility. It is at this point, however, that Stoeger identifies a limit to modern science. Modern science as science does not raise the question of existence as such. But what can? Only a science whose subject of investigation admits this kind of question. Here the notion of *creatio ex nihilo* presents itself anew. But we must be careful.

Such a notion, if it is to be conceived as a response to this further question, is, as Stoeger further suggests, of an entirely different order of causality, one more radical and basic. Why? If it itself is not to be simply a further moment in the intelligibility of contingent existence, it must not fall within contingent existence. It is that of which no further contingency is to be predicated. In other words, it is ultimate and originary cause, one which requires no further explanation and one for which there is no further reason in light of which it is to be understood. We reach the point at which theologically speaking we refer to God as Creator. Once again, in order to comprehend the deeper significance of this, it is important to keep our eye on our reflections on intelligibility and the work of meaning. Stoeger re-emphasizes the distinct kind of meaning at work here. "It should be clear, furthermore, that this primacy is fundamentally *logical* or *ontological* primacy."[58] *Creatio ex nihilo* affirms that there is no other condition, no other power, by virtue of which this act brings about our own universe. Why? Because there is no other source to the act of existence other than its own existence. Were this not so, we would fall back into contingent existence. Once again, the analogue for our understanding of *creatio ex nihilo* does not come from adverting to the findings of modern science as such; rather, it comes from adverting to the operations of understanding employed in the acts of inquiry. Our account of and reflection on retroduction has shown that existence is affirmed as a term, an end point, in the complex movement and act of inference.

Given this, Stoeger adverts to another direction of thought opened up by a reflection on *creatio ex nihilo*. It is one which affirms not only the contingency of all reality upon this ultimate cause, but also the ongoing relation of this primary cause to all contingent conditions. Our remarks on retroduction are helpful once more, for retroduction is not just another theory about the pattern of scientific inquiry. The force of retroduction is

[58] Stoeger, "Origin of the Universe," p. 258.

its capacity both to clarify earlier initiatives in the history of inference and to clarify in what way a concrete act of inquiry rises up to the standards of scientific investigation. To affirm the primacy of such a structured explanatory operation is also to see it at work in all concrete and particular investigations. Analogously, the same relation concerns the relationship between primary and secondary causality and to this topic we now turn.

(c) Primary cause and secondary causality

It is one thing to affirm that God is the ultimate cause of all that is and it is one thing to affirm that, as ultimate cause, God's creative act continues to abide with and sustain all creation. It is another thing to attempt to understand how this agency sustains the integrity of all the contingent causes known and affirmed by modern science. Ours is not the first time in the course of intellectual history this question has come to the fore. Christian thinkers throughout the early Middle Ages wrestled with the paradox of, on the one hand, affirming the integrity of human freedom while, on the other hand, affirming that God is the source of all that is good. In a formal way, the question of dual causality raised in the context of the developments of modern science brings this question into a new arena. In a masterful study on *Divine Initiative*,[59] Michael Stebbins has studied the kinds of insights and speculative achievements among the debates on freedom and grace which met the question head on and opened the avenues for deeper understanding. Given the formal similarity of the questions and the limits of this chapter, it is helpful to identify and to explore a number of key insights in Stebbins' work which identified the source of the problem and the lines of a solution. We shall take up these two issues in turn, namely overcoming commonsense thinking on causality and a clarification of the meaning of relation and movement. As we proceed, we shall begin to see the relevance of the reflections undertaken in the second part of this chapter for addressing the subject of dual causality.

(c1) An ambiguity

At the core of the problem, there remain a number of ambiguities surrounding the notion of causality itself. In spite of the refined understandings of modern science, we continue to labor under commonsense

[59] J. Michael Stebbins, *The Divine Initiative: Grace, World-Order, and Human Freedom in the Early Writings of Bernard Lonergan* (University of Toronto Press, 1995), pp. 212–252.

understanding when we imagine causality. This ambiguity is grounded in an unfortunate habit on our part of constantly imagining that causality involves an influx, or seriated and immediate relationships whereby one body impacts and has a consequent effect on another body.[60] We imagine, for example, that if *B* occurs, then there was a cause *A*. We further complexify the situation by further imagining that if *A* causes *B*, then it does so by virtue of something that happens "in between" *A* and *B*. Thus, we introduce a third link in the relation, *C*. With this in mind, then, we continue to ask, what, consequently, is the cause? Did *A* really cause *B*? Or was it *C*, which appears to be a force more proximate to *B* than to *A*? We are drawn into a tangled web of images which override in many ways the work of intelligibility to which I have just alluded. How do we refine our understanding?

Let us recall that at each step in our investigation, whether in commenting on McMullin and the virtues of retroductive inference, or whether just recently in affirming the role of ultimate cause, the emphasis was placed on a methodic issue: we are dealing with orders of intelligibility. Indeed, so significant is this for the work of modern science that Frank Budenholzer remained insistent, even in addressing scientists, that we advert to the difference between a commonsense understanding of reality – the world as consisting of smaller and smaller particles – in contrast to a scientific and explanatory understanding which relies on verified intelligibilities. Moreover, one of the keys in moving to the level of verified intelligibilities is to refine our comprehension of relations, their structured patterns (retroduction) and their recurrent schemes (verified intelligibilities).

Quite intriguingly for Stebbins, a similar insight regarding the nature of relation was what in the Middle Ages, most noteworthy in the work of Thomas Aquinas, effected a solution to the paradox and enigmas associated with claiming the integrity of human freedom in light of God's effective work of grace. The same commonsense images about influxes or imagined proximate relations continued to plague the debates. If both human beings and God cooperate in the effecting of some good, then it was thought that in some way God had to elevate human freedom (grace) in order to effect a good that was beyond the capacity of human beings to realize. But Aquinas rejected this solution since it comprised an approach that compromised the integrity and nature of human agency. Just as we today attempt to respect the integrity and autonomy and processes of

[60] On what follows, see Stebbins, *The Divine Initiative*, pp. 221–227.

nature, so too did Aquinas desire to protect the "natural" integrity of human freedom. To overcome the difficulty, Stebbins demonstrates how Aquinas reconceived the intelligibility of relations such that it was possible first to distinguish between originary cause and secondary or instrumental causes, and second to nuance the meaning of movement.[61]

(c2) Relation and movement

One of the examples provided is that of a sculptor working with a chisel on a piece of wood. What effects the sculpture? To be sure, the sculpture is realized through the work of a chisel. But, at the same time, the chisel is far from the primary efficient cause of the final work of art. The work of art itself is better the result of the artful imagination and technical skill of the sculptor. To be sure, this is a simplistic example. Nonetheless, it serves to highlight a couple of features relevant for our understanding of relations. First, it is possible to affirm that the chisel does effect the cutting of the wood such that a sculptured object begins to take form. That is, the chisel remains a tool and in no way is elevated to act beyond the intrinsic properties of its own nature. The reader should not at this point jump to the conclusion that human beings would be conceived as mere tools or instruments. Aquinas, let us recall, was attempting to preserve the integrity of human freedom as action and agency. The issue here is that whatever acts does so according to the integrity of its own nature. In our example, then, it is the sculptor who, in a real sense, is the primary cause of the work of art, although not the most immediate agent (the chisel) in a series of linkages. It belongs more properly to an artist to effect a work of art.

There is a further point. It concerns a structured pattern of relations and it serves to assist us in understanding how some agency may be said to effect what surpasses it. Here we come back to the notion of the ultimate cause as origin and the sustaining presence of that cause throughout creation. As Stoeger emphasized, God is not only the intelligible ground of what exists – God also sustains creation in its existence. In other words, in the act of creation a movement is initiated in such a way that things by virtue of their own capacity for relationships tend to promote all kinds of encounters. There is no sculpture if there is no set of conditions whereby the chisel comes in contact with wood. Fire, purely by itself, does not burn down buildings. Both fire and material have to be

[61] On the following, see Stebbins, *The Divine Initiative*, pp. 237–248.

brought into some proximity one to the other: do bring fire into proximity with wood, and something disproportionate to fire as agent occurs. Once again, these are simple examples. But at a more sophisticated level, is this not the kind of intelligibility that emerges when we advert once again to Budenholzer's account of the different sciences and their distinct explanatory conjugates?

Physics, chemistry and biology are distinct disciplines. Each possesses its own explanatory conjugates. The emergence of chemistry in relation to physics is the result of identifying a different set of explanatory conjugates that allow for the identification of different explanatory structures. At the same time, chemistry takes up within its own understandings the results of physics, and biology, for its part, takes up in its own understanding the results of chemistry. Still, in neither case is the integrity of either physics or chemistry diminished. This is validated if we look in the reverse direction: biology cannot be completely explained by chemistry, nor can chemistry be completely explained by physics. Indeed, modern science has provided us with an empirical understanding of how we constantly work with an intelligibility of relations which overcomes our commonsense notions of cause. The truth of any thing is the full and differentiated account of the total set of explanatory relations. Moreover, as science develops through the enacting of its particular disciplines, it increasingly develops a capacity to sublate such intelligibilities within increasingly complex forms of organized reality.

But there is one further characteristic about these structure patterns of relations. Whatever the distinct science adopted is, it remains a question of an insight or an intelligibility discovered in the same data. It is a remarkable thing that we can work with different levels of intelligibility when examining the same reality!

This then brings us back to the question that faces us when we take up the topic of dual causality. Is there an intelligibility, a more radical intelligibility, in light of which we can comprehend something of the fuller presence of order and intelligibility in the universe? In response, I wish to propose a qualified "yes." The qualification is needed in respect to contingent understanding. The first qualification concerns the difference between unconditioned and conditioned (contingent) reality. As Stoeger continues to emphasize, we are dealing with a notion of primary cause which is unlike any other meaning of cause identified by the investigations of modern science. *Creatio ex nihilo* refers to a cause which is the very foundation of existence itself and by virtue of which there is any existence, any reality whatsoever. In this sense, we reach a point at which explanatory conjugates are called for that are appropriate to that level of intelligibility, one radically different from those of the natural sciences. This, then, brings us back to the intelligibility of existence as such. Second, we recall that this affirmation is insufficient. The second qualification turns to the relationship between the agency that predicates existence and the secondary agencies of the "natural" structured patterns of relationships (secondary causes) which are respected in their own integrity. In Stebbins' account of the medieval Thomistic solution a key ingredient was a further precision about movement. The ultimate cause effects existence in virtue of a dynamism, a movement, integral to the operations of creation itself. All things, by reason of their own intrinsic nature, their own agency, represent a capacity for relationships which in turn becomes the fulfilling conditions for effective existence. This is what the sciences know and study.

Still, this knowledge and study constantly abide with the underlying conviction that all this is indeed and in fact intelligible. It is not scientific understanding itself which accounts for the intelligibility among the relationships or what order emerges by virtue of these relations. That is a matter of the inherent intelligibility of the order inscribed at the very heart of existence. To the extent to which such verified intelligibility is what, according to Budenholzer, is affirmed, it is also affirmed in light of an abiding trust in the presence and anticipation of order. But that order only can be found if it in turn participates in existence, for that is precisely what is affirmed. This brings us to a twofold conclusion. First, all such intelligibility ultimately has its source in what is intelligible, that is, in the source of existence. Second, the very ordering that is effected by this primary cause is effected in the very movements themselves of contingent realities. There is no third thing "in between." To the extent to which primary cause is the source of existence, it effects its own work in the actual structured patterns of relationships through which is realized the ordering of the world.[62] The universe, in the light of faith, is God's work of creation.[63] In my view,

[62] In a recent article David Burrell has made this point with respect to his reading of Aquinas, namely, that the work of creation is precisely in the ordering work itself: "think [writes Burrell] of creating as an ordering." Further, "The bestowal of being by the first cause is an orderly bestowal, yielding an inherent order structuring each existing thing so that higher levels are implicit in lower." David B. Burrell, "Aquinas's Appropriation of *Liber De Causis* to Articulate the Creator as Cause-of-Being" in Fergus Kerr (ed.), *Contemplating Aquinas: On the Varieties of Interpretation* (London: SCM Press, 2003), pp. 75–83, at p. 78.

[63] "[I]n the light of faith, originating value is divine light and love, while terminal value is the whole universe," Bernard Lonergan, *Method in Theology* (New York: Herder, 1972), p. 116.

we have the basic elements for exploring how we can identify two causes. First, the primary agency of God who, as ultimate cause, effects a universe. The work of the universe as a whole is disproportionate to any agency in the order of contingent reality. Second, we continue to affirm the integrity of the full set of structured patterns of relationships, the concrete contingent activities proper to both natural and personal agencies that give form to the order of *this* world.

CONCLUSION

I began by examining the meaning of the shift from deduction to retroduction and its impact on the notion of causality. Deductive inference's conception of a tight relationship between cause and effect anticipated a determined and necessary order. The loosening up of that relationship, first by radicalizing presuppositions inherent in deductive reasoning and second by re-establishing scientific inquiry on a methodic basis more supple, flexible and open to learning, in turn set the conditions for a heightened philosophical awareness. The suppleness and flexibility has offered new opportunities for retrieving virtues of analogical understanding and exploring its resources in the light of new challenges facing intellectual investigation and inquiry. This capacity for inquiry and learning, attuned to the complexities of the cosmos, is an anticipation of a fullness of understanding inscribed within our contingent acts of inquiry. Theological insight in the origin of such fullness and its promise takes nothing away from the integrity of scientific understanding. On the contrary, it offers a foundation upon which scientists desire to commit themselves to the integrity and virtues of authentic learning.

CHAPTER 13

God and creatures acting: the idea of double agency

Thomas F. Tracy

INTRODUCTION

One important consequence of the idea that God creates the world "out of nothing" is that no finite entity or event falls outside the scope of God's action and purpose. Jews, Christians and Muslims, each in their own context, affirm that God is at work in all things. There are of course many questions raised by this claim, including the deep challenge presented by suffering and evil. I want to focus here on an underlying issue that has implications for a wide range of theological concerns: How should we understand the relation of God's creative action and the activity of creatures? In working out a response to this question, theological discussion has given rise to the idea of "double agency," i.e., the idea that a single event can simultaneously be ascribed to the activity both of God and of a created cause or finite intentional agent. The origins of this concept lie deep in the doctrine of creation, and so we begin our exploration there.

CREATION AND DIVINE ACTION

The concept of creation has been developed in a variety of ways across its long history in multiple religious and philosophical contexts. There are, however, three key elements in what came to be the dominant formulation of this idea in Jewish, Islamic and Christian thought.

First, God's creative act accounts for the very being of the creature, and apart from this act there would be nothing other than God. This is the definitive move in the doctrine of *creatio ex nihilo*, creation out of nothing. God is not limited to working with given materials, burdened by the task of imposing order on a recalcitrant primordial chaos. Rather, the divine creative activity is constrained by nothing outside God's own nature. This stands in fundamental contrast to all creaturely creativity. Created things operate as causes by inducing *change* in other things; this is true even of the activities we typically speak of as bringing something into existence (e.g., evolutionary processes creating new species; an artist creating a painting) or as causing something to cease to exist (by bringing about destruction and death). God's creative act, however, does not produce a change in the creature since apart from this divine action there is no creature to change; it endows things with their existence. This act is unique to God alone. It cannot be assimilated into any of our familiar ways of thinking and speaking about creativity within the world, but rather accounts for the existence of the entire system of relationships within which finite acts of creation occur.

Second, creation is not a one-time event that bestows upon the creature a capacity to exist on its own. Creation is a continuous relation of ontological dependence; each finite thing, with all its essential and accidental properties, is immediately sustained, or conserved, by God at every moment. This direct giving of being is the founding relation of God to creatures, and it is independent of whether the world has a beginning. A temporally eternal world, no less than a world that is finite backward in time, depends at every moment of its history on the creative activity of God. Probably the most widespread and persistent misunderstanding of the idea of creation is that it had to do principally with how the world began.

Third, creation is a free and intentional divine act. God does not require the creature; on the contrary, God is God quite without created things. God creates for the sake of the creature, because it is good for the creature to be. God's creative action, therefore, is an expression of divine generosity, a sharing of the richness of God's being with finite things. This stands in contrast to accounts of creation as a necessary expression of the divine nature. One important historical rival to the idea of purposive creation is the Neoplatonic conception of an involuntary and unknowing emanation of being from the One source of all. In such schemes, the One does not choose and intend that there be a world of finite things, but rather gives rise to the world as a side effect of its own plentitude of being.

From this understanding of creation it follows that God is universally, continuously and purposefully at work in the activity of created things. There can be no distinction between events in which God acts and those in which God does not; God acts in every event in the world's history. Here we have the core idea of double agency; the action of creatures is also the action of God. Having said this, however, we immediately confront a tangle of difficult questions about how to understand this relation between God's creative action and the diverse activities of created things. The theological issues that arise here are of central importance and are matters of long-standing controversy. In the discussion that follows I will consider two ancient puzzles about the God–world relation and explore some of the options in addressing them.

IS GOD THE ONLY CAUSE?

The first of these puzzles concerns the causal powers of created things. It might be thought that the classical conception of *creatio ex nihilo* entails that God alone is causally efficacious, and that the activity of creatures serves only as the occasion for divine action. An "occasionalism" of this sort has been defended by various Islamic thinkers (e.g., by al-Ashari in the ninth century and al-Ghazali in the eleventh century), and most famously in the West by Nicolas Malebranche in the philosophical aftermath of Cartesian mind–body dualism.

(a) An occasionalist argument

It is not difficult to recognize the way such an argument might go. If God brings about the existence of each creature along with all its properties, then it appears that there is no role for finite causes in accounting for the way things are in the world. Consider a simple causal interaction: a stone tumbles into a pond and ripples spread across the surface. It appears that our account of creation requires that we say that God brings about the existence of the stone and each of its properties (e.g., its mass, position and momentum) and the existence of the water with its properties (e.g., its surface tension and wave structure). But then we may be forced to the conclusion that all the work has been done by God, and that the causal relation between the stone and the water reduces to a succession of changing properties each of which is the immediate effect of God's activity. In that case, the stone does not disturb the surface of the water; rather God's creative act brings it about that there is a stone with the property of tumbling into the water at one moment, and that there is a pond whose surface displays a wave form at the next moment. If God's actions are consistent across time, then events will fall into patterns of constant conjunction that we take to be causal relations, just as Hume argued. But these regularities in the order of events will be all that causality comes to on the created level.

(b) Divine action through created causes

How should we reply to this occasionalist argument? Its key inference is that, if God is the source of the being of things, then God must cause each entity to possess each of its properties. This initially sounds right; it makes no sense to say that God creates finite things without creating the various properties that make them what they are. Some caution is needed here, since we are in the near neighborhood of fundamental metaphysical questions regarding what sorts of things there can be. We should not assume an ontology that permits only fully determinate and sharply individuated objects (especially given the oddly indeterminate but well-defined entities described by quantum mechanics and the peculiar puzzles about individuation raised by the phenomenon of quantum entanglement). Whatever the shape of an adequate ontology, however, it is unlikely to include finite entities that exist but have no differentiating properties at all (not even the property of being a structure of potentialities). So let us grant that it is unintelligible to speak of God bringing about bare existents, existing things that are nothing in particular. We can accept this principle, however, and still resist the occasionalist conclusion.

Consider the following assertions:

(1) God causes the existence of an entity E (e.g., the pond).

(2) E possesses the property P (e.g., a spreading wave pattern on its surface).

Does it follow from these two premises that:

(3) God causes E to possess P?

It may appear that we must say so, since God's activity as Creator *ex nihilo* lies at the foundation of every state of affairs (such as E being P) in the world. But we also want to say that God has made a world in which created causes make a difference, e.g., the falling stone disturbs the surface of the pond.

We can reconcile these two claims by making a distinction between what God does directly without intermediaries, and what God does indirectly by means of created causes. God's action of giving being to finite things is direct, universal and unique to God alone. This act does not, as we have seen, cause a change in the creature, but rather posits in existence the finite subject of change. God could also induce changes in creatures, causing them to have their particular properties, just as occasionalism suggests. But God need not do so. Rather, God may choose to grant causal powers to created things,[1] so that in their interactions they affect and are affected by each other. As Aquinas puts it, "Divine providence works through intermediaries. For God governs the lower through the higher, not from any impotence on his part, but from the abundance of his goodness imparting to creatures also the dignity of causing."[2]

[1] For a discussion of primary and secondary causality in relation to creation *ex nihilo* see W. Stoeger's and J. Pambrun's chapters in this volume.

[2] *Summa Theologiae* 1.22.3.

This makes it clear why (3) need not follow from (1). There are two profoundly different senses of "causality" involved here. God directly causes the existence of every entity, along with all their properties and relations, *ex nihilo*. But God can indirectly cause an entity to possess a particular property through the order of created causes. So from

(1) God *directly* causes the existence of an entity E, and

(2) E possesses the property P,

it does not follow that

(3) God *directly* causes E to possess P.

This will be true even if P is an essential property of E, i.e., a property without which E could not exist. In this case, God cannot create E without P, but God may nonetheless provide that E comes to be P through the operation of created causes. Precisely this is what is involved in creation and destruction on the creaturely level, as I noted above. Within the processes of nature individuals are "created," in the sense that new configurations of matter and energy arise (and perish), but this does not involve generating new beings *ex nihilo*.

This account of the relation between God as the primary creative cause (i.e., the cause of being) and creatures as secondary instrumental causes (i.e., causes of change) allows us to clarify the idea of double agency by distinguishing the senses in which God and creatures may both be said to act in a single event. When a created cause brings about an effect (e.g., a stone causes a ripple in a pond), the action can be attributed to God in two respects. First, the Creator acts directly in and with every action of the creature as its sustaining ontological ground. This action, of course, belongs to God alone, and the creature's existence and operation is its effect. Second, we can also say that God acts by means of the action of created causes, and we can attribute the effects of these causes to God as divine acts.

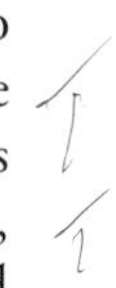

This second point deserves further comment. Intentional agents often do one thing (traveling to Castel Gandolfo) by doing another (buying a ticket, driving to an airport, boarding an airplane). Under a wide variety of circumstances we are prepared to ascribe the final effect to the agent as their act, even though there may be a number of intermediate steps between the action that the agent initiates (their basic action) and the outcome they eventually obtain. The same pattern can be applied to divine action through created intermediaries. An effect produced through the operation of a series of natural causes may also be attributed to God as a divine action; this will be the preeminent example of one agent acting by means of another. We human agents often fail to achieve what we intend, and generate instead various effects that we do not want – hence the comedy and tragedy of human action. Knowing this, we adopt as a description of one another's *intentional* actions: (a) only some of the ends we seek, setting aside those that are unlikely to be achieved through the means we have adopted (e.g., saving the whales by putting a bumper sticker on my car); and (b) only some of the outcomes that we produce, setting aside those that were not foreseen (e.g., infuriating a passing motorist who has a taste for whale meat). These constraints on the attribution of intentional action do not apply to the divine agent. God can arrange the world in such a way that all and only the effects that God intends will be produced through the operation of secondary causes, and all of these effects will be indirect divine actions.

Consider, for example, a perfectly deterministic world. According to determinism, every event throughout the entire history of the universe follows deductively from the conjunction of the laws of nature and a complete description of the state of things at any moment. By establishing the laws of nature and the initial, or boundary, conditions of the universe, God precisely specifies all that will occur. Every event in this world, therefore, will be an indirect act of God (and of course the existence of this world at every moment will be a direct act of divine creativity *ex nihilo*). The emergence of intelligent life on earth after some 13 billion years of cosmic history will be just as much an act of God as if God had "intervened" to produce this result directly, rather than bringing it about through the system of natural causes that God created and sustains *ex nihilo*.[3] This provides a simple (as we will see, *too* simple) model of double agency, a model in which created causes serve as God's instruments in bringing about the effects that God intends.

(c) *God and chance*

This account must be modified in important ways if we work with a more sophisticated picture of the world that God has made. Suppose, for example, that the world includes some events that occur by chance, where this is understood not just as epistemic chance (i.e., unpredictability) but as ontological chance (i.e., the event has necessary but not sufficient conditions in the prior history of the world). What is God's relation to these chance events? We can briefly explore two intriguing issues here.

First, chance events, like all finite things, are effects of God's direct creative agency. But a change in the properties of things that occurs by

[3] So, from this theological perspective, the debate about "intelligent design" is not so much about *whether* intelligent life is the effect of divine action as about *how* God acts to bring this about.

chance cannot, by definition, be given a sufficient explanation in terms of the operation of secondary causes (e.g., the measured spin orientation or momentum or position of an electron is not, on most interpretations of quantum mechanics, determined by the antecedent state of the system). Can it make sense to say that God causes the existence of a state of affairs (e.g., the electron being spin up) that has no sufficient cause? We can quickly dismantle this apparent paradox by recalling that "cause" is used in two quite different senses here, namely, to designate God's act of giving being *ex nihilo* in the first instance, and to indicate creaturely causation of change in the second. So we say that God creates an entity (the electron) that undergoes a transition (from a probabilistic mix of spin values to a specific measurement) that is not determined by secondary causes.

But what exactly does God create in this case? The concept of creation entails that God gives being to each entity with all its properties (to the electron in the act, we might say, of being spin up), and we have noted that God may act through secondary causes to fix those properties. In this instance, however, secondary causes do not determine the property in question. Does this mean that God's creative act specifies the property that is left undetermined within the order of nature (e.g., that God determines the outcome of the electron spin measurement, and indeed of every quantum wavefunction "collapse")? Or might God cause the existence of an entity that has one or more properties that are not determined either by secondary causes or by God? Perhaps we might think of God decreeing that there shall be an entity with one of a set of properties, and that nothing determines which member of that set becomes actual.[4] Here, causing being *ex nihilo* and causing the possession of a property are pulled apart in a striking way; God calls into being the state of affairs in which the entity possesses this property, but neither God nor creatures cause that entity to possess this property.

Second, if the world God has made includes events that are determined neither by created causes nor by God, then the ascription of these events to God as indirect divine acts will need to be qualified accordingly. The picture of indirect divine action that I first presented was deterministic, and in such a system every operation of creatures will enact God's specific purposes. Here the classical analogy of the craftsman wielding a tool is apt. But if this

[4] Peter van Inwagen suggests something like this in "The Place of Chance in a World Sustained by God" in Thomas V. Morris (ed.), *Divine and Human Action* (Ithaca, NY: Cornell University Press, 1988), pp. 211–235, at p. 229.

determinism is broken in some events, then God's intentional relation to them will be more complex, perhaps (as we just noted) taking the form of a permissive disjunction ("Let A or B or C come to pass"). And if these alternatives make a difference in the subsequent course of events, producing branching pathways that diverge over time, then the space of possibility for the world's history will be much more complex than on the deterministic account. This entire structure of possibility, of course, will be ordered by and embraced within God's purposes for creation. In a world of this sort, for example, it could be said that God makes use of both law and chance in establishing the conditions for the evolution of life. As a technique of indirect divine action, ontological chance provides flexibility and a capacity for novelty that a purely deterministic system would lack, but it also entails that God's intentions take a more complex, conditional form.

CREATION AND CREATURELY FREEDOM

We have been considering the implications of the idea of *creatio ex nihilo* for the relation of God's action and the activity of creatures. We have seen, first, that God's direct and continuous giving of existence to all finite things entails that God acts with creatures whenever they act. This is compatible with creatures operating as causes in their own right, interacting in the regular patterns that we endeavor to describe in the natural sciences. Second, because God establishes this structure of natural causality, the unfolding history of the world can be regarded as a vast and highly variegated indirect act of God carried out by means of created causes. The story we tell about the world's history as God's indirect act may need to be qualified, however, depending upon what role underdetermined chance plays within it. There is also, of course, a second important factor to consider in developing the idea that God as Creator acts by means of the actions of creatures; namely, some of those creatures may be rational free agents. The relation of divine action and human freedom is a notoriously difficult topic, and it is the subject of a long-standing debate that we cannot expect to resolve here, but we can identify some of the key issues and options.

(a) Two understandings of freedom

In contemporary philosophical discussion, there are two familiar and well-worn ways of understanding the claim that human beings are free agents. The first view holds that free action is incompatible with causal determination, and so is commonly called incompatibilism. One might be an incompatibilist and a determinist, and therefore deny that human agents ever act freely. The view that I will discuss affirms that we do sometimes act freely, and it therefore denies that our free actions are causally determined. It is important to note that the denial of determinism is merely a negative condition for freedom; roughly speaking, an agent cannot (on this account) be regarded as acting freely if causal laws and antecedent conditions entail that the agent undertakes this action. But while underdetermination is a necessary condition for freedom, it is not sufficient. Chance events also are underdetermined, but they are not free in the relevant sense. An agent's free action will be distinguished from a chance occurrence by the agent's self-determining intentional initiation of the action. The challenge facing incompatibilist understandings of freedom is to develop an account of agent self-determination and to explain its place in a world that appears to be structured everywhere else by non-intentional determining causes or by mere chance or by some combination of the two.

An alternative understanding of freedom contends that free action and causal determination are compatible. On accounts of this kind, a free intentional action just is one that comes about through the right sort of causal determination. The task for the compatibilist is to explain which pathways of causal necessitation constitute a free action. Various accounts of this can be given, but it is enough for my purposes to note, again roughly speaking, that a free action will be one that is caused (in the right way) by the agent's reasons for acting, e.g., their desires, beliefs, values and goals. The action will be free even if the mental states that cause it are themselves determined in every detail by the agent's prior history and environment. The action will be unfree if the agent is coerced, compelled or constrained to act as they do (i.e., to act "against their will").

There is a vast literature that develops and refines views of these two sorts and that carries on the debate between them. The abstract issue at stake between them, namely whether freedom is compatible with causal determination, is of central importance, but an exclusive focus on it will generate a truncated and one-dimensional understanding of human free agency. If, for example, we embrace an incompatibilist account of freedom, we must immediately go on to note the conditioning contexts within which this freedom actually is exercised. This will be particularly important in theological discussions. The concept of free will has a controversial history in Christian theology, and a simple assertion of freedom as the power of undetermined choice between alternatives will almost entirely miss the central issues that have preoccupied and perplexed the tradition as it has wrestled with these matters.[5] The moral psychology developed through the long history of these discussions has explored the ways in which our freedom is constrained and distorted in our shared, social entanglement in evil. We do not, on this account, possess an unencumbered capacity to recognize what is best, to prefer greater goods to lesser and to carry through on our moral judgments in action. While much of the theological tradition affirms that God has made us by nature lovers of the good, the mainstream of that tradition also observes that our loving is profoundly confused, misdirected and self-contradictory (and, worse, self-deceiving and perverse). We cannot readily induce ourselves to love that which is most worthy of love, even when we can glimpse it. Put in philosophical language, we could say that our first-order desires are not easily brought into conformity with our second-order assessments of them. Augustine's famous prayer makes this point well: "Lord make me chaste, but not yet." Our freedom, in short, is impaired in various ways, and it needs to be set free. So Christianity is a religion of redemption in which the free human agent is understood paradoxically to be bound and in need of liberation, of healing and of forgiveness.

The issues raised by these aspects of classical Christian theological anthropology are subtle and difficult. I think it is fair to say that, in thinking about human freedom, theologians have struggled both to acknowledge the ways in which our freedom is constrained and distorted, and to insist that individual moral responsibility is not lost. This is a difficult balance, and it would lead us far astray to explore the options in any detail here. But these issues need to be borne in mind in discussing the relation of divine action to free human action. If (and this is controversial, of course) we understand human freedom as damaged, but not altogether abrogated, then what might we say about God's relation as Creator and sustainer *ex nihilo* to the (compromised) free acts of rational creatures? It appears initially that there will be two options, parallel to the general philosophical alternatives of compatibilism and incompatibilism.

(b) *Theological compatibilism and incompatibilism*

The theological incompatibilist will hold that human action cannot be regarded as free if it is determined by God. This is not to deny, of course,

[5] This is an issue in discussions of the problem of evil, where defenses and theodicies tend to employ radically simplified pictures of the freedom of human agents. A more complex understanding of human freedom presents various difficulties for free-will arguments (e.g., considerations of moral responsibility must be more subtle and qualified), but such a theodicy will also be of greater theological relevance and interest.

that God's action is necessary for the free agent's action. As Creator, God directly sustains the finite agent *ex nihilo*, thereby acting at the foundation of that agent's every activity. God also acts indirectly through the processes of nature to bring it about that each finite intentional agent has its brief career within the vast history of the created universe. But on this view, if God chooses to make some of these agents free, then their free actions will be determined neither by the causal structures of nature, nor by God. God's goodness to creatures will include not only the gift of operating as causes in their own right (as we said in rejecting occasionalism), but also the gift of free intentional agency for finite persons. This entails, however, that they may act against God's purposes for them – or, more carefully expressed, that God's purposes include the permission of this moral freedom and encompass the tragic consequences of its misuse. In speaking not only of what God does, but also of what God permits, we introduce the idea of a free self-restraint in the uses of God's powers of action. The free actions of creatures, on this account, cannot be attributed without qualification to God as divine actions. God will act in and with the finite free agent as its Creator, but a description of what the finite agent intends cannot be taken as a description of God's act.

Accounts of this kind typically have generated theological worries about God's sovereignty and providential governance of history. One way to avoid such objections is to embrace theological compatibilism, which contends that human intentional actions can be both free and determined by God. This determination might take a number of different forms. God could, for example, so arrange the world that every action of each finite agent is determined by secondary causes. This view would combine philosophical compatibilism with an account of divine action according to which (as we noted above) the whole history of the universe is an extended indirect action of God carried out by means of establishing a deterministic natural order. Alternatively, God could leave finite agents underdetermined by the causal structures of nature, thereby securing the conditions for incompatibilist freedom on the created level, but determine action by moving the agent to their specific act. God might, for example, directly affect the preconditions of the agent's choice (e.g., their desires and beliefs) so as to assure that the agent acts in conformity with God's purposes. In this case, the finite agent is free to act on their preferences, adopting ends and choosing the means to achieve them, but what they prefer follows necessarily from God's will for them. God does not coerce the agent, but God does move the finite agent to act willingly as God intends. On this account, every free act of finite agents will be an indirect act of God.

(c) *A third way?*

There are reasons to be discontent with both of these options. If the first raises questions about God's sovereignty, the second makes God the agent of all evil. On this account, every appalling thing human beings do to each other must be attributed to God as an indirect but explicitly intended divine act. Is there a way out of these juxtaposed alternatives, a third analysis that escapes the limitations of these two?

Perhaps the idea of *creatio ex nihilo* points to a third way. The philosophical alternatives of compatibilism and incompatibilism are initially constructed in terms of the relations of intentional agents and their *natural* causal context, and we might therefore argue that neither appropriately characterizes the relation of God to free creatures. Given an affirmation of absolute creation, we cannot think of God as part of the causal nexus in which we worry about determinism and freedom. Rather, God is its source, the transcendent agent who continuously brings into being not only determining efficient causes but also chance events and free intentional agents. In "causing" these sorts of creatures to be, God does not act *upon* them, as though God were to be numbered among the forces producing change in the world. Instead, God's action *constitutes* them, bringing them about in the mode of operation appropriate to them. We might say that God's creative act posits secondary causes in the exercise of their capacity to affect and be affected by one another and, similarly, posits intentional agents in their free acts. There is, therefore, no need for God to restrict the divine activity in order to "make room" for free creatures, as the incompatibilist proposed. God acts at the metaphysical foundation of the free agent's existence; this divine action is internal to the creature's own activity, and cannot be treated as an external determining cause that interferes with the created agent's freedom. On the contrary, it is precisely God's creative act that brings it about that there is a finite agent acting freely.

Does this line of argument, which appeals to the transcendent character of God's agency as Creator *ex nihilo*, allow us to move beyond the juxtaposed alternatives of compatibilist and incompatibilist conceptions of freedom? It underscores the utterly unique nature of God's relation to the free creature, avoiding the mistake of supposing that God's action is of a piece with the secondary causal influences that provide the potentially determining conditions under which the human agent acts. It does not, however, free us from puzzles about determinism and freedom; instead, it relocates them at the level of this unique creative relation. This becomes apparent when we consider two questions.

First, we can ask what powers of action God calls into being in the finite agent. Does God's creative act fully specify the content of the finite agent's action? Or does God grant to the agent some capacity to determine its course of life? If we say the first of these things, then it is difficult to see why this does not constitute a form of determinism, albeit a distinctively theological one. Perhaps it might be replied that it is a mistake to draw a distinction between these two forms of divine action. What is specified in God's creative act is precisely the finite agent in its self-determining action. But what does freedom or self-determination amount to here? Suppose God wills that there be a finite intentional agent who freely undertakes an action. Because God's will is absolutely efficacious (indeed, God's willing is simply God's making it so), it follows necessarily that the agent freely undertakes the action. In what sense is this act free? Perhaps God creates an agent who wants to undertake this action and who does so precisely for that reason. So the action is free in the compatibilist sense. Further, it may be that the prior history of the universe up to the moment of the agent's choice is causally insufficient to produce this outcome; under just these finite causal conditions, the agent can either undertake this action or refrain from doing so. So the agent will be free in the incompatibilist sense on the created level. The agent's action, however, follows with necessity from God's creative will. It cannot be the case both that God wills that there be an agent who performs this action and that this does not occur. Of course, the agent is not compelled in any ordinary sense to act as they do, because God does not act upon them to make them perform this action. Rather God constitutes them as an intentional agent performing this action. So this is not the ordinary determination of a change in an individual through the operation of finite sufficient causes. This is determination of a distinctive theological kind, but it is determination nonetheless.

It may be helpful to consider two familiar analogies. God's relation to the finite agent has sometimes been compared to the relation between an author and the characters in the imaginative world of a novel. The author operates on a different level than the characters they create. As the author writes, the characters are constituted in their life circumstances and interactions; the author decides what scope of freedom they shall have and whether their actions will be tightly constrained by the conditions under which they act. Clearly the author's relationship to a character is not a determining relationship in the same way as the character's relationship to the narrative world may be. But surely the author–character relationship *is* deterministic, since every thought and word and deed of the character flows from the specifying creative act of the author.

Suppose we modify the analogy, and think instead of a playwright and a play. In this case, the characters that the author creates will be realized in a particular way by the actors who perform the play. A playwright might set out to specify every word and action in the production of the play and, if such a thing were possible, the dreary result would be a play that would have just one performance, however many times it was repeated. But playwrights do not operate in this deterministic way. They establish a dramatic narrative structure, and may in various degrees leave the details to the invention of actors and directors. Both the analogy of the author and that of the playwright capture the idea that the creative artist operates on a different level than the characters within the narrative, giving rise to them but not operating as one of them. Yet, in these analogies, the contrast between determinism and indeterministic freedom resurfaces, and we can ask which is more apt as an analogy for God's action.

Second, we must grapple with the troublesome fact of human sinfulness. On this third account of God's relation as Creator to free human acts, how should we understand failures of moral judgment and action, with all their disastrous consequences? It has frequently been said in theological discussions that sin is absurd, perhaps even an "impossible possibility."[6] But it is important to identify with some care what is unintelligible about sin; even among absurdities, distinctions can be made. We have, on the one hand, the inexplicable preference of the finite rational agent for a course of action that is irrational, a self-destructive resistance to one's own good. This enduring puzzle of the perverse will should not be conflated with another perplexity, namely, the self-contradiction generated by asserting that God's unobstructable will for the free creature is nonetheless obstructed. The latter is a conceptual incoherence that we would do well to avoid (though there are powerful theological considerations that may drive us toward this paradox, as can be seen, e.g., in Barth's discussion of the universal scope of God's saving action). Perhaps we could argue that sin is not so much an action as an omission, a refusal by the creature to realize in action God's will for it. But a conscious, resistant, stubborn omission *is* an action. If, on the other hand, this omission is involuntary or inadvertent or simply ignorant, then it is not culpable, and therefore is not sin. A moral psychology adequate to the actual complexity of human thought and feeling will recognize many subtle combinations of these options, as we find for example in willful ignorance or in well-defended self-deception. But the underlying dilemma will remain,

[6] As Barth puts it, for example, in *Church Dogmatics*, III/3, ed. G. W. Bromiley and T. F. Torrance (London: T&T Clark, 1960), paragraph 50.

and we can legitimately be pressed to affirm or to deny that free creatures are able to resist God's will for them.

In thinking about the relation of God as Creator *ex nihilo* to human action, therefore, we cannot avoid having to grapple with the distinction between compatibilist and incompatibilist accounts of freedom. If, in order to avoid depicting God as an intentional agent of evil, we acknowledge that free creatures can set themselves against God and their own good, then we affirm that God grants to them a scope of self-determination whose outcome is not fixed by God's creative will, and we embrace at least a limited theological incompatibilism. This does not commit us to any general claim that the action of God and of creatures is incompatible or that there is in general a "zero-sum" relation between them. On the contrary, the created agent depends utterly upon God's creative activity at every moment to sustain its being and its powers of action, including its capacity to determine some aspects of its own future. God wills that the agent exists and possesses this power of action, and God acts with the creature as it acts. But God's creative decree does not prescribe the agent's free action.

It is helpful here to note a parallel structure in our discussion of God's relation to finite efficient causes. God, we said, could bring about every change in creatures directly, but God chooses not to act in this way so that creatures may be causes of change in other creatures. So too, in creating the finite intentional agent, God could specify what the agent's act shall be. But God may choose not to do this in order that the created agent possess a limited power of self-determination.[7] The hazardous gift of creaturely moral freedom entails a voluntary divine forbearance that makes it possible to distinguish between what God does and what God permits.

(d) Double agency and free action

This will have implications for our account of double agency. We have already seen that every event, whether a deterministic causal sequence or a free intentional action, will be an act of God in the sense that God directly gives it being *ex nihilo*. We have also seen that the effects of created causes can properly be regarded as indirect acts of God carried out by means of the

[7] It is worth noting that this view does not, by itself, commit us to a Pelagian or semi-Pelagian account of the role of human freedom and divine grace in salvation. We can affirm that human agents possess the capacity to make at least some choices that are not determined by God's will, without also claiming that the creature's saving relationship with God falls within this scope of decision. It may be that in our moral choices we contribute to fashioning (and mis-fashioning) the self we become, but that the liberation and healing and final fulfillment of this self is a free gift that we receive.

structures of nature that God has established. What should we say about the free acts of finite agents? They too can often be regarded as indirect acts of God, but the relationship of divine and created agencies here will be considerably more subtle than in the case of deterministic causes. In an unimaginably rich variety of ways God will shape the conditions of free human action. God will act toward us indirectly through the processes of the natural world to which we belong and in which we live out our histories as agents. God may also act directly upon us and our world, engendering novel developments that would not have arisen had only secondary causes been at work (this may, but need not, take the form of a "miraculous intervention"). If we are free in the incompatibilist sense, then at least some of our actions are not determined by this ubiquitous divine action. But God's activity will be woven into our own more profoundly and intimately than we can comprehend, and so our actions can in various degrees properly be understood as indirect divine actions.

A number of imperfect analogies for this can be drawn from the relationships of human agents. We might, for example, think of the relation of God and free agents on the model of mutual cooperation in which two agents work together to achieve a result that can then be attributed to them both. The limitations of the analogy are obvious: The God–creature relation is radically asymmetrical, and God's action is internal to and constitutive of the creature in a way that the analogy cannot convey. Further, the analogy entails that each agent performs only part of the act, jointly applying themselves to the end they seek, whereas God as Creator is always the ground of the entire action, even when God acts through intermediaries. Nonetheless, the analogy is helpful in thinking about the ways in which God acts by means of our free actions, perhaps enlisting those actions in the services of purposes we at most dimly comprehend.

We can supplement this analogy by considering the subset of cooperative relationships in which one agent plays a primary role in enabling another to act. An interesting special case of this occurs when one person bestows on another a power of action that the recipient would not otherwise possess. I might, for example, authorize another to speak or act for me in some matter (e.g., by appointing that person as my official representative). Here the first agent's action changes the status of the second agent, and makes it possible for that agent to perform an action that would not otherwise be available to them. In one form of this relationship, the secondary agent's action then *is* the primary agent's action by proxy. (This is at work in some forms of priestly action.) In another version, the secondary agent's acts are given a standing they would otherwise lack, as in a grant of immunity. (Some theories of atonement and justification appear to involve an analogous relationship.) In either case, these analogies capture something of the constituting priority of divine action in relation to finite agents.

Perhaps the most familiar and useful analogies for subtly entangled agency can be drawn from interpersonal relationships. We recognize many ways in which our actions are deeply indebted to the actions of others. We learn from each other what we might do and become, what sorts of values might claim our loyalty, and how we might pursue the good. In these ways we profoundly shape one another's life projects. This is, of course, a morally complex and ambiguous phenomenon; we affect each other both for good and for ill and, notwithstanding our contemporary individualistic illusions, sin is a thoroughly social reality. But we also recognize that much of what is best in our own actions is made possible by the actions of others. Relationships of love are a primary instance of this; our loving is enabled by those who love us, and we may credit the generosity of the other's approach to us for evoking our response, even as we attribute our failures in love to ourselves. Something like this pattern can be recognized in discussions of divine grace and the human will, as we see for example in Augustine's *Confessions*. The God depicted here is intimately at work in every event of Augustine's life, so that the incipient love of God that takes shape in the rubble of a damaged human freedom is both God's gracious act and an expression of the human agent's own will. Here too we see the limits of analysis in philosophical theology: a well-constructed narrative can convey relationships not readily captured at the theoretical level, at least not without generating awkward antinomies.

All of these analogies inevitably fall short of communicating the intimacy and pervasiveness of God's action within and by means of our acts. When God is understood as the Creator of all things in the radical sense intended by *creatio ex nihilo*, all of our actions unfold within the universal sustaining and providential activity of God. In attempting to speak of the ways in which this ubiquitous divine action precedes, grounds and informs our own actions, we face difficult conceptual puzzles that are tied to controversial theological choices. Theological construction inevitably involves balancing contending considerations in a network of constraints of various sorts, e.g., conceptual, doctrinal, textual and practical. My aim here has been to identify some of the central conceptual issues associated with the classical theological affirmation that God's creative activity accounts for the very being of each creature at every moment. If we affirm the doctrine of *creatio ex nihilo*, then these issues will lie at the heart of our understanding of God's relation to the world.

CHAPTER 14

Thomas Aquinas on knowing and coming to know: the beatific vision and learning from contingency

Eugene F. Rogers, Jr.

(In memory of Chancellor Patricia Sullivan, with gratitude)

INTRODUCTORY REMARKS

Accounts of the history of science sometimes treat Thomas Aquinas as if he were someone interested in what we would now call natural science, but not very good at it. He does not advance an experimental method, and he is captive to Aristotle's notion of insight, or *epagoge*.[1] But Aquinas is clearly not someone who is much interested in natural science. He is not *trying* to carry out any experiments. He is not even trying to learn natural science in some other way, say by following the *Posterior Analytics*. Rather, he is supremely interested in human growth, in ethics, and therefore also in how human beings learn. He is interested in the beatific vision, in knowledge as a metaphor for complete happiness. And he is interested in the quite odd way (the incarnation) in which God graciously creates a continuity between those two discontinuous things, learning in this life and knowing in the next.[2] Learning in this life means learning from contingency. Knowing in the next life means seeing with God's own vision. They belong together only by a marvelous exchange: God enters

[1] *Epagoge* is sometimes dressed up as "induction," but in this chapter I focus on its phenomenological aspect, prominent in Aristotle and Aquinas, what we might call insight. For a survey both brief and magisterial, see Ernan McMullin, *The Inference that Makes Science* (Milwaukee, WI: Marquette University Press, 1992), esp. pp. 32–52. See also J. Pambrun's chapter in this volume. The present chapter, however, depends upon and extends the distinction among Thomistic genres offered in Alasdair MacIntyre, *First Principles, Final Ends, and Contemporary Philosophical Issues* (Milwaukee, WI: Marquette University Press, 1990). If the contribution of MacIntyre and others is to limit the relevance of the *Posterior Analytics* to textbook normal science rather than ongoing inquiry, the contribution of this chapter is to point to Aquinas' ethics for an account of how human beings learn from contingent circumstances.

[2] Aquinas, *Summa Theologiae* (hereafter *ST*), III.9.2–3.

contingency, that humans may enter beatitude; God learns, that humans may see. This is decidedly a theology of science, not a philosophy. You would not try to learn about the atom from Kuhn, or the history of science from Bohr. But you could learn a lot from both if you read them on what they are good at. What could we learn from Aquinas if we approach him on what interests him, on what he is good at? A few remarks are needed.

(a) Contingency, not *epagoge*. Aquinas is more interested in ethics than in speculative science, more interested in learning from contingency than in deduction from insight.[3] That means you might fairly develop an account of science-as-discovery not from Aristotle's *epagoge*, but from Aquinas' *ethics*, which contains his account of learning from contingency, even frailty, failure and error. In the work of Ernan McMullin, "retroduction" means the long process of thinking backwards from regular laws, by contrived experiment through new contrived experiment, to postulated entities and theories that could explain those regularities.[4] Nothing terribly like retroduction features in Aristotle's account of *episteme* in the *Posterior Analytics*. But that is not because the *Posterior Analytics* provides a rival account of scientific discovery – it is because it treats *episteme* as already established, like a textbook. Observing over a long period of time, thinking backwards from experience, and learning from contingent events do feature prominently in Aristotle, and even more in Aquinas, just not in the *Posterior Analytics*. They dominate Aquinas' psychology. It is a short step from experience to experiment, and from contingency to controlled contingency. Learning from contingency is the very part of Aristotle that interests Aquinas the most. It could be of great interest to historians and philosophers of science, because learning from contingency dethrones teleology even as it pays it lip service. Learning from contingency takes place over time; it attends to singulars; it approaches experiment. As its own subject of reflection, learning from contingency generated both Aristotle's most sustained theory, that of character, and his most elaborate theoretical entity, the habit.

For Aristotle, fortuitous happenings do not have a cause. For Aquinas, they do. When Aristotle's Fate becomes Aquinas' Providence, contingency receives a cause and an agent: God.[5] Providence becomes the

[3] This chapter depends heavily on John Bowlin, *Contingency and Fortune in Aquinas's Ethics* (Cambridge University Press, 1999). Bowlin does not apply his analysis to natural science.

[4] McMullin, *The Inference that Makes Science*, pp. 93–98.

[5] *ST* 1.93.5.

prudent law-giver whose law-giving is promulgating, making publicly known, making known to reason.[6] Anyone who reads these passages might object that they are not taking scientific laws as the model at all; they are talking about laws on the model of legislation. And yet that is the point: Aquinas supplies a wise ruler by reference to which the retroductive questions first begin to make sense. By the great metaphor of the providential ruler, we can say with modern science that "laws are the explananda; they are the questions, not the answers."[7] Aquinas' notion of Providence, unlike Aristotle's, insists that laws are not themselves the end of inquiry, but that laws too have reasons.

When Aquinas supplies contingency with an agent, he gives birth, too, to the arranger of circumstance, the experimenter, the scientist, even if – or just because – the first of those scientists is God. Here too the scientist is formed in the image of God. This is explicit and founds one of the three parts of the *Summa Theologiae*: human beings image God as masters of their acts, as arrangers of circumstances, as potential experimenters (I–II, Prologue). This is not part of Aquinas' theology of science: it is part of his theology of the human being. If we cannot imagine Aquinas saying, "God experiments," we must allow him to say, "God tests": and human beings in God's image may now, after Aristotle, do likewise. They are in God's image precisely as arrangers of circumstances toward an end, and just because, unlike God, they do not know singulars, but generalities by observation, their tests *are* experiments. A human being could not learn in the image of God without experiment: retroduction is the strictly appropriate (analogous) procedure of a creature whose nature is to be both contingent and an orderer of acts to an end. That is the innovation and the opening up of the Secunda Pars, even if Aquinas does not work out its implications for natural science. As we shall see, Aquinas' interest in contingency troubles and disrupts Aristotle's commitments to teleology at several turns. His doctrine of creation *ex nihilo* is precisely what not only allows but requires those changes of him. Aristotle's teleology cannot remain unchanged, if the creation itself is contingent. Rather, it is precisely the contingency of the world that reveals the graciousness of God. The role of contingency is to become a metaphysical revealer, both in the Scriptures, and in the world. It must be that too for physics, whether or not Aquinas himself walks through the door he has opened.

[6] *ST* I.93.1; I.90.4. [7] McMullin, *The Inference that Makes Science*, p. 90.

(b) Aquinas develops not a philosophy but a theology of science from Aristotle's account of insight. *Epagoge* does not become a font of new natural science for Aquinas: it becomes an ingredient in the beatific vision, in the science enjoyed by God and the blessed. Aquinas recognizes that there is something so teleological about *epagoge* that it is not quite human. You might read this as a critique not of science, but of Aristotle's account of science. Aquinas' theology of science deploys the *Posterior Analytics* in order to distance it. Aquinas would agree with modern philosophers of science like Ernan McMullin that *epagoge* is not how human beings learn. He might even agree that it is hopeless as a philosophy of coming to know.[8] Aristotle may or may not distinguish the logic of knowing from the logic of coming to know. But Aquinas must distinguish them as divine and human. Like retroduction, Aquinas' logic of human coming to know "settles for less" and yet "can yield practical certainty."[9] Speculative science has pretensions to know, but *coming* to know, both for Aquinas and for retroduction, is a *practical* matter. At the beginning of the *Summa Theologiae*, Aquinas insists that, in the things of which reason is capable, the truth is reached "*a paucis, et per longum tempus, et cum admixtione multorum errorum* [by a few, over a long time, and with an admixture of many errors]."[10] Rather, human beings learn by developing mental habits for dealing with contingent events. Retroduction is not a habit much practiced by Aquinas, but it fits excellently into his account of how human beings learn. Insight, on the other hand, is more like grace: a habit almost infused.

(c) Aquinas is more interested in how God can use human capacities of knowing to lead human beings to God than in how they work, although he is interested in that, too. Any kind of deep theology of science is something that modern Christianity largely lacks. Creationist versions, despite their name, undermine creation's integrity. Teilhardian versions, though profound, arouse suspicion. Rahnerian versions, despite their care, depend on a Kantianism now out of fashion. Modern Christianity needs to recover a sense that natural science can be a religious activity. That is why a theologian might turn to Aquinas here. Not because he offers a viable scientific method. Nor to open up a better place for him in its history. Certainly not to repristinate Aristotelian accounts of teleology or insight. Rather, Aquinas offers an account of all human activity as God-directed, signally human knowing. He insists that the

[8] *Ibid.*, p. 35 for quotations and discussions of *loci classici* on essences of things.

[9] *Ibid.*, pp. 95–96. [10] *ST* I.I.I.

Trinity brings human beings into participation with its own activity when they learn.[11] Science, therefore, is *divinizing*.[12] The Holy Spirit, Aquinas insists with John, will lead human beings into all truth.[13] The Spirit does not depart from the body of the Son, but befriends *matter*, in the incarnation, in the community of believers, in the sacraments – and therefore in everything that underlies those things. All things whatsoever – *omnia quaecumque*, in the sweeping phrase of *ST* I.1.8 – lie under the hovering of the Spirit on the Son. All things whatsoever lie naked – *panta gymna*, in the shocking phrase of Hebrews 4:13 – before the One with Whom they have to do.[14] Modern theologians might develop from Aquinas a Trinitarian theology of science where every instance of experiment and retroductive inference – reasoning back to causes by contrived experiment – is a form of contemplative prayer. Experiment and retroduction count as contemplative prayer not as a kind of religious complement, but for a reason that theology can specify: they attend carefully to *matter*, and in so doing they participate in the Spirit's proper office of witnessing and celebrating the Son. Trinitarian Christians need not turn to Aquinas because they want to recover Aristotelian insight. They might turn to Aquinas because theologians (if not scientists) need a Trinitarian account of scientific activity. Theologians need such an account both defensively, in order to have something better than creationism to offer, and positively, to explain why scientists have lately led the world into more truth than priests. If they have, then the Holy Spirit, who leads human beings into all truth, *must* be involved. How can theologians account for that? Reason enough for this exercise.

"*Scientia*" in Aquinas is a number of things, but among others it is a *habit*, a stable disposition of the mind. What interests Aquinas about that habit is what interests him about all habits: how finite and fallible dispositions here below become perfected and confirmed by union with the divine habits of the Trinity above. The finitude and contingency of the earthly habit, and the stability and perfection of the heavenly habit, are equally appropriate to their states. The transformation of one into the other depends on the incarnation of the Son and the grace of the Spirit. In the life of Christ, God learns as a human being in order to grant human beings divine sight. In the grace of the Spirit, human beings receive the sight of God through learning to see themselves as God sees them. The movement both defers perfect science to the next life, *and* adopts imperfect science as its predecessor. Historians of science have

[11] *ST* I.43.3. [12] Read *ST* III.9.2–3 with I–II.112.1. [13] *ST* I–II.109.1, ad. 1. [14] ST I.14.5.

noted the distancing aspect of that movement, raising the bar so as to make science all but impossible to reach in this life, without attending to the second, which elevates human learning to be a means of the divine.

THREE ARISTOTLES

Philosophers of science first criticized one Aristotle, the teleological Aristotle of the *Posterior Analytics*. That Aristotle did not have anything that looked like modern scientific method, because it proceeded by deduction from insight, a hopeless program for research. They then discovered a second Aristotle, one who worked by observation, in *Hearts of Animals*. That looked a bit more promising: an Aristotle open to evidence. But that Aristotle still did not *experiment*, did not control variables to find things out, did not exploit contingent circumstances to determine nature's secrets, did not proceed by elimination or over time: It even looked as if Aristotle would not permit that, since experiment seemed to treat nature unnaturally, to render her testimony unreliable because extracted by torture. But I want to claim that both the exponents of the *Posterior Analytics* and the exponents of *Hearts of Animals* have missed a *third* Aristotle, one who learns from contingency and advocates training in situations that make contingency revealing: the *psychological* Aristotle who read tragedies and wrote the *Nicomachean Ethics*. The *Posterior Analytics* does not describe habits of human learning: it describes a textbook. The *Hearts of Animals* does not describe learning by artful arrangement or experiment: it describes inspection, observation, taxonomy. But Aristotle, and Aquinas after him, are supremely interested in how human beings learn. Aquinas is most interested not in the hearts of animals but in the hearts of human beings. You might object that it is hard to find either thinker talking about learning from error. But that is only because by "error" they mean moral or intellectual fault. When we speak of learning by trial and error, we do not mean that our minds are faulty, we mean that we search by elimination. That process caused no problem for Aquinas, but accorded with the stepwise character of reason's composing and dividing. The difficulty is not with learning by elimination, but with making enough space in teleology for experiment's creative disruption.

But that is just how Aquinas understands the moral life. God's contingent events disrupt and re-form the finite plans of human beings. Therefore, it is to Aristotle's account of how character enables the human being to deal with the unexpected that Aquinas devotes himself. Aquinas wrote just ten pages about theology as science, citing the *Posterior Analytics* or the *Physics*. But he wrote hundreds and hundreds of pages on the *Ethics*, both in his commentary on that text and, more influential, in the entire Secunda Pars of the *Summa Theologiae*. That is his innovation, recognized as such in its historical effect, since the Seconda Pars was far and away the part most copied.[15] In Aquinas' psychology, learning from contingency is the whole point of life, and trial and error is the way of growth. And that is the part that interests him. Psychology is where his major theological innovation lies. Surely we should evaluate him on what he cares and innovates about.

What would it look like to develop a theology of science from what Aquinas says about the *Ethics* in the Secunda Pars? It might go like this. Experiment is intelligent disruption. It exploits contingency to unveil explanatory structure. Contingency reveals the hearts not just of animals, but of all created things. Retroduction, or contriving experiment, is ethics applied to matter: it tests the character of things. Both experiment and its reasoning belong to the contemplative life, and thus to prayer. Aquinas subsumes deduction, induction, retroduction and all other leadings-by-reason under another leading, one dearer to his heart: *manuductio*, the leading by God's hand. By manuduction, the Holy Spirit graciously promotes human reason to do something that it could not do by itself: lead a human being into God.[16] Some historians of science have thought that Aquinas demotes human reason by limiting it. He does not think so. He thinks he is giving it something better to do. Manuduction leads up the way that the Son descended. By the incarnation, the possessor of divine science becomes human; by God's manuduction, the possessor of human science becomes divine.

Earlier I said that Aquinas did not experiment. That goes for natural science, but not for the disciplines that interested him most. The *Summa Theologiae* – along with many of Aquinas' other works – does record textually, if it does not perform physically, the practice of learning from error – that is, it records disputations. Readers usually consult the *Summa* for its conclusions, just as students usually comb their science texts for facts. Science texts report experiments, much as the *Summa* reports disputations. Of course, that is not the same as going to the lab, and going to the lab as a student to repeat supervised experiments is not

[15] See Mark Jordan, "The *Summa of Theology* as Moral Formation" in *Rewritten Theology: Aquinas after His Readers* (Oxford: Blackwell, 2006), pp. 116–135.

[16] *ST* I.2.5; I.12.12.

the same as devising a new experiment from scratch. If you wanted the protocols of a Thomistic experiment, you would have to read a monastic rule. And yet, just for that reason, Aquinas' *Summa Theologiae* did not have to go without a practicum. In accord with Aquinas' interests, innovations, and *Wirkungsgeschichte*, the practicum was not in natural science but in human nature. The Dominican friars had all committed themselves to a new experiment, one in how human beings grow into the *scientia Dei*, one in how they might do so by begging and preaching. They had a lab: that was the monastery. Their experiment had parameters: those were their vows. They had results to retroject: those were their hearts. They had theory: that was their character. The observed regularities of human behavior provided their questions; the theory of character and the postulation of habit provided their explanations. And that is what Aquinas wrote the Secunda Pars for. He wrote it to supply theory and theoretical entities for his experiment.

You might find the comparison baroque and far-fetched, a conceit. You might find that the meanings of all the words have become metaphorical. But that would not count as a flaw for one who insists in all seriousness that theology is *scientia*. That would not count as a flaw for one who insists that reality coheres by analogy. Nor for one who integrates the learning of this life with the knowledge of God. And not for one who thinks the incarnation requires him to do so. The human being cannot come to God, unless Jesus Christ has at once the knowledge acquired by experience (*scientia acquisita vel experimentali*) and the knowledge of the beatific vision (*scientia Dei et beatorum*): so alone can Jesus offer in human words and a human life the way in the divine Word into the divine life.[17] So alone can *scientia experimentali* be led into *scientia beatorum*. If such an account integrates what modern learning divides, then that is just what a Christian scientist might want it for.

DISCOVERY, DESCRIPTION, DEDUCTION

The point of Aquinas' theology of science is to explain manuduction, how God can use things in the world to lead human beings to God. Things in the world and the human desire to know them work together to bring human beings to their ultimate happiness: science is Aquinas' major metaphor for heaven; science is a participation in divinity, because God too is a scientist. Indeed, God is a scientist who wants to know *us*,

[17] *ST* III.9.10, III.9.12, and esp. III.9.2.

us human beings, to the extent that God comes to us as a human being, as a human scientist. Thomas Aquinas is no Mary Baker Eddy, but the articles on the *scientia* of Christ (*ST* III.9) present Jesus as the scientist *par excellence*.

When, on the other hand, *scientia* remains this-worldly, it looks uncongenial to modern science. For Thomas Aquinas, *scientia* as the knowability of things is defined by form and the teleology implicit in form. For most modern accounts, teleological explanations vitiate science. What Aquinas regards as best for science, moderns regard as bad for it. The difference concerns how structures build up, how organization happens. Most Aristotelian accounts take structure immanent in things as a non-material force that works like an intention. Most modern accounts make structure contingent on random processes that build up and break down, with the result that only some structures survive.[18] The difference between Aristotle and Darwin comes down to whether *disruption* can be a good thing. In Darwin, disruption leads to both a lot of maladaptation and death, as well as to a little survival and evolution. In Aristotle, disruption is hard to square with teleology and form. Form seems opposed to randomness and disruption – evolution seems to require it. And yet form is not the place to look for Aquinas' comments on creative disruption. Look instead to his accounts of contingency and diversity.

Reading some parts of Aristotle, you might suppose that teleology goes all the way down. (His treatment of tragedy might make an exception.) But for Aquinas, contingency has equal claim to go all the way down. For, in opposition to Aristotle, he makes the world itself contingent: it *might not have been*. Contingency is not normally the subject of Aristotelian *scientia* for human beings in this life, just because we cannot pin it down. But it is part of the *scientia* for which human beings yearn, the *scientia* of God and the happy. And when Aquinas reformulates the science in which he is most interested – that of psychology, or human development – form and contingency are opposed no longer, but work closely together. It is the merit of modern science to extend to the non-human sciences the explanatory power of contingency and structure together, that Aquinas promoted in his greatest innovation. His doctrine of creation leaves room to extend that innovation also to the natural sciences. *Creatio ex nihilo* asserts both organization or form – *creatio* – and radical

[18] Though most modern accounts consider chance and probabilistic processes as important factors in the generation of structure, they are clearly not the only ones. The order and regularity in the physical interaction and in matter itself is also absolutely necessary.

contingency – *ex nihilo*. It rejects both organization without contingency – that would be Aristotle's eternity of the world – and contingency without form – that would be chaos. This is what *creatio ex nihilo* protects: the compatibility of organization and contingency.

PHILOSOPHY VERSUS THEOLOGY OF SCIENCE

As I have insisted elsewhere, Thomas Aquinas distinguishes sharply between awareness or *cognitio*,[19] of which one sort is faith, and demonstrated structure, or *scientia*, of which one sort is the beatific vision of God and the blessed in heaven. Yet Aquinas' God also destines human beings to *know*, to have *scientia*, and (perhaps shockingly) to leave faith behind. Among those knowers is Jesus, who possesses the *scientia Dei* to the extent that it displaces faith – and he *has* to have that science, according to Aquinas, both in order to bring it to human beings, and in order to know us, not just with cognition, but with *scientia*. If we want the beatific vision, Jesus has to have it; if we want to be beatified, Jesus has to know us, see us with vision. For we are beatified with the vision of the one seeing us.[20] In Aquinas (as in Rowan Williams), grace is the transformative perception of another, to use a phrase that Williams uses differently. But that is one reason why I want to use Aquinas' psychology to improve his conception of science. So here I am working rather the other side of the street from my earlier work.

One purpose of the *Summa Theologiae* is to interpret sacred doctrine as an Aristotelian discipline, or "*sacra doctrina est scientia.*" Aquinas defines an Aristotelian discipline as one that proceeds from first principles. Contrary to Thomists since John of St. Thomas, proceeding from first principles does not mean first of all an exercise in logic, unless logic means the source of structure in God's *Logos*. It means first of all a real showing or manifestation, as of a way or path, a *via*. And that showing exists both in the world and in the mind. An Aristotelian demonstration is like opening the hood of a car. To see how a car works, you open the hood and look. For that reason, a synonym for *scientia* is seeing, vision. For that reason, too, the Son may "demonstrate" the Father and be a "way" to him, where both the crucial words, *demonstratio* and *via*, are technical

[19] Victor Preller, *Divine Science and the Science of God: A Reformulation of Thomas Aquinas* (Princeton University Press, 1967), passim, but esp. p. 32. Eugene F. Rogers, Jr., *Thomas Aquinas and Karl Barth: Sacred Doctrine and the Natural Knowledge of God* (University of Notre Dame Press, 1995), pp. 17–70. The rest of this chapter follows and extends that account, which supplies more references.

[20] *ST* I.12.13.

terms in Aristotelian science – as in the Commentary on the Gospel of John. Moderns would now, after Descartes, distinguish the real and mental aspects of such a demonstration. We would now automatically distinguish the thing that demonstrates, the actually humming engine, from the one who demonstrates, the knowledgeable mechanic. We now distinguish the path that DNA follows, and a path that the mind follows. But Aquinas united what modern convention divides.[21] He had a conceptuality for keeping together the structures of reality and the structures of knowing: he called it proceeding from first principles.

If you proceeded in accord with first principles, you had a science. A first principle structured both things and minds. Unlike moderns, Aquinas distinguishes between knowers and things known precisely in order to bind them together. To hold them apart is, strictly speaking, to put Descartes before the source. A first principle of birds might be the shape of a wing. Then both the development of the wing – how it grows and flies – and that of ornithology (how Bernoulli's principle functions with feathers) belong to the first principles of birds.[22] Bernoulli's principle is a source of light both for ornithologists and, Aquinas might now say, for the random searching of protobirds' DNA.

Hearing "first principle," you may think of efficient causes, and that would not be wrong; but it would be misleading. First principles have various aspects, among which efficient causation is not left out – but for Aquinas' purposes their most important aspect is *form.* If an Aristotelian wants to refer to the first principle working itself out indifferently in things and minds, the structure demonstrating itself in both the wings of birds and the mind of Bernoulli, then form is the word that is used. A form is a followable structure, either in the building up of structures in the world or in Aristotelian knowledge. A modern Aristotelian, if there were one, might refer to form in describing electromagnetic attraction, the build-up of stars, the growth of crystals and the development of string theory. In modern parlance, we hear the quotation marks if we say that objects under gravity "know" where to go, and think of the verb as metaphorical. For Aquinas, too, such a use of "know" would be unusual. But the extension of meaning would go beyond metaphor. The world itself, for Aquinas, exhibits an ordered series of harmonious structures, repeating on different levels and in different aspects: he calls their relation analogy. If you insisted that to recapitulate in language an

[21] MacIntyre, *First Principles.*

[22] Terence Irwin, *Aristotle's First Principles* (Ithaca, NY: Cornell University Press, 1990), p. 7.

analogy between crystals and minds was to equivocate, Aquinas would reply with a distinction: some equivocations mislead; this equivocation is strictly appropriate.[23] Refuse to admit it, and you are blocking the light, the light by which things are enlightening the mind. That is the light of reason, of *ratio*, of appropriate proportion or structure in the world and in us.

For Aquinas, all kinds of knowledge – especially Aristotelian *scientia* – depend on sources of light, on smaller revelations. First principles are manifestations of forms in the world, joining in one that which idiom divides, namely the form that inheres indifferently in minds and things. Each Aristotelian science is thus originated and individuated by its formal rationale or light. If you understand frogs, then you get light from frogs that gives rise to frog science in human minds. If you understand frogs, that also shows that frogs manifest frog-light, the first principles of frog, that give rise also to followable frog-structure in frogs themselves. That is also science, the science in frogs. The science in frogs gives light, and the science of frogs appears in the light. The more you attend to the first principles of frogs, the better science you have. The more you attend to frog-light, the more scientific your discipline is. The more something is revealed, therefore, the more scientific it is. Theology is no exception to that rule. Theology exemplifies that rule. Theology is for that reason not science by disciplinary extension; theology is science *par excellence*.

I take up two objections to that account. First, you might think that theology is not really science, because science is in principle accessible to everyone smart enough, and revelation is not. Call it science accessible and inaccessible. Second, you might observe that Aquinas' account of science depends on insight and teleology, whereas insight and teleology have been more or less deservedly out of favor in natural science for several hundred years. Call it process teleological and random. I take the teleology objection first.

That objection recasts Aquinas' dependence on form as a critique. Forms build in teleology. But it is possible to take the sting out of teleological arguments in two ways. First, Aquinas' forms are not entirely fixed, but they are dynamic all the way down. Second, I think it is possible to extend Aquinas' thinking about contingency to favor arguments about how natural structures develop by random process. This means that insight gets modified by enough detail to need experiment,

[23] Preller, *Divine Science and the Science of God.*

to take time, to permit retroduction, the postulation of entities and theories to explain regularities, to extend what is. Aquinas' best example is in psychology rather than physics: "habit" is a theoretical entity invented to explain the regularities of human behavior and to bridge the gap between intention and execution when there is no time for deliberation. Habits are theoretical entities, than which nothing could be more real.[24]

Forms are not fixed. As Aristotle scholar Jonathan Lear defines them, forms are "internal principles of change."[25] They are dynamic all the way down. Evolution would seem to be written into them. It is true that they are teleological. And it looks as if their teleology is set. But the appearance of setness self-destructs by the very nature of Aquinas' teleology. In the normal sequence of how things seek their ends, every thing enjoys a movement native to it. Animals seek their good by instinct; they smell and move toward food. Plants seek their good by growing; they move toward light. Rocks seek their good by gravity. That is, the deepest desire of a rock is to reach the center of the earth. See how the rock yearns! (Push something off the table.) And yet random searching is compatible with this: plants grow toward water – by sending out roots in all directions. And further, the teleological system allows some scope for the ends themselves to develop and change. At the top of the system, human beings seek their good by reason. That means they choose their own proximate ways toward the good; they decide what to do next. Now, the hierarchy of moving creatures has strong bonds downwards, so human beings are also subject to instinct like animals, to growth like plants, even and perhaps most obviously to gravity like rocks. Does an analogous type of participation make sense also upward? Do animals in some respect foreshadow human freedom? Do plants and rocks? Aquinas does not pose that question, but he poses a close one. He asks whether reason in the human being comes superadded on top or transforms the whole organism. He answers that reason transforms the whole, at least virtually. It is not that our brain is rational and our toes are animal; our toes are rational, too. Humans have instincts "meant" to be rationalized. Fight-or-flight develops, under the right circumstances, into the virtue of courage, a habituated or sedimented rationality about when to dare and how to retreat. As humans form good habits, instincts get rational-ized.

[24] For an argument by a philosopher of science that God is a theoretical entity, see Bas van Fraassen, *The Scientific Image* (Oxford: Clarendon Press, 1980), pp. 204–215.

[25] Jonathan Lear, *Aristotle: The Desire to Understand* (Cambridge University Press, 1988), pp. 15–25.

We might now say that the brain moderates the limbic system, or the cerebral cortex retrains the amygdala. Each level recapitulates the others: the running tiger instinctualizes physics; the judo fighter rationalizes physics. For Aquinas, the whole body is proto-rational, waiting to be rationalized, toes not excepted. You can also put that the other way around: in forming habits, the considered, deliberated judgments of reason become instinctual.

As well as the human being, all creation, on a different level, is proto-rational, in that the *Logos* created it and destined its return. If that is so, human beings, with a share in the *Logos*, should be able to tell. So I think it is unavoidable for Aquinas that, if human beings are animals who can change their proximate ends by reason, then other created things can modify their ends in analogically appropriate ways. Consider how he describes mental development: "over a long time, by a few, with a great admixture of errors." Evolution of animals too takes place over a much longer time, by a minuscule few, with an enormous admixture of error. In Aristotle, none of that need imply conscious direction. Rather, consciousness itself imitates natural, unconscious process (the mind imitates crystals). But, if nature should *become* conscious, that is not inappropriate. Form comes out. For Aquinas, who does apply the tropes of consciousness to the Creator, it still marks the Creator's transcendent intimacy with creation that God can be with things in a manner appropriate to them, so that for Aquinas too it is appropriate for God to hide (or appear) under form.

Now, it marks modern science, whether in quantum foam or genetic mutation, to credit development or devolution to chance disruption. Random process sounds like the opposite of teleological process. Can an Aristotelian say that God hides or appears under randomness? Can a theologian see disruption of order as other than the chaos that God overcame? Aquinas, if not Aristotle, has positive things to say about both contingency and diversity, and he thinks deeply about how form and contingency relate. For Aquinas, God's rule over the universe does not avoid but provides for contingent events, that is, events that do not happen by created necessity. The Scriptures constrain Aquinas to think more deeply about contingent events than Aristotle does, because the Scriptures teem with contingent, historical narratives, remote from teleological necessity.

God wills, Aquinas says, that necessary things happen necessarily, and that contingent things happen contingently.[26] With that he opens a way

[26] *ST* 1.22.4, responsio and ad. 1.

for contingent, unpredictable developments, such as the evolution of stars and animals. He does little to elaborate the role of contingent or random events in the evolutionary development of irrational things. But he does a very great deal to elaborate the role of contingent events in the development of rational creatures. Almost half the *Summa* – the Secunda Pars, Aquinas' greatest innovation – insists and focuses on the role of contingent events in the development of rational creatures, human beings. In human development, contingent events provide ineliminable opportunities for the development of excellence, or virtue.[27] Contingency trains and habituates response over time. A virtue is a skill that makes the best response to contingent events, the response likeliest to conduce to happiness in the very long term. Under those circumstances, contingency provides the sort of unpredictable difficulties that expose weakness and exercise excellence. In Aquinas' hands, if not Aristotle's, form is not just dynamic, but its dynamism – its very development – *depends* on disruption. For Aquinas as for Darwin, excellence is impossible without contingency. For Aquinas as for moderns, constants keep contingency within wide bounds, which he and we call law.[28] The language of teleology may remain uncongenial to modern natural science, but under Aquinas the space for development of stable and replicating structures in response to random events has grown indefinitely large.

I have moved from the development of an individual to development of species and beyond. That road, you say, leads straight to Lamarck. But no. Aquinas would not claim that changes in individual development cause change in the species. He would just insist that a variety of developments under contingency look alike for a reason. Development is not the same process in a species and in an individual, but it is an analogous process. Little would prevent Aquinas from holding that contingent events serve to develop excellences also in inanimate structures and animals. Indeed, it would be hard for him to rule that out. Random events cause responses in animate and inanimate structures. If those responses lead to disarray or death, they count as what Aquinas would call misfortune for the star or the frog; if to success or survival, they count as fortune. Successful DNA habituates the fortunate results of contingent mutation; unsuccessful DNA kills off the unfortunate results of others. Contingency habituates, in mind and world alike. The

[27] See Bowlin, *Contingency and Fortune*. [28] *Ibid.*

mental development Aquinas taught us to call "habit"; the environmental development we have come to call "habitat."

For Aquinas, both created things in the human habitat, as an external principle, and the human habit of seeking to understand, as an internal principle, lead the human being to God. Created things lead to life with God, both by their own structure (the science in things), and by human participation in the structure of God's mind (the science in minds). Aquinas takes from Aristotle what you might call a strong anthropic principle, that things and minds are made for one another. *Entia*, things that be, just are also *intelligibilia*, things that engage understanding. (Plenty of room for theoretical entities here.) Aquinas departs from Aristotle, in supposing that there is much to be said about the maker, such as that the maker made humans and things not only for one another, but for himself; and that the maker made humans so intimately and drastically for himself, that he became a human being.[29] Indeed, Aquinas quotes the patristic axiom that God became human, that humans might become divine.[30] There is an anthropic principle for you.

To express the shock that God has fit human beings for God, Aquinas uses several metaphors, including friendship, marriage, monarchy and republic. But the metaphor that predominates recalls a natural shock, the shock of understanding. Aquinas often names the final consummation of the human being's destiny in God, by the consummation of the human desire to know: he calls it *scientia*, science. One of the best analogies Aquinas can find for the call of God and humans to one another, consummated in heaven, is the call of things and humans to one another, consummated in natural science. What makes us human is our desire to understand; we desire to understand both so that we can ourselves order our acts toward our ends, and because understanding makes us happy. What makes us perfect humans, therefore, is to understand completely (which is not to say statically), or to have science. For Thomas Aquinas, science and theology are not at odds; they are in analogy, a kind of strict harmony or ontological rhythm. To separate them would tear the human being apart. Things – matter, energy, space, time – lead human beings to virtue, and virtue leads them to God. Or better, God leads human beings to God's own self by virtue, and cultivates virtue with things. As a rule, God does not deal with human beings by bypassing things, because that

[29] These are not *entia-intelligibilia*: these are *revelabilia-credibilia*, a larger, not a contrasting, category.
[30] *ST* III.I.I.

would violate rather than perfect their nature. Bypassing things would be sloppy, and God is elegant. Creation *ex nihilo* means that nothing is in principle alien to God's purpose, and that means that no thing is immune from the human desire to know it, and no thing can finally thwart God's desire to use it to bring human beings to God's self. Aquinas finds the God-leading nature of things inscribed in a verse from the New Testament Book of Romans 1:20: "The invisible things of God can be known from the things God has made." He deploys that verse to warrant arguments both in cosmology and in Christology – since he regards them as part of the same discipline. The God-relatedness of all things, and the fittingness of the incarnation, both exemplify, on different levels, God's courtesy toward rational creatures in making the visible manifest the invisible. Indeed, the incarnation is fitting just because God relates all things to God in the Word.

I return to take up the objection about accessibility. You might think that revelation is a purely mental illumination that floats free from material particulars, and thus departs from other kinds of science. But that would be wrong. In fact, Aquinas is suspicious of illuminations that bypass the physical. He treats them under the category of "rapture." He cannot deny them, because he thinks Paul had one. But he makes much of the incommunicability of such experience. Something not first in the senses does not suit the human mind well enough to pass into language. Rapture, therefore, brings nothing linguistically stable enough to confirm or deny. Therefore, Aquinas can rule rapture out as a source of theological learning. It does not function. At best it spins, but it leaves reason unmoved.

Now there is one sharp distinction between the science that is sacred doctrine and the sciences that are natural. Both are involved in hierarchies of first principles, so that (say) chemistry depends on physics. Aquinas faces a choice about where the continuity of chemistry and physics lies. Does it lie in the things themselves, or in the scientists who know? You might say that the chemist learns his physics from other people, without having its first principles by experience in his own mind, and that therefore the continuity is personal (in the teacher) rather than principial (in the structure of reality). And in an earlier stage (in the *Contra Gentiles*) Aquinas treated theology that way. Depending on an insufficiently Aristotelian notion of revelation, he had thought that Christians believe sacred doctrine because God teaches it to them. In that case, the objection would be right: natural science was accessible, sacred doctrine inaccessible.

But later, in the *Summa Theologiae*, Aquinas abandoned that view. Now sacred doctrine is a science because it has a principial structure. It is a science, a followable structure of reality, apart from our notice, in the way that other Aristotelian sciences are: because things show themselves, manifest their form. For God as for frogs, the more the form reveals itself, the more discipline is possible. For theology as for biology, the more revealed it is, the more scientific it is. So Aquinas rejects the comparison of accessible and inaccessible: rather, all science considers inaccessible things *made* accessible. Theology is defined no longer in terms of what has been revealed, but in terms of what is reveal-able, a technical term, *revelabilia*. And all things whatsoever, *omnia quaecumque*, are revealable, lay themselves open to be known. If you think that is an extravagant hypothesis, you are right: it is a hypothesis of creation *ex nihilo* – all things whatsoever are waiting to be known, because nothing in the world escapes God's eye.

But if science is a followable structure of reality, then followable *by whom*? And if all things whatsoever are created to be known, known *by whom*? Aquinas continues to hold that the end of human existence is the saturation of the desire to understand, when we come to share God's knowledge in heaven. But now he wants to make a distinction. We cannot hold the objective, principial structure of sacred doctrine in our heads, because that would be to know the infinite and to possess God. In the *Summa*, Aquinas calls sacred doctrine a science because the discipline itself has a principled structure, but not because any living human being can have it in mind. That would blow our minds, literally. Thus this paradox: at least in this life, theology is a science without scientists. Just because the *scientia* of the next life is analogous to, and the satisfaction of, the science of this life, natural science and theology both have to be sciences – even if the scientist of each is different. The science of God satiates the science of nature, and therefore they rhyme. The difference between them is good. The light of glory shows all things at once with God's own vision; reason shows things one by one over time. Reason is nothing other than the appropriate manifestation of glory in time. The light of reason is the light of glory *created*. This is an appropriate equivocation. It is to say that the light of reason is the light of glory *shared*, shared by God with what is other than God, shared so that creatures can not only know, but desire to know, can not only desire but can stretch and run to know. In working to understand, human beings become both most themselves, and most like God.

Theology in this life is a descriptive discipline, like anthropology. It calls its practitioners believers rather than scientists, because description is only on the way to understanding. Its real scientists – its natives – are only God and the blessed in heaven. Theologians are the second-hand ethnographers of a city they have only heard about, but never visited, the City of God.

But that is not a hopeless case. Ethnographers and native informants share skills. They become like one another. If you read ethnography, you see the anthropologist looking for an informant with skills like theirs: attention to detail, a nose for meanings, skills of relative distance and translation. A certain conaturality develops between ethnographers and their informants because they share skills. Sacred doctrine has at least one native informant, one with excellent anthropological skills. Jesus Christ, according to Aquinas, actually enjoys the beatific vision, possesses the science human beings seek, the native informer about heaven. He is also God's *Logos* made *anthropos*, God the anthropologist, who attends and returns to us human beings as if we were his own first principle. Christ, for Aquinas, guarantees the hopefulness of the theological enterprise, because there is one who can, in Aristotelian language, "reduce the potential" of the human being for happiness "to act." All created things are in potential to their end: so the stone falls – if pushed. And the human being understands – if taught. The incarnation causes human understanding to fall, as it were, into place. God's Reason itself comes down, not to overwhelm human reason, but taking the form of a servant. God the *anthropos-logos* humbles himself, taking the form of a native informant, serving the subject matter.[31]

Theology does not fail to be a science, on Aquinas' account, because revelation is inaccessible; he regards all science as the making accessible of the mysterious, as the shedding of light. But there is something right in the objection, and that is this: theology is more like ethnography than natural science. Like ethnography, theology depends on particulars. As Clifford Geertz said of cultural anthropology, it depends on "exceedingly extended acquaintances with extremely small matters."[32] Aquinas would agree with that, I think; he does not regard revelation as inaccessible, but he does regard it as particular; it treats of singulars. Theology

[31] For more along these lines, see Eugene F. Rogers, Jr., "Theology in the Curriculum of a Secular Religious Studies Department," *CrossCurrents* 56 (2006), pp. 169–179, esp. pp. 171–172 and pp. 174–176.

[32] Clifford Geertz, *The Interpretation of Cultures* (New York: Basic Books, 1973), p. 21.

is not one of the natural sciences, at least to us; it is one of the human sciences. It is the anthropology of God.

God can use science to bring human beings to God, by involving them in the Trinitarian structure of the Spirit resting on the Son in the love of the Father. The Son and the Spirit indwell a human being in a way specific to rational creatures: as the thing known in the knower (*cognitum in cognoscente*) and the thing loved in the lover (*amatum in amante*).[33] Anything structured or lawful belongs to Christ, the *Logos* or Word of God, which both structures like a *ratio* and saves like a *sermo*. So science is Christology waiting to happen. Anything involving human desire belongs to the work of the Holy Spirit, the Gift of God, which both manifests like a fire and reveals like a lover. So science is also pneumatology resting on matter. The Holy Spirit, the Gift of God, is characteristically looking for a gift to give the Son, who already has everything. So God finds new and creative ways for the Son to receive what he has. The Son loves matter so much that he has inscribed himself into the natures of things, into their *logoi*; and even so much that he has taken on a material body. The Spirit, in leading, following, accompanying and resting on him, also befriends and accompanies things, working as it were paraphysically, alongside matter.[34] The deep Trinitarian principle of the Spirit celebrating the love of the Father and the Son repeats and reflects in creation and therefore in human beings. So the scientist wondering at the structure of creation reflects, at a distance, the Holy Spirit igniting love for the Son. The Father sends Son and Spirit into creation to return it to himself, involving them with the utmost intimacy in created things. By the Word and in the Spirit, God comes closer to things than they are to themselves. God conforms the structures of things to God's Word and moves the hearts of things by God's Spirit.[35] Therefore, the more a science attends to the structure of things, the more Christocentric it is, and the more scientists are led by the things in the world, the more they are filled with the Spirit. The *Summa* places its teaching on creation *ex nihilo immediately* after the question on the sending of the Son and the Spirit in part to protect the claim that God so *differs* from creation, as to love it more than it loves itself.[36] Indeed, it is just because God *transcends* the world, and

[33] *ST* 1.43.3.

[34] A thesis of Eugene F. Rogers, Jr., *After the Spirit: A Constructive Pneumatology from Resources Outside the Modern West* (Grand Rapids, MI: Eerdmans, 2005), esp. pp. 99–104.

[35] *ST* 1.45.6. [36] *ST* 1.45.1.

differs from things, that God is able to come closer to them than they are to themselves. If creation's difference from God were *alien* to God, rather than *given* by God, its intimacy with the Word would be *less* than that of the creature to itself, and its bearing into God by the Spirit would be exile rather than homecoming. The doctrine of creation *ex nihilo* has a soteriological purpose and a Trinitarian deep structure.[37] It expresses the intimacy of God to things without compromise, as befits the incarnation of the Word. It expresses the orientation of things to God without compromise, as befits the consummation wrought by the Spirit. It insists that a God-relation is built into the creature (1.45.3) without rival.[38]

The best glimpse at this is in Romans 8, where Paul describes Trinitarian relations as contemplative prayer. In Romans 8, the Spirit leads human beings into the Son's relation to the Father. Aquinas elsewhere describes that relation as *scientia*, consummated contemplation. In Aquinas' commentary on Romans, even cosmological arguments for God's claim on creation get assigned to the persons of the Trinity. This is a cycle from science to science. Not that natural science leads to God without help. But it is characteristic of the Holy Spirit to use it. The Holy Spirit has to engage the intellectual faculties sooner or later. The Holy Spirit does not have to begin with science, but has to end with science. Science, too, is Trinity-shaped contemplative prayer.

[37] *ST* 1.44.1 and 1.44.4; 1.45.7.

[38] And Aquinas refers his reasoning about relations existing in creatures (*ST* 1.45.3, ad. 1 and 2) to his reasoning about relations among the Trinitarian persons (*ST* 1.13.7; 1.42.1, ad. 4).

Index